"Robert Gerst has written a one-of-a-kind book that brings alive the challenges of film directors over the evolution of moviemaking and inspires readers to create their own films sparked by the solutions to these challenges. Following in the tradition of famous painters learning from imitating others, *Make Film History* will fire-up student filmmakers and re-energize and stimulate experienced filmmakers."

— Gael Chandler, author: *Film Editing – Great Cuts Every Filmmaker and Movie Lover Must Know*

"Robert Gerst has created a wonderful, and sometimes astonishing, new way to study the history of movies and, at the same time, learn moviemaking techniques. The sum total is an exciting experience like no other book I've ever read."

— Paul Chitlik, Clinical Asst. Professor in Screenwriting, Loyola Marymount University; Member, WGAW and The Academy of Television Arts and Sciences

"A stunning accomplishment. Robert Gerst has transformed the story of film history into a personal hands-on filmmaking experience. And that experience is unforgettable. *Make Film History* paints the vivid, colorful chronicle of cinema history in a totally new way."

— Eric Edson, professor, screenwriter, author: *The Story Solution – 23 Actions All Great Heroes Must Take*

"Fascinating! A brilliant way to learn filmmaking and film history. Robert Gerst's *Make Film History* is an instant classic. A must-have resource. I know of nothing like this book, anywhere. Congratulations Robert!"

— Tony Levelle, author: *Producing with Passion, Digital Video Secrets*

"This book gives the filmmaker and film lover a remarkable opportunity to re-visit the great classics of the cinema, gain fresh insights into the circumstances under which they were made, and test these new insights by actually handling the footage oneself! We hear a great deal about 'r nication. Here's an example that truly works."

— Charles Wilkinson, director: *Peace Out, Down Here*; author: *The Working Film Director*

"Ingenious! Professor Gerst is brilliant. He distills film history into 25 game-changing discoveries. Whether it's Muybridge and intermittency or Murch and sound mixing, each advance is placed in historical context and then put at the center of a hands-on exercise for readers to try. Each practicum is cleverly designed to show us why pivotal innovations like montage or storyboarding were significant, and how to reproduce them. You don't need to buy additional equipment to do the exercises. If you have a computer and an Internet connection, you're good to go. *Make Film History* is a beautifully illustrated, instructive guide that makes some of the most awe-inspiring moments in film history easily reproducible for even the most novice of filmmakers. Highly recommended!"

— Jennifer Van Sijll, author: *Cinematic Storytelling*

"A treasure trove of filmmaking in a book. Working with an easy-to-use website, this book takes you step by step into the filmmaking process, allowing you to work hands-on with film classics from the history of the cinema. A new kind of filmmaking learning experience."

— Tom Lazarus, screenwriter, author: *The Last Word – Definitive Answers To All Your Screenwriting Questions*

"Learning the techniques of filmmaking has just taken a great leap forward. Robert Gerst's new book, *Make Film History*, combines the act of filmmaking (using your computer) and studying the work of many past masters of the filmmaking process to create a hands-on method for learning the *reasons* behind the techniques — by getting the student to 'walk in their shoes.' Amazing."

— Richard La Motte, author: *Costume Design 101 – 2nd Edition*

"*Make Film History* puts theory to practice in a book that's essentially a portable film school. Through chapters that delve into film concepts from *mise-en-scène* to jump cuts, author Robert Gerst examines the seminal works of directors like Chaplin, Griffith, Godard, and many others to show today's filmmakers how yesterday's greats pieced together the world's most memorable movies — so they, too, will be able to craft a more cinematic tomorrow."

— John Trigonis, author: *Crowdfunding for Filmmakers*

"In this 21st century treatment, film history and filmmaking become participant activities. A beautifully written, invaluable addition to the literature on the history of film."

— David L. Brown, three-time Emmy Award-winning documentary filmmaker

"Skip film school. If you do all the exercises in this book, you'll learn at least as much as you would at film school — at one-thousandth the price."

— Alex Epstein, screenwriter: *Bon Cop/Bad Cop*, *Naked Josh*; author: *Crafty Screenwriting*

"Unlike any film book on the market, Mr. Gerst's perspective on the history of film and his encouragement to explore will give you a completely new understanding of how cinema started and continues to be created today. If you call yourself a fan of film, you need to have this book in your collection."

— Matthew Terry, filmmaker, screenwriter, teacher, reviewer for microfilmmaker.com

"Whew! At last a book to re-awaken students and teachers of cinema studies and moviemaking."

— Richard D. Pepperman, author: *Illuminations – Memorable Movie Moments*, nominated 2011 Best Moving Image Book Award

"The structure of *Make Film History* — a unique connection of book and website — reveals for students everything about cinema: its methods and goals, its development, and its masters. A much-needed work!"

— Inga Karetnikova, Former Associate Professor and Director of the Screenwriting Program at Boston University, author: *How Scripts Are Made*, *Seven Masterpieces of 1940s Cinema*, *Mexico According to Eisenstein*

"Robert Gerst's *Make Film History* is an exciting project! Great fun for everyone who aspires to make movies or just loves to watch them."

— Leon Steinmetz, artist, author: *The Magic Life of Madame Tussaud*, co-author (with Peter Greenaway): *The World of Peter Greenaway*

"What a terrific approach to learning filmmaking! Bob Gerst has given us the opposite of a dry, academic introduction to film mechanics and language. By examining the history of film as the history of *problems and their solutions*, he is able to show the development of film technique in the most sensible and meaningful way. And by re-encountering these problems and finding solutions to them in practice, this book will really help young filmmakers to learn the craft, as well as the history, of this most wonderful art."

— Sheldon Mirowitz, Professor - Film Scoring Department, Berklee College of Music, Emmy-nominated composer

Rewrite, Reshoot, and Recut the World's Greatest Films   ROBERT GERST

MAKE FILM HISTORY

M I C H A E L   W I E S E   P R O D U C T I O N S

Published by Michael Wiese Productions
12400 Ventura Blvd. #1111
Studio City, CA 91604
(818) 379-8799, (818) 986-3408 (FAX)
mw@mwp.com
www.mwp.com

Cover design by Johnny Ink. www.johnnyink.com
Cover photo: Ren Hui Yoong, www.renhuiyoong.com
Interior design by William Morosi
Printed by McNaughton & Gunn

Manufactured in the United States of America

Library of Congress Cataloging-in-Publication Data

Robert, Gerst
 Make film history : rewrite, reshoot, and recut the world's greatest films /
Gerst Robert.
     p. cm.
 ISBN 978-1-61593-122-4 (pbk.)
1. Motion pictures--Production and direction--Study and teaching. I. Title.
 PN1995.9.P7R53 2012
 791.4302'3071--dc23
                                    2012016311

Printed on Recycled Stock

For Angela, my eyes, now and always

Table of Contents

How To Use This Book

In this book, you read about moments when great filmmakers made revolutionary advances, and you learn by **doing as they did**. Working with *Make Film History* you learn the history of the movies by **actually redoing the history of movies**. You rework their footage or make rudimentary movies of your own. Read it. Learn it. Do it. It's études for the movies. You learn what makes a great movie. You learn how the magic started and where it's going.

1. **Follow these steps.**

● Read a chapter. Each focuses on a great filmmaker in the act of transforming movies. No chapter takes longer to read than an old-fashioned two-reeler movie (roughly 20-24 minutes). At the end of every chapter is a film-making exercise—many offer two—where you work out for yourself whatever the filmmaker at the center of the chapter was wrestling with.

● View the film clip or clips for that chapter on the *Make Film History* website (http://makefilmhistory.com). The clips demonstrate what you just read about. The clips set before your eyes—from the filmmaker's point of view—what the challenge was... and is.

● Download the exercise file from the website.... and do it. There's an exercise for every chapter, and some chapters offer several. Work through the exercise using your computer's digital editing software. Repeat the exercise as many times as you like. Play with it every which way. Run it double speed and slow motion. Filter it so that it looks like a movie made on Mars or a hundred years ago. No one is watching—go crazy! Try anything.

Each exercise is a scale you practice before you make your masterpiece. When you're satisfied, you can advance your skills by making another similar movie of your own invention. The book offers numerous suggestions.

The payoff to this reading, viewing, and making is huge. When you finish the book, you'll have learned how movies developed from

1880 to today. You'll have learned and practiced the rudiments of making movies. You'll start seeing and hearing as filmmakers do. You may find yourself reading those names at the end of a movie—writer, producer, associate music producer, color timer, telecine operator. You may start envisioning your name among them. You'll have learned movie history the way the great filmmakers learned it—by making it.

2. **What equipment you need.**

If you elect to try the exercises, you need only the media-making software pre-installed on your computer. iMovie is perfect for Macintosh. Movie Maker or Live Movie Maker works for Windows. Advanced editing packages like Final Cut Pro or Avid Studio are fine if you're already comfortable using them. The exercises work in any operating system. Computers and hand-helds come with video editing software already installed, even hand held devices like iPod Touch 4th generation, iPhone 4, iPhone 4S, and iPad 2. Whatever software you use, you focus on basic principles, not advanced techniques. For a couple of exercises, you many find a digital camera or a cell phone camera helpful.

You don't need anything more to work through *Make Film History* For that matter, you don't need more to make engaging movies. "You can basically edit, color, mix and score an entire film on a laptop computer," says Scott Franklin, who produced *Black Swan* (2010). In 1995, filmmaker David Lynch made a continuous take, fifty-five second movie, *Premonition Following an Evil Deed*, employing nothing but the hand-cranked camera the Lumière brothers used to shoot their first movie in 1895. You need an inquisitive mind, a curiosity about how movies evolved, and a willingness to experiment with things. The one essential need is a love of the movies.

3. **What this book explains about movies.**

If you think of the history of movies as itself a movie, *Make Film History* is a series of freeze frames from the film. We advance the projector, speed through the reel, then stop at turning points when something especially crucial happened: How motion stirred in still pictures. How sound came into movies. How editors learned to structure action. How the voice-over turned movies into Möbius strips that, ever twisting, turn outward while turning inward. This book focuses on turning points in the history of movies.

4. **How to use this book as a text for a class in movie history or movie viewing.**

Working with peers or a teacher brings other eyes and ears to your movies, and the sharing process demonstrates how most filmmakers collaborate. With friends, with peers, or in a class with a teacher, you can collaborate in numerous ways. You can save an exercise—finished, unfinished, or somewhere in between—on a web-based file sharing service (such as Dropbox) where everyone in the group accesses it. There everyone can change it, or complete it in stages. Create alternate versions. Create a single master file that everyone, in sequence, changes. Give everyone a time period—say, twenty minutes—to ring a change, add a feature or a title or a sound. Run a "virtual" film festival there, awarding prizes. Review. Talk about everybody's movie. Redo. Discuss. Redo the redo. One movie grows out of another.

You can create a private YouTube channel for all members of the group. You can set up a group blog, a Facebook page, or a Google+ circle for posting video exercises and exchanging feed-back comments. You can mix and match all of the above.

5. **How to use this book as a self-paced guide to the history of movies and to moviemaking.**

Proceed at a pace that suits you. Read the text. Nothing requires weekly meeting in a room. Try the "You Did It Then" exercises. Then move on to "You Do It Now" exercises, shooting original footage with your point-and-shoot or your DSLR camera. Post your work to YouTube or Vimeo or anywhere videophiles gather. Join a group. Share, upload, and comment. Create your own group. If you do eventually feel the desire to work intensively with others, hundreds of schools, colleges, and educational programs offer programs in film making or courses in appreciating movies, both of which *Make Film History* teaches you.

You can create your own exercises even without shooting a foot. You can mashup public domain movie footage available, among other places, at the Internet Archive (www.archive.org).

The Internet Archive moving image library now contains 680,000 items, including 4,900 full length and short feature movies. Footage for your next filmmaking exercise may be in there some-where. No one's home in the house of alone anymore.

I wrote this book to inspire you to find your inner filmmaker. You can reach me at robert@makefilmhistory.com.

Robert Gerst
Boston
August 5, 2012

❶

INTERMITTENCY:
Eadweard Muybridge (1872)

The path from photography to motion pictures in the nineteenth century may now seem obvious, but cul-de-sacs, dead ends, and byways obscured the way. Artists, businessmen, scientists, and magicians inched towards something they sensed but could not name, often using old tools in new ways. Cardiologist and physiologist Étienne-Jules Marey used a photographic gun that spun a photosensitive disk to record sequential events on a single plate. So did Ottomar Anschütz in Germany. Thomas Eakins, a Philadelphia painter, traced photographs to canvases, anticipating what Max Fleischer in 1915 dubbed the "rotoscope." Photographers like William Mumler in Boston, Frederick Hudson in London, and Édouard Isodore Buguet in Paris purported to photograph "energy fields" and record ghosts to hoodwink credulous spiritualists in the late nineteenth century. Created for various purposes, their images are accidentally poetic, as suggestive as figures on an ancient Greek amphora, but they did not lead directly to movies.

Few photographers sensed the greater magic—that flights of projected photographs compounded in darkness could constitute an entirely new time-based art. Most nineteenth-century progenitors of movies had little idea that they were incubating a new art. Cramming glass plates coated with wet or dry collodion into their

Étienne-Jules Marey in Paris called images like these in the 1880s "chronophotographs." His photographic gun captured motion at 12 frames per second.

cameras, they tinkered with shutter springs and emulsions, hoping to reduce exposure times from minutes to fractions of seconds. They saw photography pragmatically. "Instantaneousness" was their goal—a way to extract splinters of time with a tweezers.

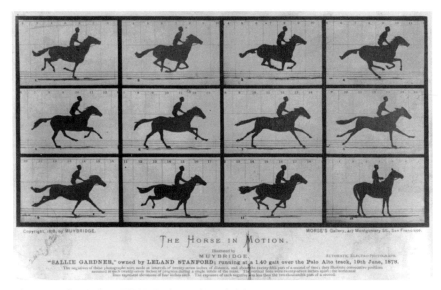

The Horse in Motion (1878). Eadweard Muybridge.

"Photographed by MUYBRIDGE in less than the one-thousandth part of a second, while the horse was trotting at the rate of thirty-six feet per second," the legend says below the drawing. Muybridge's art dealer commissioned this card in 1877. When a fire destroyed the dealer's gallery in 1878, Muybridge lost much of his photographic inventory.

Then in 1872, photographer Eadweard Muybridge devised a way to represent movement as a series of photographs recording successive stages of an action.

It all started with a horse, Occident, then the world's fastest trotting racehorse. Hired by industrialist and horse breeder Leland Stanford to find out whether a trotting horse's hooves ever simultaneously leave the ground, Muybridge set up a bank of cameras along a makeshift racetrack. As Occident successively tripped each shutter, one image Muybridge made in 1877, now lost, settled the question. The answer was "Yes."

If Muybridge first considered himself an anatomist using cameras attached to wires to tease out details of horse physiology by capturing a series of still images, he later saw himself as a showman. Muybridge the showman diverted audiences with a device of his own invention, a kind of projector he called a "zoöpraxiscope." He lectured in packed opera houses to audiences eager to listen, learn, and be entertained. By affixing his zoöpraxiscope to a magic lantern to project serial drawings on a rotating disc, Muybridge the showman created the illusion of movement.

Although numerous others in the 1880s sought, as Muybridge did, to capture time with a camera, their inventions did not lead directly to the movies. The zoöpraxiscope did. Muybridge is a progenitor of movies precisely because he conceived of taking his serial photographs off the page and into the projector, where horses, dancers, and animals of innumerable sort gambol and cavort. He had discovered the fundamental feature of what eventually became the movies. He had discovered how to *project* intermittency. Within the intermittent light of Muybridge's zoöpraxiscope, movies begin.

Intermittency is the essence of the motion picture. A movie is a series of slightly differing still images. When viewed with human eyes, the images seem to stream continuously. Images that change less rapidly than twenty times a second appear distinct to the human eye and may seem to flicker. Changed twenty-four times a second or faster, the images appear to flow seamlessly. Changed seventy-two times a second, they seem entirely free of flicker. The eye endows these intermittently changing similar images with apparitional motion. The brain reads this apparent motion as real. We construct a film as we see it. This may be why movies feel so hallucinatory. We help shape what we perceive.

Muybridge advertised his zoöpraxiscope exhibitions as entertaining but authoritative demonstrations of physiological science. He compared his "accurate" renditions of animals in transit with "erroneous" versions created by earlier artists studying motion only with eyes, not photographs. In his zoöpraxiscope, drawings

made of photos unleash imagination. Muybridge's device was slide-ruler geeky. A glass disc rotated before a magic lantern projector. On another disc, this one metal, slots functioned as shutters. Illustrators painted the glass disc with silhouettes of animals

Zoöpraxiscope glass disc. Muybridge projected not photos but drawings derived from his photos, reasoning that audiences saw them more clearly and preferred them. At the dawn of movies, observation and imagination were twins.

or humans that they traced from Muybridge's photos. When projected through the counter-rotating metal disc shutters, these hand-drawn figures quicken with apparent motion. Muybridge used drawings, not photos, because projection introduced distortion and because drawings, being more visible, appealed more strongly to audiences. American poet Marianne Moore defined poetry as "imaginary gardens with real toads in them." When thought about in Moore's way, the zoöpraxiscope made poetry, initiating the history of animation and realism in film simultaneously.

Paraphernalia for shooting and projecting what we might now call movies then proliferated. (Chicago or New York street people may have slipped the term "movie" into English in 1906 or 1907.) Inventors of shutter mechanisms, looping systems, emulsions, and

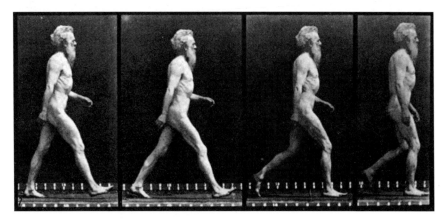

Muybridge secreted this portrait of himself into *Animal Locomotion* (1887), his publication of 20,000 sequential images captured by three banks of cameras rendering quarter turn, profile, and three quarters turn exposures of countless moving subjects. Three plates depict "an ex-athlete, aged about sixty."

cranks filed rival patents, aiming them like pistols at each other. Thomas Edison and Muybridge conferred in 1888 to discuss pairing Muybridge's zoöpraxiscope with Edison's phonograph "to do for the Eye what the phonograph does for the Ear." Judging that he could not synchronize sound and image reliably, Edison ultimately declined Muybridge's proposal and in 1889 filed his intention to secure a patent application for his own silent Kinetoscope exhibition device.

Others started down different paths to challenge Edison. In 1888, Louis Le Prince fed photographic paper film George Eastman had patented into a handmade camera to create what some regard as the world's first movie, *Roundhay Garden Scene*. On the verge of patenting his invention in America, where Edison would soon be contesting all rivals to his own movie inventions, Le Prince mysteriously disappeared from a Paris-bound train September 16, 1890, never to be seen again.

Edison's patented Kinetoscope—his Cyclops—required a half-ton of wing nuts and gears to titillate viewers with peepshows of biceps and butterfly dances. In 1892, a 20-year-old Parisian named Léon Bouly filed a patent for a rival device—a hand-cranked, portable camera Bouly called the cinématographe. When Bouly failed to pay the fee required to maintain his patent, Auguste and Louis Lumière bought his patent for their photographic dry plate-manufacturing firm. In 1894, they converted the cinématographe into a projector as well as a camera, using it to shoot, develop, and project the films they exhibited in their "first" public showing of movies in 1895. Projected movies then slipped into the world like fireflies at dawn, pulsing intermittently.

Above, left; the man views a twenty second Kinetoscope movie in 1895 while he listens, through headphones, to the accompanying phonograph cylinder. Edison called this combination the Kinetophone.

Above, right; Peter Bacigalupi's Kinetoscope Parlor, San Francisco, 1894 or 1895. The sign on the window said, "Kinetoscopes and Phonographs," and legends on the machines said, "Edison's Latest Invention The Kinetoscope." Every other word inside the arcade said, "Edison." Electric bulbs (marketed by Edison) gleamed in the chandelier, and signs on the wall said, "Edison Kinetoscopes and Phonographs for Sale." The brass peacock conveyed, as djinn in a fairy tale might, that what the machines contained was apparitional and splendid.

EXERCISE ONE: INTERMITTENCY

What this exercise teaches:

● **How to create the illusion of motion from a series of still images**

● **How fast images must change to simulate motion**

● **How to create slow motion, normal speed, and time-lapse shots**

● **How the movie you see begins as the movie you imagine**

From *The Photographic News*, March 17, 1882:
"I should like to see your boxing pictures," said the Prince of Wales to Mr. Muybridge on Monday at the Royal Institution, when the galloping horse, the running deer, the trotting bull, the halting pig, and the racing dogs had successively crossed the screen in life-like measure.

"I shall be very happy to show them, your Royal Highness," responded the clever photographer; and promptly there was thrown up on the screen two athletes, who pounded away at one another right merrily, to the infinite delight of the audience in general and the Prince of Wales in particular.

Mr. Muybridge, in this case, had taken rapid successive pictures of a pair of boxers as they assume one fighting position after another, and then these photographs were rapidly thrown on the screen in the same order by means of his zoöpraxiscope. This is a boxing-match reproduced in all its photographic reality. "I don't know that pictures teach us anything useful," said Mr. Muybridge, "but they are generally found amusing."

You Did It Then: **Rediscover intermittency as the matrix of movies by constructing a two-second "movie" out of photographs of boxers that Muybridge published. Motion is the primary "special effect" of the movies. Step by step instructions and the image sequence are in the *Make Film History* digital cutting room: http://makefilmhistory.com.**

You Do It Now: **Shoot an object in motion using the continuous shooting function (burst mode) of your digital camera. From your image sequence create a two-second "movie." Find the frames per second rate that works for your movie.**

PRODUCTION **Make Film History**
DIRECTOR _____
CAMERA _____
DATE   SCENE   TAKE

1

❷
"REALITY":
The Lumières (1896)

The man in the bowler hat has just emerged from a crowd exiting the theater when, unexpectedly, his companion appears. They greet with affection and they walk off together. The frame belongs to a Lumière film running forty-seven seconds that likely soon played inside the theater. The theater—2,000 seats—filled nightly for eighteen consecutive months with people who had never before seen a movie. Imagine these men as the realist and expressionist filmmaker and you perceive with your own eyes the similar but different faces of realist and expressionist filmmaking.

Realism and expressionism are the poles of moviemaking. Realists see the world as a scene in a snow shaker. They view it from outside. They may nudge the shaker to set it undulating, but they never attempt to pry it open for fear of destroying it. Expressionists see the same world from a different perspective—from inside the shaker. They send messages out from the center. Realists depict while expressionists offer witness. Realists see naked what expressionists see nude. Realist and expressionist movies are fraternal but not identical twins. They enable us to see different aspects of the world, as the photo and the x-ray do.

Realist movies and expressionist movies entered history more or

The gentlemen in the foreground of the film frame above seem captured in the act of acknowledging kinship. They are meeting before the Empire Theater in Leicester Square in London during the premiere exhibition of movies there by Auguste and Louis Lumière in 1896.

less simultaneously. On December 28, 1895, Auguste and Louis Lumière, pioneer film realists, exhibited a program of short movies, the first commercial showing of a film in France. The first of the

-7-

films they projected depicted workers—women in aprons, men in hats, bicycle riders, dogs that gamboled—exiting the Lumière factory in Lyon. The projectionist intentionally paused at the initial frame, and then cranked the movie forward to its conclusion. The transformation of a moment of stillness into 55 seconds of motion conveyed the essence of films—motion transfuses illusory life into images. What moves seems to live.

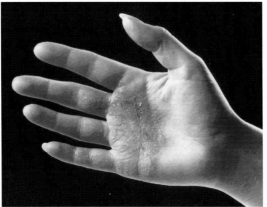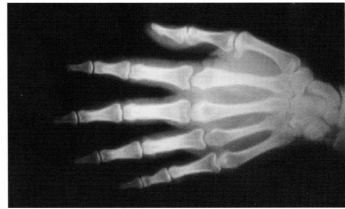

The dermatologist's photograph, left, documents an epidermal condition. The radiologist's x-ray, right, reveals the hand's metacarpal and phalanx bones. Where the realist documents surfaces, the expressionist looks inward. Each method can inform. The truth of the photo does not dispute the truth of the x-ray. The realist gaze and the expressionist vision are reciprocal versions of each other.

Among the Parisians in the audience was Georges Méliès, a stage magician who thereafter put the movie camera to a different use—to visualize phantasms in dreamlike expressionist movies. December 28, 1895, when the Lumières first showed their movies to a Parisian audience, was also the day Wilhelm Röntgen in Vienna published a report of his discovery of x-ray. We can think of the x-ray as a photographic process akin to expressionism in its attention to interior structure rather than visible surface. Realists and expressionists moved film art down parallel but different paths—realism, towards the freedom from distortion that nineteenth century photographers so often coveted; expressionism, towards the vision-in-depth offered by the x-ray. Which mode of sight seems superior depends on what your mind needs to see.

Consider the first-born twin, realism. Realist filmmakers fanned out from cities in Europe and America in the last days of the nineteenth century carting the camera invented or refined by Auguste and Louis Lumière. From Saigon, Egypt, and Lyon they documented, sent back, and preserved forever the transient reality of pagodas, railroads, parades. Of 2,113 items in the Lumière catalogue listing cinématographe movies available for sale in 1903, Auguste or Louis Lumière themselves shot just 50. Itinerant Lumière employees created the vast majority. Their movies ran for forty seconds, slightly longer than a sigh. A few were comedies—some contrived; some acted in makeshift studios—but mostly Lumière cameramen recorded the world unstaged. To machinists in Grenoble and farmers in Saskatoon, these filmmakers sought to bring back evidence of the "real."

What the early realists and their audience meant then by "real" varied. "Reality" is a steamer trunk word missing a label. We probably understand it differently than film viewers did in 1902 when, for instance, Enrico Caruso recorded operatic arias by bellowing them into funnels leading to a stylus. Those recordings strike most living now as acoustically distorted. But in 1909 New York schoolteachers regarded them as transcendently real, angelic enough to

Realists may seem guileless, but they, too, suffuse their images with a purpose. Cameraman Félix Mesguich shot cinématographe footage in America, western Europe, Russia, and Asia, first for the Lumières between 1896 and 1898 and then for other firms. In North Africa, he said, he sought to capture "the divine atmosphere of the captivating and mysterious" Sahara. This frame appears in a Lumière cinématographe, but Lumière records do not identify the cinematographer.

wean children "away from moving picture evils to all good music." Early reviewers of Lumière films regarded the background rustling of leaves and the tread of horses down a street as wondrous. Auguste and Louis Lumière advertised the films they first screened in 1895 for a paying audience as "actualités," meaning, more or less, "that which is." In the view of many first viewing them, eternity moved in the transient wings of these movies. "You'll see people and things as they are," *The New York World* testified about a movie by Woodville Latham in 1895. But most of us now perceive them otherwise, our context being very different. You see only what your experience enables you to see.

Consider *L'arrivée d'un train à La Ciotat,* renowned as the first masterpiece of film realism. Louis Lumière shot it the summer of 1897 and exhibited it in Lyons on October 10, 1897. When he showed it that night the film had no name. (Movies first bore titles in 1902.) The film records a train pulling into a station. Films like this allegedly frightened early viewers out of their seats, but modern viewers often wonder, "That's it?"

Arriving from screen right, a train approaches the train station at La Ciotat, the seaside town near Marseilles where, among palms and statues, the Lumières maintained a Tuscan style family-compound villa. Without a pan, tilt, or dolly, the cinématographe records the incident. The action is elemental. A porter dragging a luggage cart enters the frame and quits it. The train approaches on a diagonal that renders the action dynamically. Hundreds of subsequent films have represented an arriving train from exactly this perspective. Doors swing open when the train stops. Waiting passengers include the mother and wives of Auguste and Louis Lumière and Louis's daughter, niece and nephew. The women and children, intending to board, thread their way through men getting off. Abruptly, the shot breaks off. Writing in colonial Vietnam in 1899, an anonymous journalist perceived all provincial France in this 50-second titrate of reality:

> **The arrival of a train, classic tableau that we all hold in memory and that reminds us of the country; travelers pale enough to be sea-sick; we do not recognize individuals but familiar types; the little maid, the butcher boy, the young man looking for work and leaving his village with his bundle of clothes; maybe he has come to look for his fortune in Tonkin, the awkward movements of the children perfectly rendered.**

L'arrivée d'un train à La Ciotat is, however, the second time Louis Lumière depicted this scene, not the first. The previous year he had filmed a similar but different train dropping off passengers at La Ciotat, and in 1935 he returned there again, this time using a stereoscopic camera of his own invention to document an arriving train. There may have never been a director satisfied with just one take. In *L'arrivée d'un train à La Ciotat* Louis Lumière believed he was depicting unmanipulated reality, but reality diffuses, spreading like watercolor pigment through a glass of water, taking uncountable shapes.

In the first version of the arrival, the train pulls up a little further down the platform, which this time swarms with men. Among them

L'arrivée en gare d'un train à La Ciotat (1896), dir. Louis Lumière. **The man in the deerstalker cap exits from his compartment.**

is a traveler sporting the tweeds and deerstalker cap of Sherlock Holmes. (This classic tableau is repeated time after time in film history. Seven years later, 1902, in *The Great Train Robbery* an identical looking man in tweeds and deerstalker cap exits from another passenger train coach. Another similarly disembarks from a steam ship docking in Constantinople half a century later in the *Earrings of Madame de....*) The disembarking traveler seems to embody enigma, ever ready to walk across the platform of reality. The door separating imagination from reality is never locked.

Realism can travel perfectly happily with imagination: comings and goings on a train platform can seem banalities or intimations of the spiritual, depending on how a filmmaker renders them. Once Louis Lumière set up his cinématographe beside the rails, the arrival of a train at a train station became a turn-of-the-century film staple and a commonplace of a century of movies—the train platform as portal to the soul. See in *Casablanca* (1942) Rick squeezing Ilsa's rain-spattered letter between his hands on a train platform in Paris, or, in waltz-time, the rush of the Orient Express from the platform like a grand dame gathering her petticoats in *Murder on the Orient Express* (1974). The

Harry Potter and the Sorcerer's Stone (2001), dir. Chris Columbus.
"All you've got to do is walk straight at the wall between platforms nine and ten."

motif persists today. In *Harry Potter and The Sorcerer's Stone* (2001), Harry awaits the train to the magical Hogwarts School of Witchcraft and Wizardry at London's King's Cross Station. It arrives at the secret Platform 9¾. Even the primitive realism of *L'arrivée d'un train en gare de La Ciotat* expresses visions and inspires dreams.

No single feature of a movie determines what is realistic since "realism" is a set of ideas about movies that have changed over time. As early as 1901, a time-lapse movie by American Mutoscope and Biograph showing the demolition and apparent resurrection of a theater in Manhattan turns a realistic record into an act of imagination. By 1908, Pathé newsreels running eight minutes showed horse-drawn sleds crisscrossing Moscow streets. In the wake of

the Second World War, the Italian neo-Realist filmmaker Cesare Zavattini defined realism in movies as movies showing real people doing real things. Zavattini derided as "fakery" the competently crafted but studio-bound films of the Italian 1930s. In the 1960s, Bernardo Bertolucci, speaking like an expressionist, reversed Zavattini. "Realism does not consist in reproducing reality, but in showing how things really are," Bertolucci maintained, quoting playwright Bertolt Brecht.

The Lumières saw themselves as rational investigators, chemists who made products and happened to produce movies. The Lumière firm sold 15 million dry photographic plates in 1895, the year before the Lumières entered movie exhibition as a sideline business. (In 1921, Auguste Lumière wrote a monograph, *The Role of*

Pescadero Pebble Beach (1871) Stereoscopic image. Eadweard Muybridge.

Colloids in Living Things.) At least at first, the Lumières envisioned the cinématographe as a tool for geographers and physicians.

L'arrivée d'un train en gare de La Ciotat shows the realist preference for clarity over suggestion, for holding a mirror up to the world, for "nature caught in the act." Location shooting, non-professional performances rendered in authentic clothing rather than by professional actors in costumes contribute to what movie lovers generally mean when they call a movie "realistic." Narrative running from start to finish with little diversion of sequence and time, minimal transformation of the image shot by the camera, minimal reliance on thematic montage and attention-getting shot-to-shot transitions contribute to what movie lovers generally mean when they call a movie "realistic." Tracks of synchronous sound mixed simply rather than multi-layered mood-transforming constructions and characters who seem to emanate from the street, not the inkwell, all contribute to what movie lovers generally mean when they call a movie "realistic."

But "realism" is finally an act of assessment. Viewers gazing at stereograms through stereoscopic viewer images "saw" in three dimensions because the brain interprets the slightly offset images as the perspective of the left eye and right eye respectively. The images are almost exactly identical, but the eye perceives and the mind resolves the difference. Movie realists like Auguste and Louis Lumière and movie expressionists (like Georges Méliès) initiated that kind of tension at the dawn of the twentieth century. They continue to do so today. Reality is a costume imagination wears.

EXERCISE TWO: FILM REALISM

What this exercise teaches:

- **How to adjust film clip exposure, brightness, contrast, and saturation levels**

- **How to use and layer sounds**

- **How to create a plausibly "real" moment that never existed**

- **How much can be evoked within the limits of film "realism"**

Louis and Auguste Lumière hustled you off to the Nile with a cinématographe in 1897 to capture street scenes, pyramids, and railroad trains. You already have filmed one train arriving (in Ramla) and three departing (from Cairo, Benha, and Toukh), and now you are making your way south, past the falls of the White Nile into Mahdist Sudan. You are Alexandre Promio, luxury-loving Lumière *opérateur*. Crank your cinématographe. Pans, tilts, and dollies are forbidden.

You Did It Then: Evolve the realist film of the Lumière era into something approaching contemporary realism. Use one shot to depict a train approaching a station. Overlaying sound, adjusting lighting, and reversing action (tools unavailable to the Lumières), build your shot into a movie suggesting the passage of time. Using no more footage than the single shot, evoke a mood. Step by step instructions and the shot to use are in the *Make Film History* digital cutting room: http://makefilmhistory.com.

The word "fact" derives from the Latin word for action, "factum." Facts, the language tell us, are not what we find in the world. They are what we do.

You Do It Now: To the "movie" you created using the burst mode shots of your digital camera, now add sound, modify exposure, contrast, and other effects of your choosing. Suggest with these new elements the passing of time.

PRODUCTION **Make Film History**
DIRECTOR _____
CAMERA _____
DATE   SCENE   TAKE

2

❸

IMAGINATION:
Georges Méliès (1896)

The first expressionist of the movies, Georges Méliès, was the third son of a self-made Paris manufacturer of elegant footwear. In 1884, he fled the footwear business to perfect his English in London, where he fell under the spell of stage illusionists Maskelyne and Cooke. When his father retired in 1886, Méliès sold his stock in the firm to his elder brothers and used the proceeds to purchase the Robert Houdin Theater, then the leading Paris stage magic venue. In plumes of steam, extricating rabbits from hats, he there began his transformation from manufacturer to magus.

What Méliès began on stage as magician he continued on the screen: a new kind of seeing—the movie not of sight but of inner vision. Where the films of the Lumières showed railroad platforms and elephants in procession, the films of Georges Méliès looked into dreamland, suggesting the spiritualist séance and the worldview of Sigmund Freud. Méliès and Freud were actually mining similar veins. By 1899 Freud was proposing in *Interpretation of Dreams* that dreams manifest distorted and disguised unconscious wishes; that same year Méliès was shooting *Cinderella* and 43 other works of dream-like fantasy. Méliès's movies lead, through many intermediate stages, to the digital special effects of contemporary cinema.

Four Hundred Tricks of the Devil (1906), dir. Georges Méliès. The man in the middle, surrounded by imps, is Georges Méliès.

Méliès was smitten by the movies at the Lumières' first screening at the *Salon Indien du Grand Café*, and he offered to purchase a ciné-matographe on the spot. Since the Lumières planned to operate cinématographes and never sell one, Antoine Lumière, father of Auguste and Louis, rejected Méliès' offer. He informed Méliès

20,000 Leagues Under the Sea (1907), dir. Georges Méliès. As much the octopus (right) as the bearded face behind the propeller (left), Méliès pervades every aspect of his movies. He directed, acted, and painted sets for almost all of them. Only fragments of this movie remain.

that movies would soon fizzle, according to Méliès. (The Lumières rethought the commercial viability of movies by 1897, when they offered a catalog of 1,619 cinematographic "actualités" for sale to exhibitors.) Rebuffed, Méliès purchased a 35 mm Theatrograph projector in London from Robert Paul, an inventor and film pioneer. Méliès nicknamed his device "the machine gun" in recognition of its explosively sputtering shutter, and he set about to try his hand at modifying it for moviemaking.

Several months later in 1896, Méliès stood on a traffic island in the *Place de l'Opéra* extricating film from the gears of his handmade

motion picture camera. The camera held 65 feet of film, but Méliès had mismeasured the distance required to separate the sprocket holes he had hand-punched along the edge of unexposed Eastman film stock. A dexterous tinkerer, Méliès fixed the jam in a moment and resumed shooting without a change of angle. But when he developed and then spliced together the frayed ends of exposed negative, the scene had altered. Two minutes of action was missing. The change was startling. At the splice, men turned, mid-stride, into women. The Madeleine-Bastille carriage proceeded down the street, transformed abruptly into a horse-drawn hearse. From this

Place de L'Opéra, Paris. (1895).

From simple stop-action shots, he moved rapidly to double exposures, action reversals, superimposition, miniatures, false perspectives, dwarfs, and moving backdrops. These movies show actions created by the camera recording them. They put perception in the service of imagination. They look inward, turning what we might dream into what we might see.

Méliès might be the original film impresario. With family members, he started up Star Films in 1896, the first commercial entity focused exclusively on producing movies—movies as legion as his love affairs. Star released a total of 503 films; Méliès starred in most of them. Scenarist, producer, actor, in the morning he painted gray backdrops at his suburban Montreuil-sous-Bois studio. Afternoons, he acted out his stories before the camera. Evenings started with invoicing clients and shipping prints. He wholesaled *A Trip to the Moon* prints in 1902 for roughly $155; for hand-colored prints he asked double. Then he rushed next door to the Théâtre Robert Houdin to supervise the nightly magic show. He exported his movies to the fairgrounds and eventually the nickelodeons of the world. The Star logo proclaimed his artistic mission: "The Whole World Within Reach."

accident, Méliès asserted in 1907, he conceived the stop-action photography that became the heart of his theater of the magical.

Méliès' first intentionally distorted film was *Escamontage d'une Dame Chez Robert-Houdin* (*The Vanishing Lady*, 1896). First draping his assistant Jeanne d'Alcy with a cloth, he stopped the action and replaced d'Alcy with a skeleton. When he lifted the cloth, he "discovered" the skeleton. His conceit is obvious: within and beneath the visible lies another reality. *Escamontage* was the initial iteration of Méliès's favorite theme—the illusion of "reality."

Like leitmotifs in opera—Méliès adored the operas of Jacques Offenbach—certain features recur in Méliès films. A bounding, dancing, pointing, gesticulating character scurries through many. Méliès played that man, and *was* him. He cast himself as a magus in countless films and as Mephistopheles in twenty-three. Characters

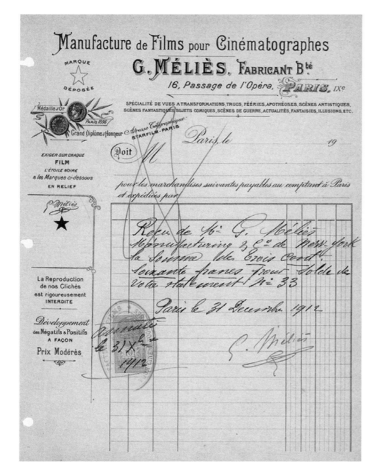

"We specialize in transformations, fairy tales, manifestations of gods, artistic scenes, fantastic comic subjects, war scenes, news clips, and fantasies," the Méliès Star Films receipt form (above) stated in 1912. In this year-end transaction, Méliès in Paris issues a receipt for 360 francs worth of sales to his brother, Gaston, representing Star Films in New York. A sidebar message declares, "Reproduction of our negatives is strictly forbidden."

Transferring these funds to his brother, the equivalent of $70 in 1912, Méliès might have felt particular emotion. On behalf of Star Films, he filed for bankruptcy in 1913, ending his filmmaking career.

divide, multiply, rise and fall through the agency of multiple exposures, stop-action photography, hoods black as backdrops, and trap doors. Stars and extraterrestrials of various sorts rise or divide on backdrops hand-painted by Méliès and his assistants.

Méliès films distill that moment at the end of the nineteenth century when science looking out enabled art to look in. They portend the paintings of Henri Rousseau and Marc Chagall. They ventilate dreams of theory-spinning *fin de siècle* scientists—Percival Lowell's 1895 argument for extraterrestrial canals on Mars, for instance, and his argument for individual imagination as the engine of human progress. They recall the stagecraft of nineteenth-century French opera-ballets, called *féerie*. Méliès' films are haiku, not novels. The shortest ran little more than 45 seconds. Few ran longer than 12 minutes. Colorists wielding sable brushes hand-painted many Méliès films. Projected roughly 16 frames per second, a film of three minutes could be, in essence, 2,880 paintings executed serially on rectangles one and three eighths inches wide by one inch. In these films, the camera never moves. From a central seat where Aristotle's unmoved mover might sit, the viewer sees all.

Beneath caricatures he drew in 1889, Méliès signed not his name but the English word, "Smile." Nearly an anagram, the name change expresses the joy pervading his movies. Some Méliès movies suggest the Paris of Toulouse-Lautrec; some, fairies on dewdrops. Many featured fairy tales, and most, magic; some, actualités, others docudramas, advertisements, even turn-of-the-century peep shows. All exemplify Méliès' impulse to reconstruct the world he felt rather than the surface of the world outwardly seen.

For Méliès, magic was a star that shone just once. Movies like *Voyage to the Moon* (1902) won plaudits. But circulating prints were largely counterfeit. His movies earned him less than he anticipated. His printed invoice hissed at would-be dupers—"Reproduction of our negatives is strictly forbidden"—but a French magician's threats were risible. American courts issued contradictory rulings on protection for foreign books and films even after legislators revised copyright law in 1909. That year, when American and European filmmakers acceded to Edison's Motion Picture Patents Company diktat establishing an international standard film gauge (Edison's) and a rental revenue model (also Edison's), Gaston Méliès, Georges Méliès's brother and producer in America, turned his hand to shooting Méliès Star-Films cowboy movies, attempting to revive the firm. He shot westerns first in a studio in Brooklyn, then Texas and California. Then he traveled further west to catastrophe. When he sailed off in 1912 to the South Seas, freighting his pedestrian oeuvre with the signature, "G. Méliès," the tropical climate destroyed most of his negatives.

By then, Méliès was in debt to Pathé Frères, the Parisian movie equipment manufacturer, film exhibitor, and producer. Audiences for his films had vanished. Imitated and pirated, fantasy films were old hat. Méliès gave up film production in 1913. In 1923, then a forgotten bankrupt man facing eviction, he incinerated such negatives as he still possessed, perhaps including the original stop-action splice of footage that had jammed outside the Paris Opera House. From 1925 to 1932 he pedaled toys and candy in a Paris railroad station kiosk operated by his second wife, Jeanne d'Alcy, the assistant he had transformed into bones in his first magical movie. Freud died in 1939 and Méliès in 1938. They were companions in dreamland who passed through life without recognizing each other. Freud detested movies. Freud sought to understand unconscious experience. Méliès sought to free it.

The central ideas of Georges Méliès were the metronome of his movies. He had no interest in reportage—you can view all his films without ever encountering, for instance, the slightest note of the sudden spike in leather prices at the dawn of the twentieth century that bankrupted the Méliès family footwear firm. Méliès shows not market forces but maguses, goddesses, and demons raveling and unraveling the world. Even his "realist" films abound in fantasy: his "underwater documentary" of the USS Maine sunk in Havana harbor records, literally, a toy boat submerged in a fish bowl.

Poets sometimes speak of "pure poetry," meaning a lyrical arrangement of words that is translatable into no other language because in no language but the original do the sound of the verse and sense of the verse identically coalesce. "Fuzzy Wuzzy was a Bear/Fuzzy Wuzzy had no hair/Fuzzy Wuzzy wasn't fuzzy, was he?" is pure poetry. It could mean nothing in a language other

At this kiosk (above) run by Jeanne d'Alcy, his former assistant and second wife, the editor of a French film journal rediscovered Méliès in 1929. In *Hugo* (2011), director Martin Scorsese treats this phase of Méliès' life—in 3D. Scorsese slips himself into Hugo as a photographer (below).
Film restorer Serge Bromberg similarly created 3-D versions of two 1903 Méliès movies in 2010. Synchronizing French and American versions of *The Infernal Boiling Pot* and *The Oracle of Delphi* (each shot with a pair of adjacent cameras operating simultaneously), Bromberg put Méliès into 3D.

than English. Méliès's movies are the "pure poetry" of film. They could not exist, except by operation of a motion picture camera. Of the movie camera's defects Méliès made virtues. In its stuttering and starting he discovered phantasms, especially those he himself played.

Virtually every successive expressionist filmmaker learned from Méliès. The seven hundred double exposed sketches of Emil Cohl's first movie—*Fantasmagorie* (1908)—derive from Méliès double exposures and announce the birth of animation. Méliès's magic passed through double exposures of Mary Pickford playing two roles in *Stella Maris* (1918) and to the cantilevering sets of *The Cabinet Of Dr. Caligari* (1920). His movies prefigure the films of the 1920s and 1930s German abstract expressionist filmmakers like Walter Ruttmann and Oscar Fischinger and countless others who followed. His dancers foreshadow the geometrics of the white piano Busby Berkeley musicals of the 1930s. Méliès anticipated contemporary technology. His stop-action effects lead to the morphs, chroma keys, and CGIs of *Adaptation* (2002) and the 3D CGI effects of *Avatar* (2009).

On the first of each year during the 1960s, Henri Langlois, spiritual father of the French New Wave, would extract from archives at the Cinémathèque Française one original nitrate print of a Méliès movie to screen privately for employees. They were "pure movies," he said. They trace in light what angels might see.

Fantasmagorie (1908), dir. Émile Cohl.

The Cabinet of Dr. Caligari (1920), dir. Robert Wiene.

Stella Maris (1918), dir. Marshall Neilan.

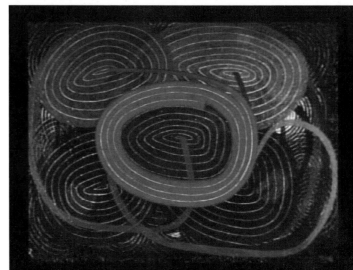

Motion Painting No. 1 (1947), dir. Oscar Fischinger.

Gold Diggers of 1937 (1936), dance numbers by Busby Berkeley.

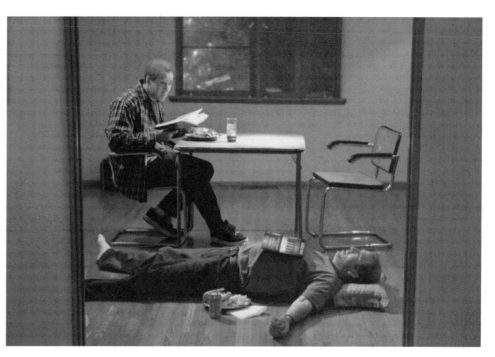

Adaptation (2002), dir. Spike Jonze.

EXERCISE THREE: IMAGINATION

What this exercise teaches:

● **How to create illusion with stop action, superimposition, and matte shooting**

● **How Méliès made movies out of impossible actions**

● **How "special effects" are as old as the movies**

The French army melted down numerous Méliès negatives during World War One to use as feeder stock for military boot heels, and Méliès himself destroyed others in 1923. 379 of the 552 movies Méliès created are lost, and those not lost often descend from release prints or pirated films. Méliès movies, long thought lost, continue to reappear and vanish: film restorers erroneously believed they had discovered *Cléopâtre* (1899) among Méliès movie prints inside an auctioned chest of drawers.

Imagine this: In the back of a breakfront in the Chateau d'Orly near Paris, where Méliès died in a retirement home among faded stars of the French film industry, you have just discovered a canister the size of a hockey puck. A phrase is written in ink on the canister: 1897: *Le Coeur d'un Homme* (The Heart of a Man). Opening it, you discover exposed but unedited lengths of 35 mm film showing a man in cutaways. You hold the shots to your eye and discern what Méliès must have intended to have happen: a man is releasing a menagerie of flying beasts from a canister that could not possibly contain them.

You Did It Then: **Finish what Georges Méliès started. From this footage—at long last—make the "lost" Méliès movie, *Le Coeur d'un Homme*. Step-by-step instructions and shots you can use to channel your inner Georges Méliès are in the digital cutting room at http://makefilmhistory.com.**

You Do It Now: **Return to the burst mode images you created in the first exercise. Do something different with them. Unleash your imagination. Zoom in? Animate them? Turn them into pictures within pictures? Double or triple expose them? Try absolutely anything.**

CUTTING TO CONTINUITY:
Edwin S. Porter (1903)

"The future had no end."
Bronco Billy Anderson

To edit a film to continuity is to flow action continuously through successive shots, linking those shots meaningfully in time, trimming each back to essential action. This way of handling action is the glue stick of movies, the film editor's commonest tool.

Compared to more conspicuous showings of the editor's ability to build a world out of film clips—for instance, "classical cutting" and "thematic montage"—cutting-to-continuity is Plain Jane slicing carrots in the kitchen. But Plain Jane is essential. Cutting-to-continuity, an editor trims away footage that seems unnecessary, links trimmed action shots into scenes, and assembles scenes. Cutting to continuity lends velocity to action by streamlining it. Action cut to continuity gains complexity and takes on significance. Cutting-to-continuity, an editor condenses, but unobtrusively. In four shots, she pushes her hero from start to finish of a marathon. In seven shots, she disintegrates his marriage. In three, she reunites him with his long-lost love. Cutting-to-continuity turns footage into action.

"Match cutting" is continuity cutting that transpires at the level of the film frame. Match cutting joins shots of an action at that frame

The Great Train Robbery (1903), dir. Edwin S. Porter.

in each shot where the action has identically advanced. If cutting-to-continuity builds scenes, match cutting makes them seem to flow. We scarcely recognize these related cutting room actions as the feats of imagination they are. They are the invisible stitching of

This sequence from *Murder On the Orient Express* (1974), dir. Sidney Lumet, treats a train's departure in five cut-to-continuity shots. Cutting-to-continuity lends cadence and drama to a commonplace event. It can expand but more often contracts time.

Spider-Man 2 (2004), dir. Sam Raimi.

Right arm down and left arm akimbo in both shots, Spiderman looks towards screen left where he stares down the gunman. We are closer to Spiderman in the second shot, and camera angle and depth of field differ, but we perceive Spiderman's action as continuous because the editor has joined the shots where the action is identically advanced in both. This is match cutting.

9192—Gold Miners and Packers on Dyea Trial, Alaska.

"Four masked men last night held up the watchman of the Featherstonhaugh mines in Atlin, Alaska, and stole nearly $20,000 worth of gold dust... The watchman was caught from behind, pinioned and gagged, and in 20 minutes the big clean-up was in canvas sacks which the robbers brought. They fled in darkness."

New London (Connecticut) *Day*, August 26, 1903

movies. But someone did first try these techniques and saw that they were good—quite possibly, that someone was Edwin S. Porter.

In 1903, Edwin Porter labored at a workbench at Thomas Edison's new film studio in Manhattan. At that time, America abounded with rotund men sporting pocket watches striding forth into a world they felt destined to remake. Miners combed the Klondike searching for mother lodes. President Teddy Roosevelt was debating whether to set off an expedition to confirm the existence of a monster amphibian reputedly "swimming in the waters of a Southern Andean lake." Enrico Caruso was premiering in *Rigoletto* at the Met. Edwin Porter was another of these people. He was short, stooped, stout, a mechanically inclined former projectionist who downplayed his inventiveness and hid his imagination behind a walrus mustache.

But Porter taught himself the essence of film editing: less is more. In *A Grammar of the Film: An Analysis of Film Technique* (1935), film director/producer Raymond Spottiswoode dubs this essence the practice of "cutting at the peak of the content curve." A shot in a film, Spottiswoode meant, should run as long as it takes an audience to absorb it, and no longer. Duration must match complexity. Assembling *The Great Train Robbery* (1903), Porter groped his way to this understanding. The result continues to engage most viewers now as a genuine 13-shot movie, albeit an archaic one. Characters race with energy and purpose through scenes that change. Action flows across the splices.

Before he joined Edison Manufacturing, Porter's dexterous hands had led him first into work as a telegraph operator, then as an electrician, then most consequentially for the history of the movies, as an itinerant film projectionist. He operated the Vitascope projector at Koster and Bial's Music Hall in 1896 the night Edison finagled the first commercial showing in America of projected movies—dancers, surf on a beach, a comedy boxing match, eight marching band musicians and a conductor from a Broadway revue, and a skirt dance, all half life-size on a screen "framed like a picture." *The New York Times* took note of the exhibition, describing "two precious young blonde persons of the variety stage, in pink and blue dresses, doing the umbrella dance," adding that "long before this extraordinary exhibition was finished... vociferous cheering was heard."

In 1896, Porter purchased a Vitascope projector from Edison and set off on his own from a foothold in Costa Rica. He and a business partner barnstormed the West Indies for three years, showing Edison movies. Projecting movies in the Caribbean may have served as a film school where Porter learned what to cut by observing where audiences fidgeted. He exhibited the Edison movies under the assumed name of "Thomas Edison, Jr." It was simple to advance claims then regarding an Edison picture. Edison permitted no credits except those identifying the films as Edison movies, and the Motion Picture Patents Company he established in 1908 with other producers to control the world film industry forbade the practice. Not until Carl Lemmle's *The Broken Oath*

(1910) would an actor—Florence Lawrence—have her name affixed to a movie. When Porter returned to New York in 1899, Edison rehired him to turn out product serviceable to vaudeville theater managers who, by 1900, punctuated their stage shows with movies. Between 1899 and 1910, when Porter eventually set up a rival production company, Porter directed 136 movies for Edison.

In most movies he created in 1902-1903, Porter imitated others, sometimes slavishly. Trick photography and comic costumes, not cut-to-continuity action, are the major interest in his imitation of Méliès, *Jack and the Beanstalk* (1902). In *Life of an American Fireman* (1903), Porter recreated James Williamson's *Life of a London Fireman* (1901). There he succeeded in telling a story but handled action on a ladder awkwardly, entirely repeating in an exterior shot a rescue he had already fully depicted in a previous interior shot.

In *The Great Train Robbery*, however, Porter got continuity and virtually everything else closer to right. The movie inspired an industry. Across America, entrepreneurs opened thousands of nickelodeons to exhibit it. By 1909, more than one hundred thousand ushers, piano players, drummers, and men tending projectors and their assistants were earning livings screening movies. "Nearly every other person in the United States" attended a movie show each week, *The New York Times* reported in 1909. More than any other picture, *The Great Train Robbery* ignited that fervor for movies.

This melodrama written for the stage in 1896 by Scott Marble, *The Great Train Robbery*, inspired the movie.

Europeans like Méliès assumed movies are works of art created by artists. Americans such as Porter saw them as products. The title card asserting Edison's copyright for *The Great Train Robbery* ignores Porter, who wouldn't have dreamed of claiming a credit. He was small-town America. His work cranking movies in dim beer halls would have taught Porter how to pace, crosscut, and shape the movie. In *The Great Train Robbery*, he set out to tell to beer hall audiences a then-popular story.

Porter was uncertain of his creation until he test-marketed it. He screened it first at Huber's Museum—in 1903, a Manhattan dime museum for the gullible, "home of the bottled snakes, the stuffed

lizards, of the fat women, and of Bosco, who ate them alive…" *The New York Times* remembered when it closed in 1910. Then Porter brought *The Great Train Robbery* to the similarly down-market Eden Musée, a Madame Tussaud Waxworks-style emporium in Manhattan that had formerly employed him as projectionist. Max H. Aronson (later famous as Bronco Billy Anderson, silent movie cowboy star) played a bandit, a dude, and a passenger in *The Great Train Robbery*, and described the Eden Musée preview:

The audience didn't seem to take to the idea very much, and then it started. They all started to get boisterous, and yell and shout 'Catch 'em! Catch 'em!' and different kinds of epithets, you know. When the picture was over, they all stood up and yelled and shouted 'Run it again, run it again.' So they did run it again, and then they wanted to run it again. Finally they turned on the lights and they had to put them out. And then on the outside there was a big gathering, that had got wind of it all, ready to come in again. I think they ran it for a couple of days. They then ran it to get the reaction of a better class of audience up at Hammerstein's at 42nd and Broadway. That was a vaudeville house. I was a little dubious about how it was going to go with that audience. When the picture started they all started to get up as usual and walk out, but then turned back to look at it, and they all, slowly, as the picture went on, went back to their seats. And they sat there, stupefied. They didn't yell, but they were mystified at it. And when it was over, with one accord they gave it a rousing reception. I said to myself then, 'That's it. It's going to be the picture business for me.' The future had no end.

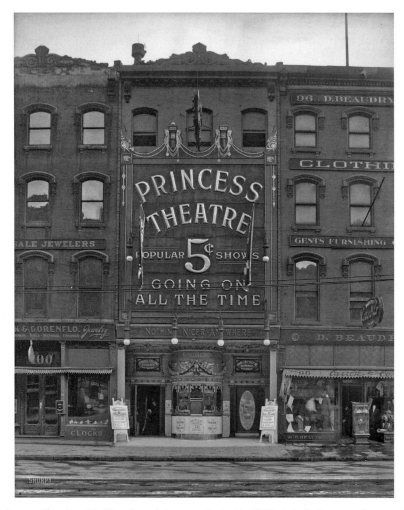

Princess Theater, 98 Woodward Avenue, Detroit, 1909. Admission was five cents. The show played continuously. "Nothing nicer anywhere," the sign proclaimed. On exhibit that day were two Vitagraph films, one Pathé fantasy, and a singer singing two ballads.

Harry Davis had opened the world's first nickelodeon in Pittsburgh in 1905. Four hundred fifty patrons showed up the first day to view *The Great Train Robbery*.

The story that *The Great Train Robbery* relates is elemental—robbers strike and are apprehended. But the storytelling is complex. From his story (what happens) Porter built a plot (how the storyteller structures the story to lend surprise, pace, and tension). In the first shot, robbers bind and gag a telegraph operator in a railroad station. Action then rises and falls in eight different settings. The thieves rob and murder in a baggage car. They struggle atop a moving locomotive. When the train stops, they fleece passengers and gun one down, then drive the detached engine to their waiting horses—before Porter brings in the telegraph operator's daughter in the tenth shot to rescue her father back at the station. We hurtle through New Jersey from the tender of a moving locomotive. Design governs the flow of action. Characters enter shots through doors on screen left. The train moves always leftward.

To 1903 eyes, this sequencing of shots moved the action vividly. In *A Trip to the Moon*, Méliès sequences shots as if he were stringing a strand of pearls. Each shot in the Méliès film is self-contained and gleams but derives no luster from the shot that follows or precedes it. In *The Great Train Robbery,* the train that fires up in one shot rumbles to a stop in another. Shots seem therefore to flow. As the engine moves the train, cutting-to-continuity moves the movie. Not pearls joining pearls at knots, the shots seemed, to audiences then, interlocking links of a golden chain.

Porter makes other consequential choices. He introduces the conventions of the western movie. His bad guys in black form

The Great Train Robbery (1903), dir. Edwin S. Porter.

the prototype of countless western movie bad guys to follow. He utilizes numerous other cinematic effects—for instance, matte shots, dissolves, pans. Except for one close-up of a bandit firing a gun at the camera—the last shot or the first, depending on exhibitor's assessment of his audience—action plays entirely in long shot.

When judged by contemporary practice, Porter cut imperfectly. He misses chances to match cut where editors now would match cut. A fuller alphabet of movie language was still to be worked out by Griffith and others in the decade that followed. But Porter gave storytelling movies a template. His story construction chisels time, joins actions, creates tension, and resolves it. It propels the film through the classic stages of drama. As exposition, robbers waylay the telegraph operator. Action rises when when they steal, kill, and flee. The film climaxes when pursuers apprehend the robbers. Since Porter's time, nearly every narrative movie has passed through these stages.

Once Porter cut to continuity, filmmakers everywhere did. The "story movie" since Porter uses cutting to continuity as a primary way of assembling shots into sequence. In the twenty-first century, this method of joining shots into story-length sequences seems as natural to us as using nouns and verbs to express whole thought. Porter's scientist contemporaries might have used the language of science to express what he achieved, but, machine oil in his veins, Porter had few words for the process. He simply stumbled on it. A Darwinist might have expressed the technique biologically. Cutting to continuity, Porter transformed single-cell organisms—that is, individual shots—into a higher organism encompassing them all, a movie. Before Porter, as a chemist might have put it, shots were inert. After Porter, they were reactive and compoundable. They combined, forming new worlds from old.

EXERCISE FOUR: CUTTING TO CONTINUITY

What this exercise teaches:

● **How to assemble shots for a rough cut**

● **How to cut a film to continuity**

● **How editors say more with less**

At Mr. Edison's rooftop studio at 41 East Twenty-first Street, Mr. Porter has written you a note. "I'm having lunch with Marie Murray over at the Players' Club. Assemble this *Great Train* footage. We had to shoot the New Jersey scenes before we came back and shot the other scenes here in the studio. I think you can cut out some of it. I don't know what we should do with that shot Blair made of Justus shooting at the camera. Use your judgment."

You Did It Then: Preview the four studio shots and the nine location shots Edwin S. Porter made into *The Great Train Robbery*. Then recut the movie, doing whatever seems useful to narrate a story with tension, interest, and significance. Feel free to delete elements (such as excessive footage), add elements (such as sound, visual effects, or transitions), or otherwise modify these shots for contemporary viewers. Step by step instructions and the component shots are in the *Make Film History* digital cutting room: http://makefilmhistory.com.

❺

Mise-en-Scène:
Charlie Chaplin (1914)

"The shapes a bright container can contain!"
Theodore Roethke, "I Knew a Woman"

Mise-en-scène is a French term meaning "put in scene." The English equivalent is "composition." Theatrical directors in France used the term first to describe the arrangement of features on a stage. In movies, mise-en-scène means visual style, the

arranging of lights, shapes, props, distance and characters within a film frame. *Mise-en-scène* lends meaning to movies as composition contributes to painting.

Elements of a movie shot take on significance, in part, from how and where on screen they appear. When you sense that the telephone on the right side of the screen is about to ring, you are

Twenty-one in 1910, Chaplin (above left) set foot on the American stage with a troupe of British vaudevillians. By late 1913, at Mac Sennett's Keystone Studio (above center), Chaplin had entered the movies. By twenty-eight, he had become the world's most recognized celebrity, as above (right) in *The Adventurer* (1917). In a long shot in *Kid Auto Races at Venice* (1914), Chaplin's transformation began.

Creation and Fall (1513-1515). Mariotto Albertinelli, Oil on panel. 564 cm x 165.4 cm.

In Renaissance Europe, even the physical dimensions of a canvas could suggest something. For example, in *Creation and Fall* (1513-1515) above, Mariotto Albertinelli maximizes distance from creation to man's fall in a horizontal canvas that is, for symbolic reasons, three times wider than it is tall. The foreground reads from left to right as sentences do, beginning with creation and ending with the fall. Hand raised in the center, God stands equally close to the beginning and innocence's end. Renaissance painters could fit image to content because, unlike filmmakers, they had no need to conform the dimensions of their image to industry format standards.

Shooting Zampanò's act in medium shot when *La Strada* begins, Fellini conveys Zampanò's virility and vainglory. In an extreme long shot near the film's end, the identical gesture expresses Zampanò's disintegration. A circus ring now encloses him. Small and distant as the light dims, Fellini's muscleman descends soon into grief. Zampanò recalls Maciste, the muscleman of Pastrone's *Cabiria*. But Fellini employs *mise-en-scène* as novelists once used a pen.

Zampanò begins the movie on one beach in sunlight and ends it on another. Distance and darkness diminish him.

likely responding to *mise-en-scène*. *Mise-en-scène* leads your eye around the frame. In shots created by visually inventive directors, where characters appear suggests what they signify. Fellini's protagonist of *La Strada* (1954) flexes his muscles in ever-longer (more distant) shots as the movie progresses because Fellini is using the long shot to enfeeble him. (Smaller is weaker in the shorthand of movies.) *Mise-en-scène* works best when least perceived. Like a pen writing on the surface of a lake, it leaves its mark in circles spreading outward imperceptibly to the farthest reaches of the water.

Even the earliest filmmakers could use *mise-en-scène* imaginatively, as *The Big Swallow,* a one-minute film created in 1901 by British filmmaker James Williamson illustrates.

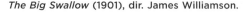

The Big Swallow (1901), dir. James Williamson.

When *The Big Swallow* begins, a man is standing outdoors in long shot, perusing a hand-written letter. He raises his cane and scuttles angrily towards us when he notices the camera through which we view him. "I won't! I won't!—I'll eat the camera first!" he enunciates for lip readers. (A music hall comedian plays the role.) His protestations voice the thought, evidently, that the camera will reduce him to an object.

In the next shot, his lips stretch to the margins of the film frame, engorging it in an extreme close up. In shot three, in a netherworld suddenly, we *are* the irate man, somewhere inside his mouth, regarding the world from the point of view of his tonsils. Between us and the exterior world is the cameraman, cranking his camera and looking ahead, as we do, into darkness. His camera preceding him, the cameraman then raises his arms and disappears down into oblivion.

The last shot of the film returns us to the outer world of sunlight again. Acknowledging our presence, the outside man cracks open a huge suggestive grin. He now recognizes us. *Mise-en-scène* moves us from *seeing* him to *being* him and back again. The movie is primitive but, in it, subject and object turn into one another. Ingmar Bergman returns to imagery like this in *Persona* (1966).

This primitive movie suggests what Escher depicts in his famous lithograph of hands drawing each other—by picturing the world, imagination appropriates it. In this movie, the ruthless camera seems to stand for imagination. It objectifies us even as we welcome it. *The Big Swallow* may be movie's first haiku, being suggestive without being entirely comprehensible. This pure movie is an exercise in *mise-en-scène*.

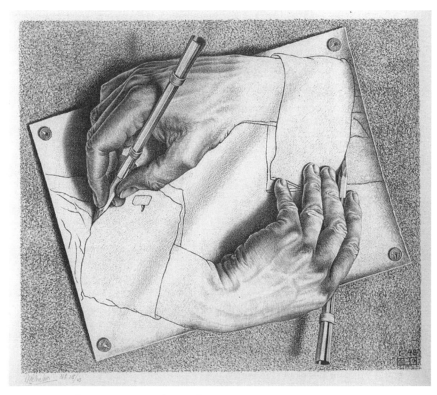

Drawing Hands (1948) M.C. Escher. Lithograph.

The Return (2003), dir. Andrei Zvyagintsev. In pattern, color, light, and shape, mise-en-scène says to us here, "This boy could survey the world from atop a tower, but he feels closed-in and afraid." *Mise-en-scène* runs ceaselessly through all the frames of a film, each arraying visual elements in ever-changing patterns. (A 90-minute movie is 129,000 individual frames.) Freeze a frame to study its mise-en-scène and you see into the essence of a film.

Prix de Beauté (1930), dir. Augusto Genina. Louise Brooks plays a typist who wins a "Miss Europe" beauty pageant. Try spelling out the plot of this film from the *mise-en-scène* of this single frame from the last scene. Your eye enters the film where opposites (big/small, dark/light, moving/still) most visibly conjoin. Where it moves then establishes the frame's "meaning." The chart below puts in words what your eye wordlessly tells you.

	Characters who face the camera reveal themselves	Characters who face away from the camera keep something unknown or unsaid
	Characters who move through empty space seem unconstrained, autonomous, and free	Characters jammed against each other, dwarfed by backgrounds, or confined to small portions of the frame seem entrapped
Lighting	Low key (low intensity) suggests mystery, religiosity, or uncertainty	High key (high intensity) light conveys joy, energy
	Flat lighting conveys low conflict or low energy	High contrast lighting conveys high conflict
Camera & Stock	From above, we sit in judgment on the characters	From below, we sit in thrall to them
	From afar, what's at issue is the character's place in the world	From close, what's at issue is the inner life of a character
	Seen though a wide angle lens, the world expands	Seen through a telephoto lens, the world contracts
	Monochrome (Black & White) film stock abstracts	Color film stock excites emotion
	In a shallow focus shot (where the depth of field is small), viewers see clearly only what the cinematographer selects. Shallow focus isolates and confines subjects	In a deep focus shot (where the image appears sharply focused almost everywhere), foreground and background seem comparably important. Deep focus grounds subjects in their setting
Framing	Borders of an open form shot enclose action that continues beyond. They are fence posts in a world of accident and chance	Shapes and actions inside a closed form shot seem balanced, organized, and intentionally designed. Borders delimit a world of purpose and order
	What's close and large almost always dominates, but a background can comment on a foreground	Shots with detail in foreground, midground, and background feel "denser" than shots with detail on just one of them
Characters	Side-by-side, embracing, close together characters share an intimacy	Separated by considerable space, characters are opposed, unrelated, or estranged
	Characters atop the frame dominate characters below them	Characters at the center of the frame dominates those at the periphery

Dimensions of the film stock itself help define *mise-en-scène*. Gauges narrowed and widened at first like the railroad tracks they resemble. Competitors marketed competing stocks. Purchase orders, not aesthetics, determined the film gauge that came to prevail—rolls of film Edison purchased from George Eastman in 1889 were box camera film rolls 70 mm wide split down the middle into 35 mm-wide ribbons. When, in 1895, William K. Dickson started up American Mutoscope in competition with Edison, Dickson stopped splitting the film stock and produced a wide-screen 68 mm film stock that advanced without sprocket holes to avoid Edison patent infringement lawsuits. In France, Gaumont-Demeny stock for amateur cinematographers shrank to 15 mm to operate in smaller cameras. By the 1930s, some stocks for professionals anticipated the anamorphic (horizontally compressed in the camera lens and expanded in the projector lens) wide-screen formats such as CinemaScope reintroduced in the 1950s.

In December 1908, the free-for-all for a standard gauge effectively ended. The Edison Trust comprising the nine major American film producers—Edison, Biograph, Vitagraph, Essanay, Selig, Lubin, Kalem, American Star, and Pathé—then designated Edison's 35 by 25.4 mm film gauge as the international theatrical release standard, which it remained for four decades.

Early ideas about film strike many now as more sophisticated than the movies themselves. But Charlie Chaplin's first "Little Tramp" film—*Kid Auto Races at Venice* (1914), directed by Henry

Charlie Chaplin (center), Henry Lehrman (right), and Frank Williams (left) gather at the Keystone camera in this undated publicity photo, most likely created in early 1914. Lehrman directed *Kid Auto Races at Venice* (1914), Chaplin starred in it, and Williams cranked the camera that actually recorded the action.

Lehrman—illustrates what *mise-en-scène* contributes to even a primitive film with a sophisticated premise. The Little Tramp may seem to have been Chaplin's alter ego from birth. In reality, he emerged from Chaplin's psyche while Chaplin worked out gags for *Kid Auto Races at Venice,* a self-referential movie about the making of a movie. Chaplin improvised the action on location. Henry "Pathé´" Lehrman, a former streetcar conductor employed by Mack Sennett as an actor/director at Keystone Films, transported a film crew to nearby Venice, California. When the Little

Tramp showed up while the camera cranked in Venice that day, no one was expecting him, perhaps not even Chaplin.

Lehrman shot on Saturday and Sunday, January 10 and 11, 1914. That weekend, Pancho Villa was driving 4,300 Mexican federal troops across the Rio Grande to surrender to soldiers on the American side of border and, in Los Angeles, 10,000 spectators were viewing a 14-year-old boys' homemade car race and the soapbox derby that followed it. In a long shot, the Tramp emerges from a knot of spectators lining the curb at the intersection of Main and Westminster Street in Venice, California.

The movie then becomes the story of "an odd character" who obtrudes relentlessly into the field of view of the motion picture camera purportedly recording the movie Lehrman purportedly directed. In 13 of 18 shots, Lehrman shoos the Little Tramp off camera while Chaplin inserts himself back into the camera's line of vision. "In picturing this event," the first Keystone intertitle reads, "an odd character discovered that motion pictures were being taken and it became impossible to keep him away from the camera."

The Little Tramp is the antitype of the man in *The Big Swallow* who exclaims, "I won't!" As "the odd character" closes in on the camera, *he* seems to say, "Yes, "I will!" In the final shot, the Little Tramp peers into the camera from a distance of six inches. The close-up serves as thesis statement concluding a paragraph: as dreamer is to dream, camera is to Little Tramp. He is looking into his maker.

Mise-en-scène begins with camera placement. In *Kid Auto Races at Venice,* a second camera, of course, is recording this action from behind Lehrman and his cameraman. The camera-in-a-camera motif is not unprecedented. Operators shooting a parade for the

Bangville Police (1913), dir. Henry Lehrman.

The "Keystone Kops" appeared first, without uniforms, in this farce about a girl, a calf, burglars, and the world's most hapless police force.

Keystone directors like Lehrman at that time eschewed studios and scripts. They went for belly laughs, crashing cars and setting comics sliding around corners. Keystone Kop comedies say, in effect, that searching for dignity in people is as futile as trying to net starlight.

But the Little Tramp seems to assert the opposite—that even the least of us aspires somehow to realize himself.

Lumières in 1896 had already created a movie showing a camera shooting a movie. The second camera here, however, shoots from a spot behind Lehrman for the purpose of depicting the action as a contest between the man inside and the man outside Lehrman's camera. The second camera might have shot this action from else-where—from the point of view of a bystander on the sidewalk, for instance. But the movie then would confine the obtruding man and the camera shooting him to the single distant plane of a long shot. Their dance would sink into insignificance. The point from which we see an action determines what we see *in* it. Camera placement is the prime element of *mise-en-scène*.

Chaplin entered this zone of inspiration first for *Mabel's Strange Predicament*, shot by Lehrman two days before he shot *Kid Auto Races at Venice* and released by Keystone two days after it in February 1914. While selecting his wardrobe for those two movies in a dressing room, Chaplin discovered the antithetical strains of his character. His shoes belonged to Keystone actor Ford Sterling. His trousers were Keystone actor Fatty Arbuckle's. The cutaway belonged to actor Chester Conklin. He devised a mustache out of crêpe hair belonging to actor Mack Swain. Except for his walking stick, which resembles the caduceus carried by Hermes, the ancient Greek god of poetry, thieves and boundaries, Chaplin's character derives entirely from the trappings of other actors. The Little Tramp is the self-reflexive misfit everyone is. When he looks into the lens of the camera in the final shot of the film, he is looking for a face recognizing his.

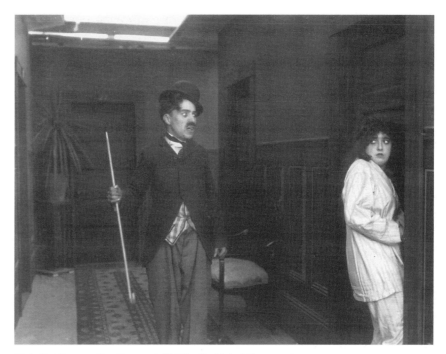

Mabel's Strange Predicament (1914), dir. Mabel Normand.

Kid Auto Races at Venice plays almost entirely in long shot (action 8 to 15 feet from the camera). In movies he directed starting in 1914, Chaplin favored this *mise-en-scène*. Long shot action is suffi-ciently far from the camera to isolate actors from one another but close enough for actors to signal feeling in gesture and facial expression. Close enough to represent the tramp as one among others, it is distant enough to show him as fundamentally alone. Shabby-genteel, instinctual, greedy and giving, confabulated out of mismatched parts, his natural environment is the long shot where

Kid Auto Races at Venice (1914), dir. Henry Lehrman.

he is close enough for us to read his eyes and far away enough for us to judge him. Albertinelli would have understood this distance perfectly, had he lived to make a movie showing Adam's place in God's eyes.

Mise-en-scène invests images with significance. In the frame above, for instance, the tramp creates the point of dominant contrast.

Your eye gravitates to him first because his waistcoat and trousers contrasts most starkly with the "white" of the macadam. In the street rendered white by the orthochromatic (blue sensitive, red insensitive) negative, he stands alone. The rightmost leg of the tripod and the Little Tramp's cane create sides of an incomplete equilateral triangle. The partial triangle suggests equivalence between the men. (In real life, Chaplin detested Lehrman.)

We perceive director and tramp as identically slight men of average height, upright as exclamation points. Frock coats, mustaches, and hats accentuate their resemblance. They are counterparts, head and tail, inside man and outside man respectively. If one embodies the neediness of the tramp, the other portends Chaplin the perfectionist director.

The director imploringly looks back to us from the margin of the frame. Closer to us, Lehrman might exercise first claim on our attention—proximity to the camera can turn a pebble into a meteor. But seeing him at the margin of the frame, we attend to him less. The cameraman and the crowd behind him blot him away. Lehrman matters, but Chaplin himself centers the shot as God does in Albertinelli's painting. In even a hastily shot movie, *mise-en-scène* leads you through the visible. *Mise-en-scène* is the rip tide that sweeps beneath the surface waves. You start to think about it when you feel it.

EXERCISE FIVE: *MISE-EN-SCÈNE*

What this exercise teaches:

- **How to preview the setup of a shot**
- **How to position your camera**
- **How to choose light levels**
- **How to think about where characters stand, look, and move**

"I found that I could say things with color and shapes that I couldn't say in any other way, things that I had no words for."

Georgia O'Keeffe, Foreword in the catalogue of her show at the Anderson Galleries in New York, 1926

You Did It Then: Change the look and feel of *Kid Auto Races at Venice* by modifying elements of *mise-en-scène* using your editing software. Step by step instructions and the component shots are in the *Make Film History* digital cutting room: http://makefilmhistory.com.

You Do It Now: Create a scene with three elements (a foreground subject, a midground subject, and a background). Photograph the scene twelve times. Making each photo, change the foreground subject position, the midground subject position, and the camera angle, lens setting, and/or distance. Then analyze how each change affects the mood and feel.

MOVING CAMERA:
Giovanni Pastrone (1914)

"You must let yourself go along in life like a cork in the current of a stream."
Painter Pierre-Auguste Renoir to his son,
filmmaker Jean Renoir

Tracking shots are shots made from a mobile camera mounted on tracks or wheels. They are the pencil of the subjective camera. As it moves across the dance floor with a masked man in the *Le Masque* segment of Max Orphul's *Le Plaisir* (1952), the moving camera pulls viewers into the movie. Moving cameras make their destinations matter by virtue of moving there.

In *Shadows of Forgotten Ancestors* (1965), Sergei Parajanov uses tracking shots to show the world from the point of view of angels. In *Taxi Driver* (1976), Scorsese tracks to unbalance Travis while he telephones Betsy. In *Shadow of a Doubt* (1943), Hitchcock tracks toward a man conducting the air with a cigar while lying on a bed, and the glide itself conveys the threat in his reverie. The longing that pervades the films of Max Ophüls—all those women in white in his movies ascending and descending opulent stairwells—derives from Ophüls' discovery that the stationary camera merely reveals what a tracking camera seems to feel. Other techniques to simulate motion can certainly move the viewer's eye. In *pulling*

focus, a cinematographer adjusts the focal point of the camera—where the shot appears sharpest—to maintain focus on a subject moving closer or farther away. In *racking focus*, a cinematographer adjusts the focal point not to follow a moving subject but, instead, to nudge the viewer's attention from an element at one depth to a different element closer or further away. But the tracking shot—called also the dolly shot or the trucking shot—transports the viewer's psyche to a rendezvous with feeling.

Tracking shots entered movies during the second decade of the twentieth century, the decade when astronomers photographing a 1919 solar eclipse proved that light bends around the sun, as Einstein's general theory of relativity predicted. Tracking shots are comparably magical-seeming and disorienting. They underline, undercut, or undertake action by advancing towards a subject, retreating from it, or traveling beside it.

Earlier filmmakers had certainly shot film from cameras in motion mounted on moving vehicles. Lumière cameraman Alexander Promio filmed Venice from the deck of a rightward moving vaporetto in 1896, inspiring a Lumière product line called "Panoramas," the world seen as 30-second cinématographe "postcards" sent from rickshaws, steam

Shadow of a Doubt (1943), dir. Alfred Hitchcock. The camera tracked in as Joseph Cotten arrives at the station. Hitchcock told his associate art director what he wanted from the numerous tracking shots in this film: "I want the camera to go 'Ahhh!' like an intake of breathe..."

From the tracking cameras and massive Moloch set (above) of *Cabiria* (1914), dir. Giovanni Pastrone, came the moving cameras and massive Babylon set (below) of D.W. Griffith's *Intolerance* (1916). Griffith inspired the montages of the Soviets.

Le Plaisir (1952), dir. Max Ophüls.

engines, street cars, and palanquins. Other cameramen then filmed wharves from steamboats or railroad switching yards from the cowcatcher of an advancing locomotive. By 1903, movies were already offering virtual tours. Amusement park and storefront theater simulating railroad cars—so-called Hale's Tours—projected "phantom rides" from an observation car or a locomotive to 72 "passengers" while a pretend track bed clattered and the virtual carriage tilted, rocked, and vibrated. But audiences lost interest in ersatz trips during the second decade of the century when movies grew more ambitious and moviemakers began to use motion for the purpose singers use vibrato—to suffuse notes with feeling.

By 1912—while Griffith was still cranking out one-reelers for Biograph—filmmakers in Italy were shooting and shipping around the world three-hour epics of passion and bondage in ancient Rome. Kohl-eyed heroines in stolas, papier-mâché miniature volca-noes, and slaves wringing hands before painted backdrops seem risible to many contemporary viewers, but these films—especially *Cabiria* (1914)—intrigued filmmakers such as Griffith. Shots in them where the camera glides towards and away from action engrossed audiences. The camera had functioned as a courtroom stenogra-pher in the Lumière era, dispassionately recording the proceedings. It now took the stand to bear witness.

Historians identify Giovanni Pastrone as the originator of the story film tracking shot and point to his epic *Cabiria* (1914) as the first feature film to track a camera in order to express feeling. Since

Tracking shot c. 1933 Cosmopolitan Productions. Mounted on a dolly, the light and the blimped sound camera lead Marion Davies across the set.

"All right, Miss Davies, when you come through there, stay right there...and then right through that door. You understand?" the director shouted while the camera rolled rightward.

Solar eclipse, May 29, 1919, Sobral, Brazil. Photo by the Royal Observatory, Greenwich, England/UK.

the streets of Dunkirk that year, half a dozen boys gamboling before his invisible trolley in a take running five continuous minutes.

On the other hand, most early movies were flammable and as brief as love notes. In archives, in trunks, and as ghosts in contact paper prints submitted to the Library of Congress for copyright protection, just 3,000 of 17,000 pre-1909 movies survive. Nitrate prints run through a hundred projectors seemed worthless and were indeed dangerous. Producers burned negatives before they combusted spontaneously. Typical are the 75 American "lost" silents rediscovered in New Zealand in 2009. They survived because producers judged them less valuable than the cost of shipping them home to Hollywood. Other nitrate prints from 1919-1925—including Rex

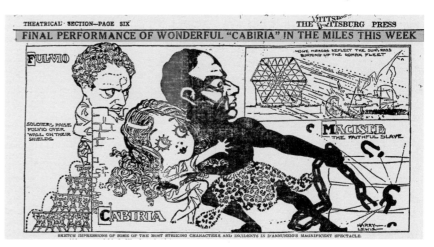

"The run of Cabiria will end this Saturday evening to make room for... D.W. Griffith's great photo drama, *The Avenging Conscious*," the *Pittsburgh Press* wrote on May 17, 1915.

Pastrone registered a patent for a dolly device in 1912, the attribution seems deserved, although ambiguity pervades the history of motion in early artisanal movies. Still cameras attached to the breasts of French carrier pigeons were photographing enemy positions in 1914. Movie cameramen were certainly shooting from vehicles wending through city streets by 1913. One anonymous cameraman traversed

Ingram's *The Arab* (1924)—went unnoticed for decades in Soviet film archives that happened to retain them and returned to America as digitals in 2010.

Cabiria was Pastrone's tenth, most ambitious, and most risky movie. Shot while colonial administrators were consolidating the 1911-12 Italian conquest of Libya, the movie returns to an ancient precursor war, Rome's conquest of Carthage during the Punic Wars of 264-164 BC. Production costs were reputedly 1,000,000 lire—perhaps $200,000—when the norm for Itala Films was 50-60,000 lire. Moving a vast cast through gargantuan sets was an expensive undertaking. Segundo de Chomón, whose hand-painted shorts of acrobats and enchantresses resemble those of Méliès, shot the film. Ildebrando Pizzetti, a well-known symphonic composer, produced just nine minutes of the commissioned three-hour score, leaving someone else to complete the bulk of the music. The world-famous poet Gabriele D'Annunzio wrote the dialogue or narration that explains the action—intertitles.

The film runs roughly three hours. The set of Moloch is jaw-dropping: Maidens are fed to the maws of a glowering idol. Hannibal crosses the Alps with live elephants. A leopard laps milk from a tamborine in a seraglio. After countless deaths and escapes, a muscleman named Maciste—reincarnated in 48 subsequent movies—rescues Cabiria, a Roman girl abducted and enslaved in Carthage. The film concludes with a swirl of nymphs, aloft in a darkening sky, whirling in circles above lovers in the prow of a stage-set boat.

Giovanni Pastrone was a slight, intense man, a natural engineer who as a music student hand built cellos and, after he quit the film business, went on to construct medical x-ray devices. Opera was Pastrone's first love, and he played second violin at the Theatre Reggio Opera House in Turin before he entered the film business, first as accountant, then as a director for Itala Films.

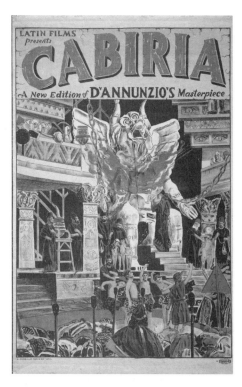

Dolly shots in *Cabiria* draw the eye to action in a number of scenes, identifying what matters. They attract the eye as magnets draw iron filings. Consider this scene. Princess Sophonisba (see the nine frames below) feeds the birds and prepares herself for marriage in a seraglio that resembles a birdcage. Her father betroths her to a warrior she reviles, and during the seconds before her wedding she expresses her unwillingness to marry him by lifting and releasing a dove. A feather headdress and a layered sheer gown give her the

Cabiria, 5th Episode. Sophonisba girds herself to marry a man she reviles.

look of a goddess entrapped among real and imaginary birds. She trudges to her wedding with the grimace of a sacrificial victim.

The obvious way to shoot this action in 1913-1914 would have been to take it in a single long shot. A long shot would certainly have rendered all the action. Maids-in-waiting would come and go. A

woman would rock on a hammock in the background. Sophonisba would pass to and from the window. But Sophonisba's passage across the set, represented that way, would signify nothing of particular moment. We would simply pass along to the next scene, where Sophonisba collapses while holding aloft the ceremonial vessel that consecrates her marriage, just as she had held aloft the dove and released it in this scene.

The classical cutting solution to shooting this action—that is, breaking sub-actions into separate shots to build tension and to lead the viewer through the event by passing from wide shots to medium shots and close-ups—had not yet entered every filmmaker's vocabulary. (See the next chapter.) Pastrone's way was neither of those methods. He renders this action by dollying almost imperceptibly slowly to the right and left, into the set and out of it, as Sophonisba passes toward and leaves the window. This tracking draws a line under Sophonisba's emotion, intensifying it.

Pastrone uses tracking shots sparingly, perhaps because the dolly—Italians called it a *carello*—was then an untried device in story films and he may not have wished to wager his movie on a device of unproven effectiveness. No tracking shot in *Cabiria* runs longer than the forty seconds of a cinématographe shot.

They are soft pencils that shade characters' actions without dominating them. They approach, treat with, and ultimately back away retreating from the actors. They move into action and out of it, never across it. The chief characters in *Cabiria* are potentates and princesses, so the fifteen or so tracking shots Pastrone works into the movie seem to importune without intruding, like minions arriving in slippers and departing into silence. The cinématographe of the Lumières had presented life as a parade best witnessed by a spectator on the sidewalk. The dolly shot introduced by Pastrone joins the parade and, moving with it, looks back at the sidewalk. Tracking shots in *Cabiria* were the first steps towards the gliding camera of German expressionist directors of the 1920s and the steadicam invented by Garrett Brown that Kubrick uses in *The Shining* (1980).

After Pastrone introduced them into a story film, tracking shots and similar crane shots became common. Griffith cranes in on the vast set of Babylon in *Intolerance* (1916), and Murnau tracks with a protagonist to an illicit assignation in *Sunrise* (1927). Later twentieth-century directors created tracking shots of vastly longer duration. A tracking crane shot at the start of Orson Welles' *Touch of Evil* (1958) simultaneously follows a couple through a crowded border checkpoint and the suspenseful planting of a car bomb. In the penultimate shot of Michelangelo Antonioni's *The Passenger* (1975), a subjective camera affixed first to a ceiling and then to a crane tracks out through the bars of a hotel window to return back there through the same bars seven minutes later. Robert Altman connects writers, producers, and staff in a studio with an eight-minute tracking shot at the start of *The Player* (1992). These later directors understood what the tracking shot could suggest. Pastrone merely invented it.

Dolly shots perform three main functions. They express a point of view. They express a desire. They assess a statement or an action. They can dominate a movie or just connect elements that cutting would otherwise separate. They are wishes progressing in stages towards objects of desire. They say "I" while showing "It."

The Earrings of Madame de... (1953), dir. Max Ophüls.

If Pastrone was the progenitor of the tracking shot, the master was Max Ophüls (1902-1957). Consider, for instance, a railroad station scene in *The Earrings of Madame de...* (1953) that Ophüls constructs out of five successive tracking shots. In the first, the estranged General and Madame de... trudge towards screen left down a train platform, the direction in which the train will ultimately depart. In the second, the general settles his wife on board. In the third, the general exits the train, and from the platform clasps his wife's hand and kisses it. Now looking towards the camera, he raises his right hand to suggest a salute. Train, wife, and the general's shadow on the railroad cars vanish together. He trudges away in darkness.

We dissolved into this scene from a prior tracking shot that showed fire consuming Madame de...'s lover's gift box, and we exit from it dissolving into yet a final tracking shot. The last track enters into Madame de...'s sleeping car through the curtain of her window, where, head to pillow, she is raising and letting fall her right hand in delayed response to her distant husband's gesture. If there is something naturally affecting about a husband and a wife separating on a railroad platform, Ophüls uses tracking shots to distill that feeling into universal grief.

EXERCISE SIX: MOVING CAMERA

What this exercise teaches:

● **How to use an animatic to prevision action in a movie.**

● **How to pace a tracking shot.**

This shot never existed, but picture it as if it did:

SHOT ONE. TRACKING SHOT. INTERIOR OF ITALA FILMS STUDIO. APRIL 17, 1913.

We track ahead as hammers smack into plywood in darkness. Saws cut, lathes turn, voices shout. We advance while arc lamps near the roof of the studio light up like airplane portholes. We track past plaster elephants, hieroglyphs, and extras in desert robes. We dolly into the center of the set, closing in on four men who are attempting to rotate a wheel beneath a cart-like contraption. When we are close, one looks quizzically towards the camera. This is the man we have come to see—the minority shareholder of Itala Films, the producer, director, writer and creative force behind *Cabiria.* Wiry, intense, 30 years old, he is a small man wearing an overcoat and a fedora to ward off the cold. He has bet the future of Itala

Films on this sandals and toga movie. We continue to track towards him until his eyes fills up the entire the screen. He regards us curiously. Music rises. This is GIOVANNI PASTRONE.

You Did It Then: **View an animatic (sketch simulation) illustrating the tracking shot described above. Adjust the "motion" to a pace that seems right to you. Compare this "tracking shot" to other animatics covering the same material using a camera that does not move. Choose the approach that seems best for your "movie." Step by step instructions and the component shots are in the *Make Film History* digital cutting room: http://makefilmhistory.com.**

You Do It Now: **Create a scene of your own choice using at least one human actor. Shoot it first with a stationary camera. Then shoot it with moving camera. Keep all other elements the same. (You don't need to get fancy. Jean-Luc Godard rented a wheelchair to shoot the dolly shots in *Breathless*.) Consider how the moving camera changes the feel of the film.**

PRODUCTION **Make Film History**
DIRECTOR _____
CAMERA _____
DATE   SCENE   TAKE
6

7

CLASSICAL CUTTING:
D.W. Griffith (1915)

"How was I to know that...he was intending to use only the shortest of flashes, measured in frames and not feet, and that he had to punch everything possible into these shots? The heart of his craft was in what we fumblingly called cutting, or editing."
Karl Brown, *Adventures with D.W. Griffith*

Editors transform "rushes"—uncut footage—into movies by ordering them in sequences, creating a narrative trail in what is otherwise a thicket of exposed film. Editors move eyes across screens by joining shots and pacing them. They usually attempt to cover their tracks, so editors are the least recognized creators of movies. They work in shadows. They dissolve into the movies they cut, most present when they are least visible. You can learn the mechanics of editing, but *how* you edit expresses who you are. D.W. Griffith directed, but, by supervising editors—"cutters," he called James and Rose Smith—he also cut his movies, too. In effect, a Griffith movie is the world seen through Griffith's eye and cut by his hand.

Moviemakers discovered editing incrementally. Lumière employees made no edits beyond cuts to excise "flash frames"—overexposed frames at the head of a shot—or to join frames ripped by the

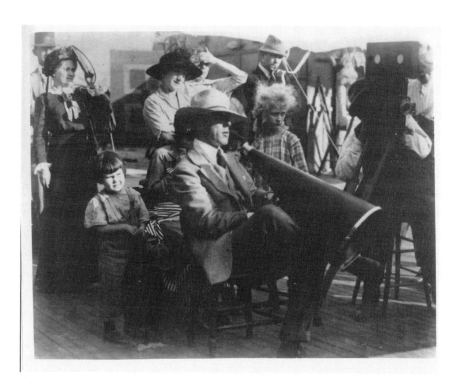

D.W. Griffith directing *Hearts of the World* (1918). The megaphone, the straw hat, the right leg dangling on the left knee were emblems of Griffith as familiar as the face on a penny to those who repeatedly made movies with him. Child actor Ben Alexander follows the action over Griffith's shoulder. Billy Bitzer, Griffith's cameraman from 1908 to 1929, cranks the camera. It was Bitzer who implemented the fade-outs, iris shots, soft focus, and close-ups Griffith combines as elements of the "classically cut" scene.

projector. While the Lumière cameraman cranked, he might pause and therefore abut one image to another. Except for these functional edits, a cinématographe was single master shot. For a snowball fight in a gag film in 1897, the cameraman positioned the cinématographe to anticipate the approach of a bicyclist. But no editing signals that the rider is heading for a pummeling. (A close or medium shot detailing the rider before the event could have signaled what was coming.) In a Lumière cinématographe, the scene, not the shot, is the smallest unit of action.

Twenty years later, most filmmakers had learned to convey judgments and feelings by sequencing and pacing shots assembled into movies that sometimes ran for hours. Most learned crucial lessons in shooting and cutting from D.W. Griffith. "The basic ingredient is the image," Henri Langlois, spiritual father of the French New Wave, explained much later in the 1960s. "Let's call it a diamond. An uncut diamond already gives off light, but improves when polished. Griffith cut facets into the diamond."

Griffith's life recalls a line from Percy Shelley's "Ozymandias," exactly the kind of nineteenth century verse he loved to read—"Look on my works, ye mighty, and despair!" He was a 32-year-old playwright and stage actor when he arrived in New York from Kentucky in 1907. A middling actor, his baritone voice boomed. That same year, Edwin S. Porter, turning out Edison movies in The Bronx, rejected a movie script Griffith attempted to sell him but cast him in *Rescued from an Eagle's Nest*. Griffith then began film acting.

In 1908, Griffith began directing for an Edison competitor, American Mutoscope and Biograph. The company produced movies *in* the marketplace *for* the marketplace—10 vaudeville houses and nickelodeons competed for movie patrons within 400 feet of the studio Biograph had opened in 1903 at 11 West Fourteenth Street. Biograph had introduced large-format (68 mm) movies in 1895 to evade Edison's incessant patent claims. By the time Griffith joined them, Biograph producers were cranking out 83 one-reel—10 to 15 minute—story films per year under arc and mercury vapor lights. Biograph eschewed the "high culture" competitors were pedaling—for instance, Adolph Zukor's "Famous Players in Famous Plays"—in favor of merchandise for Main Street.

Griffith cranked out 450 Biograph one-reelers, roughly two a week, some in studio, and some on location. He learned movie making at Biograph as original artists inevitably do—by inventing, improvising, and copying. If a Pathé film of 1907—*The Runaway Horse*—crosscuts (alternates actions in different places to show them happening simultaneously), Griffith crosscut two years later in *The Curtain Pull*. Eventually he bridled. Once he viewed Giovanni Pastrone's *Cabiria*, he aspired to make an epic. When he overspent the $36,000 Biograph reluctantly budgeted for *Judith of Bethulia* (1914), a 61-minute biblical epic that he shot in Biograph's new studio in the Bronx, Griffith and Biograph parted ways. In a 1913 trade publication ad, Griffith's personal representative lauded him for "revolutionizing Motion Picture drama and founding the modern technique of the art." Griffith, the ad states, introduced "the large or close-up figures, distant views...the 'switchback,' sustained suspense, the 'fade out,' and restraint in expression."

A few years earlier in 1910, Griffith had shot *In Old California* on location for Biograph at Sunset and Vine in Hollywood. In 1913, Griffith relocated to Los Angeles. Eastern filmmakers had, since 1911, been shooting movies in new studios there. Griffith and partners bought one. There, in 1914, he directed and produced *The Birth of a Nation*—the start of a 30-year Hollywood career in which he arrived as emperor and departed as pariah.

Most viewers in 1915 saw *The Birth of a Nation* as inspired. It toured as a special event road show with a crew of 100 stagehands, electricians, and musicians. Tickets sold for $2 when other movies fetched five pennies. But the success undid Griffith. If the movie's dynamic cutting, original orchestral music, wide sweep, and focus on the Civil War during the first half mesmerized audiences, civil rights groups of his day roared their disapproval of the second half. There the movie, grotesquely, portrays Klu Klux Klansmen as agents of justice and mercy. It depicts a South after the Civil War as Griffith may have seen it but as it never was. Black state reps with their feet on their desks gobble peanuts, swill whiskey, and voice-vote legislation that never was. Pursued by a villainous ex-slave, a white girl protects her virtue by leaping to her death from a mountaintop. Civil rights groups denounced *The Birth of a Nation,* picketed it, and implored boards of censorship to cut shots. Many did.

Griffith next made *Intolerance: Love's Struggle Throughout the Ages*, a film that earned less than it cost to produce and exhibit. Griffith absorbed much of the loss himself, and by 1918 Triangle Studio, which he had founded in 1915 with Thomas Ince and Mack Sennett, passed to Samuel Goldwyn. The next year, with Chaplin, Mary Pickford, and Douglas Fairbanks, Griffith started up United Artists, only to quit Hollywood for New York in 1920 to produce and direct independently.

The tone of Griffith's public statements now turned plaintive. "Motion pictures must obey the economic laws the same as any industry...Those who trespass beyond it may find a heavy burden from their experiment," Griffith opined in a film industry almanac in 1924.

Griffith lurched through the 1920s. *Broken Blossoms* (1919), *Way Down East* (1920), and *Orphans of the Storm* (1921) succeeded brilliantly. *America* (1924) failed. In 1925, he released an old-fashioned coincidence-filled comedy with W.C. Fields, *Sally of the Sawdust*, while in Paris the avant-gardist Tristan Tzara was publishing *Seven Dada Manifestos*. In 1931, he directed his last film, a talkie, *The Struggle,* in which, seeking to reform, a drunk fails. In 1939, Griffith returned to Hollywood to help make *One Million B.C.*, a low-budget second feature "B" movie featuring a caveman and cavewoman grunting at the dawn of time. Unable or unwilling to contribute much, Griffith eventually expunged his name from the credits.

He was by then a forgotten and unem-
ployable man, passing like a wraith
through 1940s Hollywood. In restaurants
frequented by Hollywood celebrities, he
waylaid those who had learned from him
enough to now scorn him. He said in the
end that he had never meant to direct
movies at all. In 1948, he died in a hotel
in Hollywood, where he lived alone in a
furnished room. "My life time ambition
has been to write," an obituary reports
him saying.

Griffith never saw himself as a rule maker.
Instead, he pictured himself as men of his
generation often did. He saw himself as
a knight-errant as Conan Doyle or Robert

Sir Nigel Sustains England's Honor. N.C.
Wyeth. Oil on Canvas. Illustration for
Arthur Conan Doyle, *The White Company*
(Cosmopolitan 1922 edition).

The Birth of a Nation (1915). The Little Colonel (Henry B. Walthall) rallies the
Klan to rescue Elsie Stoneman (Lillian Gish).

Lewis Stevenson would have pictured one, a man engaged in a
struggle to defend the pure and uphold lost glory. "When he came
on the set," Griffith's assistant remembers, "he would take off his
coat and he would start shadow boxing, and he would have a fine
time throwing whistling rights and jabbing lefts and ducking. He
always defeated the invisible man."

Griffith's vision of himself engaged in invisible struggle pervades
his way of making movies. He infused creative tension into the
smallest fabric of his movies. Griffith's way of building tension and

purpose in movies endures and seems so natural now that we
strain to recognize its inventiveness. He read verse and fiction of
the nineteenth century voraciously and gave movies the structure
and pace he found in novels and short stories. Griffith derived
"parallel cutting"—cutting that shows action in separate locations
happening simultaneously—from novels of Charles Dickens, he
told his first wife, Linda Arvidson, and others on a set in 1909. The
assembled actors were nonplussed. Nobody else on the set had
ever read a sentence of Dickens, his wife confessed.

Dorothy Gish, D.W. Griffith, Lillian Gish c. 1922.
Shooting *The Birth of a Nation*, Griffith would sing arias from *Pagliacci* fortissimo and dance with Lillian Gish, says his assistant then, Karl Brown.

Griffith's filmmaking principles seem now as natural as breathing. Expressed in words, Griffith's cutting rules would be something like this: A scene should excite emotion. A standard pattern organizes it. The scene begins with an establishing shot, a long or full shot that places action in a setting. A sequence of shots then successively reveals, through medium, close, or close-up shots, emotionally compelling details. From different positions, running

many seconds or just a few, the shots convey action, reaction, and emotion. Pace matters. Shots must play long enough to engage the attention of a viewer—but no longer. They should show actions in the order they occur, but whenever possible, they should convey what action *signifies* to characters.

Griffith's cutting practices gave film a grammar.

- Scenes are paragraphs.
- Shots are sentences.
- Actions within shots are words.
- Paragraphs begin (or sometimes end) with a fundamental assertion.

Griffiths' grammar makes it possible for movies to express complexity. Augmented with match cutting—Griffith rarely endeavored to match frames in 1914—the Griffith technique of constructing scenes remains the default way to join shots into scenes and scenes into movies. He never used the term, but today we call Griffith's practices "classical cutting."

Viewers can grasp how classical cutting works by comparing a segment of *The Birth of a Nation* to uncut footage from which, in concept, it derives. The frame below comes from a screen test for *The Birth of a Nation*. Actors George Siegmann and Lillian Gish gesticulate and crisscross the set in a scene showing, as Griffith would have imagined it, innocence responding to villainy.

George Siegmann (left) and Lillian Gish (right) work out blocking in a screen test for *The Birth of a Nation*. While the camera cranked, Griffith would rumble out instructions, giving words an intonation of his own. "Show that you're horrified, Miss *Geesh*," he would have called.

During the reconstruction period following the Civil War, the newly elected Lieutenant Governor of South Carolina is proposing to the daughter of his mentor, an abolitionist senator. Actor George Siegmann plays the lieutenant governor, purportedly a mixed race character. Actress Lillian Gish plays the woman.

The screen test shot seems a parody of nineteenth century melodrama—Siegmann lacks only a villain's mustache to twirl. Taken from the point of view of a stationary camera, the test is a master shot, complete with mishaps, recording thwarted embraces, rolling eyes, chases through the furniture. Actress Lillian Gish

erupts with exaggerated horror to Siegmann's marriage proposal. Powder makeup accidentally wafts out of Siegmann's costume while he pounds his chest. As he moves, Siegmann's waistcoat splits. The actor playing Gish's father misses his cue. In response, the confused Siegmann swivels to face the camera. A mustache of makeup powder that Siegmann accidentally acquired when he kissed Miss Gish now whitens his lips. Gish crumples as he lugs her closer toward the camera. Siegmann glances screen right, still anticipating the actor playing Gish's father. Then Siegmann lugs Gish back through a door on the left. He returns to the set from screen left as the third actor at last arrives. The men are gesticulating when Griffith presumably rumbled, "Fade out."

The screen test shot ran two minutes. No cut interpreted the action. Each stage of the action weighed equally. The stationary security style camera missed nothing—except everything that makes film scenes memorable. For that reason, Griffith did not use, and would never have expected to use, the action of this screen test in exactly the way this screen test recorded it. Griffith understood—some say he invented—the first rule of editing: *When everything counts equally, nothing does.*

(*opposite*) Griffith classically cuts here—we experience the action in bits and pieces, sequenced to make us feel what the heroine feels. As the screen test does, this sequence runs approximately two minutes. It covers the same action Griffith covered in the screen test. But Griffith treats it differently here. The action transpires in phases, one to a shot, staged to convey Gish's escalating panic. While Seligmann continues to importune Gish, the camera increasingly isolates her. The last shots are closer than the first. In crosscuts, the threat inside meshes with the threat of troops outside. The screen test shows what the audience attending a stage performance might see. Classical cutting shows what the heart feels and the mind sees.

The following title cards appear within the image:

¶ Lynch's proposal of marriage.

¶ Lynch's reply to her threat of a horsewhipping for his insolence.

¶ "See! My people fill the streets. With them I will build a Black Empire and you as a Queen shall sit by my side."

Instead of employing a single take to cover this action, what Griffith *did* do with the action of this master shot was to "classically cut" it. He did not cover the entire action in one long take. He broke the action into parts—beats, screenwriters call them—and reassembled the parts. He sequenced action photographed from various different perspectives in order to excite not thought but emotion.

Griffith assembled *The Birth of a Nation* without a shooting script. He utilized in the final cut barely 1% of the negative he shot. Conferring with his "cutter," Rose Smith, Griffith spent three months assembling *The Birth of a Nation* intuitively. Griffith and Smith continued to tweak the ride-to-the-rescue scene even while he and she previewed the movie before moviegoers in Riverside, California.

Griffith rehearsed his cast and crew for six weeks—an eternity by the standards of 1914—and shot the screen test primarily as sketchpad for motions, props, and costumes. In the movie as he ultimately released it, iris shots, cutting, and crosscutting, "meanwhile, back at the ranch" segue cutting, all vastly complicate the action. The camera tracks. Intertitles give words to the inner and outer turmoil.

In the released movie, 36 shots treat Seligmann proposing and Gish fainting. But interspersed between and among them are shots and sequences showing soldiers outside firing in the street, Klansmen galloping in the fields, minions scurrying about the house, and eventually Gish's "father" arriving. So one shot of action swells to 66 interrelated shots depicting different stages of the rescue.

This is classical cutting. It is the blueprint for making movies. If anyone invented it, Griffith did.

"Come, little pussy-cat," Griffith once told an aged lion that he grabbed by the mane and led away from a conversing actor and a director. Griffith was directing *Intolerance* then, a man of forty-one at the height of his powers. The elder Griffith, holding the lap cat above, collapsed beneath the chandelier of the Hotel Knickerbocker in Hollywood on July 23, 1948.

EXERCISE SEVEN: CLASSICAL CUTTING

What this exercise teaches:

- **How to crosscut action to build tension and suspense**

- **How to select shots for their emotional significance**

- **How to compress minutes of action into seconds**

D.W. Griffith is conferring with his six-foot tall red-headed negative cutter, Rose Smith, at a temporary editing table set up in the Loring Opera House projection booth in Riverside, California.

It's January 1, 1915, and their movie continues to defy all attempts to give it a final shape. Having culled 13 of every 14 feet of *The Clansman* Griffith printed since shooting concluded late October 1914, Griffith and Smith are still feverishly cutting, taping, untaping and recutting the ride-to-the rescue scene between previews. "I would come into the projection booth,

and the next day I'd see a lot of the film she'd cut on the floor. Then they'd show the picture at the next regular performance, and maybe cut some more and sometimes put back some that had been cut," the local projectionist remembered.

You Did It Then: **Help Griffith analyze and then compress the ride-to-the-rescue scene, but not by accelerating the projection speed (Silent-era projectionists sometime cranked films faster to lend them an air of frenzy.) First view the *Make Film History* clip collection of some—but not all—shots Griffith included in his ride-to-the-rescue sequence. Then create your own cut. Griffith's crosscut sequence finishes nineteen minutes after it begins. Whittle yours down to less than four minutes. Step by step instructions and the files you'll use are in the digital cutting room at http://makefilmhistory.com.**

PRODUCTION **Make Film History**
DIRECTOR _____
CAMERA _____
DATE   SCENE   TAKE
7

8

MONTAGE AS AGITPROP:
Lev Kuleshov (1920)

"Now I have a close up. Let me show what he sees. Let's assume he saw a woman holding a baby in her arms. Now we cut back to his reaction to what he sees, and he smiles. Now what is he as a character? He is a kindly man. He is sympathetic. Now let's take the middle piece of film away, the woman with the child, but leave his two pieces of film as they were. Now we'll put in a piece of film of a girl in a bikini. He looks—girl in a bikini—he smiles. What is he now? A dirty old man. He's no longer the benign gentleman who loves babies. That's what film can do for you."

Alfred Hitchcock,
TV interview with Fletcher Markle (1964)

Sequences of shots assembled to excite emotion are montages. Griffith used montage to ratchet up tension and to suggest, especially in *Intolerance* (1916), that seemingly unrelated actions can join like the blades of a scissors. Soviet filmmakers studied *Intolerance.* In the aftermath of the Russian Revolution of 1917, they saw in Griffith's crosscutting a way to direct the course of history—or so they thought. One of them, Lev Kuleshov, taught filmmakers that assembling shots into montages imbues them with meaning they cannot alone possess.

At that time a 21-year-old art student, Kuleshov made his discovery about montage in an experiment he conducted in 1920 working

While czarists and Bolsheviks clashed, Lev Kuleshov conceived how context—and conflict—is the mother of meaning in movies. Above, former soldiers of Czar Nicholas, now taking up arms for the Bolsheviks, assemble on Liteiny Prospekt, Saint Petersburg, Russia. Their banner says, "Down with the Monarchy" and "Long Live the Democratic Republic." They are a motley crew of soldiers, junior officers, Cossacks, and sailors. It was early March 1917, the start of the revolution.

on scraps of film left over from pre-revolutionary movies. Joining shots, Kuleshov perceived, creates meaning. Spliced together, shots

Beat the Whites with the Red Wedge (1919) El Lissitzky.

The apparition of these faces in the crowd:
Petals on a wet, black bough.

The lines inspire the thought that each of us emerges from a universal source—when the poet combines them. The combined lines excite a thought that neither by itself would provoke. "In a poem of this sort," Pound explained, "one is trying to record the precise instant when a thing outward and objective transforms it, or darts into a thing inward and subjective."

Pound's assessment of his poem explains Kuleshov's discovery of how montage works in movies. Shot A and Shot B are distinct from one another. Joined by an editor into a sequence, they transfuse each other. Viewing a movie, you see them with the eyes an editor lends you.

Lev Kuleshov had entered the film business in pre-revolutionary Russia as a set designer and actor for director Evgeni Bauer. Barely eighteen years old, he stepped into Bauer's role in *For Happiness* (1917) when Bauer sustained the broken leg that led to the pneumonia that killed him. When the Bolsheviks overthrew the czar, Kuleshov soldiered on in the film business, now cutting and shooting news for the Bolsheviks—that is, recording events as the revolutionaries saw them.

By 1920, revolution seemed ready to spread. Kuleshov enlisted in this activity. Lenin, who insisted that movies should be machine guns for revolutionary thought, had already established the Moscow

assume meanings they do not in themselves possess. Meaning in movies is contextual.

To understand Lev Kuleshov's experiment with montage it helps to think first of poetry. In 1909, American poet Ezra Pound stepped into the sunlight from the métro station at *Place de La Concorde* in Paris, compressing that moment over the course of the following 16 months into a two-line poem (*In a Station of the Metro*):

"The road is covered with snow-drifts. The telephone wire buzzes. The air is so clear. The night is transparent."

"Days of Revolution. Automobile-sledge of the former Czar Nicholas II."

Kuleshov conducted his experiment with montage while opposing armies advanced and retreated during the civil war in Russia that followed the overthrow of the czar. America and European nations were then embargoing shipments to revolutionary Russia, so unexposed film stock was scarce. Kuleshov therefore used old movies to practice cutting while he squinted at the light table in the Re-Editing Department of the Moscow Film Committee. While he was recutting pre-revolutionary films into new ones—"making new subjects from old films"—a splice he

Lenin's two-tone private Rolls Royce Silver Ghost, above, had been fitted out by Czar Nicholas II in 1914 with half tracks behind and wheels with skis in front for winter driving. In its Rube Goldberg way, it illustrates what Kuleshov discovered about montage in movies. One thing joined to another creates something different than either or both. The vehicle resembled a firefly tugging a caterpillar.

H.G. Wells, "Russia In the Shadow," *The New York Times*, November 21, 1920.

Film Committee for creating and exhibiting agit-prop (agitation and propaganda) movies to the millions of Russians unable to read. With other young filmmakers—Dziga Vertov and Eduard Tisse, for instance—Kuleshov ventured out of Moscow riding in Lenin's customized Rolls Royce to shoot agit-prop footage with a Debrie-Parvo camera. He returned from these sorties to assemble footage into movie in the two—story bungalow that housed the Moscow Film Committee and its successor from 1917 to 1929.

A Bolshevist Propaganda Train. Characteristic Picture Depicting the Red Army Hunting Down Capitalists and Anti-Bolshevist Generals.

made with a single shot of pre-revolutionary star Ivan Mozzhukhin taught him what he called "the laws of editing."

In the shot Kuleshov was using, Mozzhukhin gazed at the camera. Mozzhukhin revealed no emotion. But he would begin to "change his emotion" when Kuleshov spliced the shot to other actions. Soviet filmmakers like Eisenstein and Pudovokin who studied with Kuleshov created an aesthetic from his experiment. They were inspired to regard the cutting room as the creative center of a movie and to regard a shot not as a sentence in a paragraph but as a beam intersecting others in a structure. Move one and your building slips off its foundation. Excise a shot from a sequence where it belongs and you maim your movie. Considered this way, sequence and pace matter more than any given shot or cut. In this new aesthetic, plot diverts, but montage *is* the story.

Kuleshov's own early films such as *The Extraordinary Adventures of Mr. West in the Land of the Bolsheviks* (1924) made little use of inventive cutting, but colleagues and students at the Moscow Film Committee built masterpieces of montage inspired by the Kuleshov experiment. Classically cutting editors cut to make movies flow; montage-oriented filmmakers who succeeded Kuleshov cut to make them explode.

Kuleshov's influence is obvious in the work of the more militant and gifted Sergei Eisenstein, who attended Kuleshov's filmmaking workshop in 1923. In *Strike* (1925) and *Battleship Potemkin* (1925), Eisenstein cut to express conflict. He described his method as

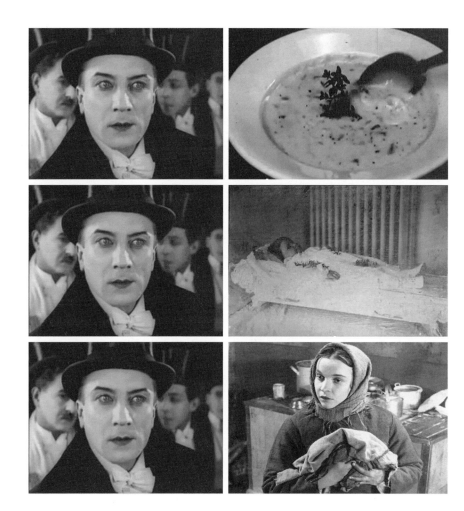

Kuleshov preserved none of the shots he used to create his experiment. But this frame of Ivan Mozzhukhin playing Detective Z in *Le Braiser Ardent* (1923), a movie Mozzhukhin directed and acted in in Paris, can illustrate the Kuleshov effect. The shot precedes a shot of a soup bowl, a child in a coffin, and a girl at play. Audiences perceived Mozzhukhin as hungry, grieving, or gleaming with fatherly solicitude, depending on which shot followed the shot of Mozzhukhin. But the shot of Mozzhukhin was identical in every case.

dialectical materialism made visible—opposites in conflict colliding to create a synthesis. Instead of match cutting to flow action across cuts, Eisenstein often did exactly the opposite. He joined black to white, large to small, moving to still, so that sequences played like combat and expressed revolutionary fervor. This approach to montage gives Soviet movies of the early 1920s, particularly Eisenstein's, vivacity and pugnacious energy. They spew out in quickly changing flows of particulate fragments. They are visual machine guns. They pop on screen. By formal means, they seek to express that conflict, especially class conflict, moves history forward. These are movies intended to reshape minds and memories.

Most movers of twentieth century history looked to movies to shape values and influence popular actions. Griffith served up *Hearts of the World* when Prime Minister Lloyd George beseeched him to aid the British cause in World War I. World War II filmmakers strove to influence public opinion with movies. Ever defamatory, Goebbels produced *The Eternal Jew* (1940). Churchill

Battleship Potemkin (1925), dir. Sergi Eisenstein. Nine shots appear and vanish in this 20-second fragment of the Odessa Steps sequence of *Battleship Potemkin*, the last shot playing less than a second. Shot conflicts with shot as soldiers conflict with civilians. Eisenstein cuts here to disrupt and assail. Form communicates the story. Kuleshov praised the montage in this movie. Censors see things differently than artists do, however. The Motion Picture Commission of New York, for instance, required New York exhibitors in 1926 to excise six shots from the Odessa Steps sequence, including the 7th and 9th above.

allegedly deemed William Wyler's *Mrs. Miniver* (1942), "more important to the war effort than a flotilla of battleships."

But it was Lenin in the Soviet Union who most centrally saw truth as malleable—"we must not regard our knowledge as ready-made and unalterable," he wrote as an exile from Russia in 1908. Lenin therefore unabashedly embraced movies as instruments of war and montage as a weapon. "Cinema is the most important of the arts for us," Lenin told his commissar of education. In 1922, he instructed his commissar for entertainment to classify Soviet films as either "films of entertainment" produced "for purposes of advertisement and commercial purposes" or, preferably, "films with exclusively propagandistic content," every film to be litmus-tested for Marxist orthodoxy by functionaries wielding ideological dipsticks. "Propaganda and pedagogical films must be submitted to experienced Marxists and literary men for evaluation, in order that we never once find ourselves in the unfortunate situation where propaganda achieves results exactly opposite to those intended."

Especially in movies cut by editors influenced by Kuleshov, the first years of Soviet filmmaking were imaginative and inventive. But turning movies into machine guns proved tougher than Lenin and Stalin, his successor, imagined. Once Stalin in 1932 required Soviet art, including movies, to celebrate heroes of labor in unambiguous terms, Soviet movies lost vigor. To survive as an artist was to embrace orthodoxy. In the mid-1930s the arts magazine *Iskusstvo* sounded the requisite note: "Our art is our Communist philosophy

This 1937 drawing depicts an imaginary moment from Russian civil war of 1917-1923. Slightly bowed, Lenin reports a ticker tape dispatch to the larger Stalin. Lenin is the civilian; Stalin is the commander. That Stalin played a negligible role in the civil war was immaterial to the artist, T. Vasilev. Soviet realist style is not necessarily realism.

expressed in visual form!" Show trials that began in 1936 to condemn to death commissars and factional leaders completed the process of silencing the original and terrorizing the inventive.

Kuleshov's ideas for movies failed to match Stalin's and his summons to account for vaguely identified ideological failures arrived in 1935. His crime was "formalism." In his apology to the Union of Soviet Film Workers for his "very many bad films' resulting from ideological error, Kuleshov offered the kind of statement a totalitarian state inevitably requires. "In order to make good films, one must observe funda- mentals, and a fundamental truth is that art must be Party oriented. A director must be a Party person from head to toe, wholeheart- edly and wholemindedly," he testified in a show of abject self-criticism. He made his last movie in 1943, when he became the director of the Soviet film school and wrote unpro- duced screenplays until his death in 1970.

But the Kuleshov Effect—the juxtaposition of images to create meaning that derives from the difference between constituent elements— remains a principal maker of meaning in movies, especially for formalist directors like Alfred Hitchcock who use montage to serve imagination. In *Saboteur* (1942), for instance, Hitchcock's villain seems to smirk sardonically at the hulk of a ship sunk at a pier in the Hudson River. The ship was the French liner Normandie, sunk by accident at Pier 88 in Manhattan on February 9, 1942. The actor was Norman Lloyd, glancing at nothing whatever on a Universal Studio soundstage in Universal City, California. A perfect example of the Kuleshov effect, the splice joins shots made on opposite coasts.

When the Normandie sank unexpectedly in February 1942, Hitchcock dispatched a newsreel crew to film the sunken ship from the point-of-view of a speeding car window. Hitchcock fabricated purpose out of the accident, imbuing the newsreel footage with "meaning" by sandwiching it between shots of the "smirking" saboteur played by actor Norman Lloyd. The script of *Saboteur* included no shots of sabotaged ships.

Norman Lloyd turns his head slowly as he plays a scene in an ersatz taxicab on a soundstage in Universal City, California. Visible through the window, a rear projection shot creates the illusion of Manhattan traffic. Lloyd's "smirk" in a studio 2,450 miles from the ocean liner submerged in Manhattan is an act of conjury. Lloyd "reacted" without ever laying eyes on the ship.

EXERCISE EIGHT: MONTAGE

What this exercise teaches:

- **How to give "meaning" to shots by linking them**
- **How Kuleshov discovered the essence of Soviet montage**
- **How, making movies, combining shots makes them into something new**

"If we change the place of one particle in one problem we alter the past as well as the future..."

A.S. Eddington quoted in R.D. Carmichael, "Einstein's Third Victory: Red-Displacement of Spectral Lines Regarded as Completing Proof of Relativity Theory," *The New York Times*, March 28, 1920.

***You Do It Now*: Re-run Kuleshov's experiment, this time using contemporary footage. You find step-by-step instructions and the shots you'll need in the digital editing room of http://makefilmhistory.com.**

INTERTITLES:
Manuel Orazi (1921)

For *L'Atalantide* (1921) Manuel Orazi designed title cards, costumes, sets, and posters such as these three.

"Do not worry. You have always written before and you will write now. All you have to do is write one true sentence. Write the truest sentence you know."

Ernest Hemingway, *A Moveable Feast*.

Above: American expatriate writer Ernest Hemingway (left), resident of Paris, in Pamplona, Spain, July 1925.

Paris of the early 1920s, where Hemingway wrote the words under the photo, was as close to representing the antipode of Moscow (where Lev Kuleshov intercut shots) as absinthe is to altar wine. Paris was then awash with hookahs, Arabists, discharged French Legionnaires, hoochie coochie dancers, jazzmen, surrealists, Freudian dream analysts, most converging on the idea that reality begins in dreams. To Paris drifted Gertrude Stein and James Joyce and Pablo Picasso. Paris was where the pre-revolutionary actor Ivan Mozzhukhin (whose face Kuleshov was so fatefully splicing) fled. Russian artists of every sort fled Bolshevik Russia for refuge in western capitals, especially Paris, as did millions of counts, smugglers, Jews, and orthodox Christian faithful.

FLEEING RUSSIA WITH GEMS.

Profiteers and Deserting Bolsheviki Tax German Guards' Resources.

BERLIN, Dec. 23.—Russian smugglers are taxing the resources of the customs officials and guards on Germany's eastern frontiers. Large quantities of precious stones and gold rubles have recently been confiscated from shabby looking individuals seeking entrance into Germany.

One of the smugglers had a black bread sandwich studded with diamonds, valued at millions of marks. Another had a large diamond buried in the heel of his boot. Yet another was munching a loaf of bread, which was discovered to be filled with gold rubles.

The majority of the smugglers are said to be profiteers or officials deserting the Bolshevist cause.

The atmosphere in Europe on Christmas Eve, 1921. AP dispatch to *The New York Times*.

While Kuleshov in Moscow in 1921 was teaching himself that the essence of movies is cutting, Manuel Orazi, an Italian lithographer in Paris, was advancing moviemaking in a radically different direction. Orazi was not joining together picture to picture as Kuleshov did. He was joining word and picture. Movies had certainly used titles for decades before Orazi. Before Orazi, however, most silent movie intertitles—those words inserted into scenes to explain action—were essentially black on white cards, one second per word, with five more seconds for slow readers. After Orazi, intertitles, and their sound-era descendents, movie titles themselves, took on shapes and sometimes moved in ways that express the nature of the movie.

In a sense, intertitles of silent movies prefigure the contemporary "tweet" (140 characters or less). They could compress, exhort, suggest, assess. Sometimes they did. "War's peace," judges a title in *The Birth of a Nation* before Griffith moves to shots of the battlefield dead. But usually they didn't. Most simply delivered dialogue or jokes. "To think that I held Paradise in my arms—and didn't know enough to keep it!" winks an intertitle card in *Don't Change Your Husband* (1919). Intertitles might describe a movie's setting—"A Farm in Patagonia"—or the passage of time—"Twenty years later." Most simply wrote out the words a character delivered, as this from *Souls for Sale* (1923) does: "Is there anything about you that *is* real? You-actress!"

Even during the silent era purists argued that silents shouldn't need intertitles because the silent film's story ought to play out plainly before our eyes. Murnau employs just one in *The Last Laugh* (1924), inserted before the ending to point up the ending's absurdity— "Here the story should really end, for, in real life, the forlorn old man would have little to look forward to but death. The author took pity on him and has provided a quite improbable epilogue."

But audiences wanted intertitles, and to guide them, title writers delivered. By the '20s, almost every movie employed intertitles. "Pago Pago-in the sultry South Seas-where there is no need for bed clothes-yet the rain comes down in sheets..." Anita Loos (or someone who shared her Jazz Age sass) intertitled to introduce *Sadie Thompson* (1928).

IL PLEUT

il pleut des voix de femmes comme si elles étaient mortes même dans le souvenir

c'est vous aussi qu'il pleut merveilleuses rencontres de ma vie ô gouttelettes

et ces nuages cabrés se prennent à hennir tout un univers de villes auriculaires

écoute s'il pleut tandis que le regret et le dédain pleurent une ancienne musique

écoute tomber les liens qui te retiennent en haut et en bas

Parisian poet Guillaume Apollinaire (1880-1918) called this 1918 composition, "Il Pleut" (It Rains). It's a poem that begins, "It's raining women's voices as if they had died even in memory..." Shaped poems like this were Apollinaire's most personal creations. He called them "calligrams," meaning words that take on, as octopuses do, the look and shape of whatever they describe.

Orazi carried this idea of his Parisian neighbor to movie titles.

In absinthe-green Paris of 1921, Manuel Orazi hand-painted intertitles to do in a movie what Apollinaire did in *Il Pleut*. In Orazi's intertitles for Jacques Feyder's *L'Atalantide*, word and image fuse. Orazi's intertitles are concrete poems disguised as narrative bridges. They shape words into forms conveying the Orientalist sensibility of Feyder's movie. In the '20s, Hollywood called titles like this "art titles."

THINK AHEAI

Since the layout expresses the difficulty of doing what the word exhorts, the effect is humorous. Orazi brought this kind of word and image interplay to his titles for *L'Atalantide*.

Once Orazi created intertitles like this, other graphic designers, for instance, Saul Bass, created main titles as riveting as the movies themselves. "So important have the titles become that they can be a menace to the movie itself. The titles for the 1962 production of *Walk on the Wild Side*, for example, were so arresting and so widely acclaimed that the film is remembered for little else," a *Life* writer remarked in 1964. Orazi did all this first in 1920. Designers like Kyle Cooper continue the practice today.

A lithographer from Rome, Orazi had worked and lived in Paris since 1896. By 1921, he was known for book and journal illustrations, for jewelry designs and, most of all, for theater posters rendering in *art nouveau* swirls the motion and the dark narcotic smoke of the occult. Through Orazi flowed all streams of Parisian avant-garde thought.

Saul Bass titles for *Anatomy of a Murder* (1959), dir. Otto Preminger.

Masculin féminin: 15 faits précis (1966), dir. Jean-Luc Godard.

Kyle Cooper titles for *Se7en* (1995), dir. David Fincher.

The *L'Atalantide* title cards he produced in the aftermath of World War One evoke the mythic lost Sahara city of Atlantis. The cards are Art Nouveau calligrams that express the mood of a mystical movie.

Orazi brought his taste for tajines and hanging lanterns to his titles for *L'Atalantide*. The movie derives from a 1919 fantasy novel by Pierre Benoît that combines four themes—drugs, sex, death, and a land

beyond time. Feyder shot the film in North Africa. In the story, two French legionnaires, lost in the desert, encounter Antinea, the queen of lost Atlantis. Alive but exempt from time, Antinea is a goddess of voracious sexuality. In her Atlantis, camels sleepwalk across the horizon. Harem slaves drift across the screen. A panther purrs with his head on his mistress's lap. When one of the legionnaire spurns her,

Above left, Orazi poster for the premier of Massenet's opera, *Thaïs*, 1894. Above right, Orazi illustrations for a 1905 French language edition of *Last Days of Pompeii.*

Orazi's poster work put him in contact with impresarios and divas: Loïe Fuller, for instance, whose "serpentine dance" on an Edison film of 1901 enthralled early movie viewers. Orazi's poster of Fuller (above) shows her as a dervish whirling by imperceptible gradients into nothingness.

Orazi's *Le Calandrier Fantastique*. This was a limited edition arts nouveau calendar spoofing black magic that, in 1896, Orazi lithographed for a Paris art gallery. Fusing text into image, Orazi's pages prefigure the astounding sets, costumes, posters, and most of all, the intertitles he designed to express the sleepwalking atmosphere of Feyder's movie, *L'Atalantide*.

NAPIERKOWSKA

2636-4

On the left, a movie theater advertises *L'Atalantide* in Auckland, New Zealand in 1923. A doorway flanked by fluted columns with tapering shafts lent this Fullers' Theater then—as now—the escape-from-reality look perfect for an exhibition of *L'Atalantide*. North Africa was, in the early 1920s, a source of popular fantasy. At Fullers', "I've Seen the Harem," is next week's "brand new shriek."

Above, Stacia Napierkowska, who plays the enchantress in *L'Atalantide*, as she appeared in publicity shots circa 1910-1915.

Antinea induces the second to murder him. Crazed with remorse, the second man escapes but ultimately feels driven to return to Atlantis.

Feyder's movie played in Paris for months. Retitled, it toured America and other English-speaking nations as *Missing Husbands*. After *L'Atalantide*, Hollywood producers sent divisions of French Legionnaires into battle formation on back lots up and down southern California—according to the Internet Movie Database, since 1921, 105 movies or TV episodes have depicted activities of the French foreign legion, and 314 movies or TV episodes have treated Atlantis. *L'Atalantide* inspired countless "me-too" sex-in-the-desert fantasies—for instance, Paramount's *The Sheik* (1921) starring Rudolph Valentino and, eventually, Bernardo Bertolucci's *The Sheltering Sky* (1990). G.W. Pabst shot English, French, and German versions of *L'Atalantide* in 1932. Edgar Ulmer, Giuseppe Masini, and Frank Borzage reshot *L'Atalantide* in Technicolor in 1961. A French-Italian consortium did it again in 1992.

Above left, opening night at Grauman's Egyptian Theater, Hollywood Boulevard, October 18, 1922. Above right, Howard Carter and assistants open King Tut's tomb February 16, 1923.

Viewers around the world were acutely smitten then with Egyptomania: the excavation of King Tut's tomb in 1922 and the allegedly resultant "curse of the pharaohs" created box office magic.

Souls for Sale (1923), dir. Rupert Hughes.
"Are you real or a...mirage?" she (Eleanor Boardman) asks the sheik (Frank Mayo). "Neither. I'm a movie actor," he replies.

Comedy producer Joe Rock and a crew shooting *Mummy Love* in late 1925. Their "location" is the forecourt of Grauman's Egyptian Theater.

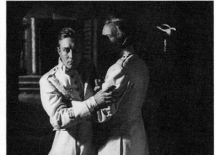

The 23 intertitles that Orazi drew in Paris for *L'Atalantide* using word as elements of design express the wish for rapture that suffuses the movie. Orazi's hand-drawn words make white lines among images of lynxes, peacocks, ibises, and palm trees. Red colors almost every card, signifying, perhaps, blood or dust or moments when sunlight cedes to starlight. Art Nouveau motifs appearing first in the intertitles spill into and out of sets and costumes (also created by Orazi). Words in the titles speak mysteriously and suggestively. In the dark corner of a Paris café, a Dada poet could have written them.

In effect, *L'Atalantide* is where the movie title takes on its modern character. Kinetic titles—titles that move—began soon after Orazi and continue today what Orazi began. Orazi's process was laborious. You can more quickly create a kinetic title today with motion graphics and compositing applications. You'll create one in the exercise for this chapter.

L'Atalantide (1921), dir. Jacques Feyder.
The birds, cats, and arabesque shapes of Orazi's intertitles pervade the film—Orazi designed the sets and costumes, too. A narcotic haze drifts through the movie.
The titles above exemplify the titles of *L'Atalantide*. The first says, "Tell your mistress that I want to see her! I want to see her across this door, this instant!" The second says, "And not a day passed without Saint-Avit dreaming of his companion." The third asks, "Where is my companion?"

EXERCISE NINE: INTERTITLES

What this exercise teaches:

● **How and where to insert film titles**

● **How long a title or an intertitle should remain on screen**

● **How titles interpret silent films and lend tone and meaning to talkies**

● **How fonts & other design elements can enrich your movie**

"Did you tell her about love, travel, moonlight, Italy... that on the other side of the world the sea is phosphorescent, and that there are hummingbirds in flowers, and that you make love under gardenias beside water fountains?" Sidonie Gabrielle Colette, *Gigi*

You Did It Then: **On Orazi's backgrounds for *L'Atalantide* intertitles, "move" the meaning of** the on-screen action in a set of "new" titles. Select fonts and title style consonant with Feyder's Orientalist aesthetic. Then, once you've got the hang of intertitling, write a new intertitle. Step-by-step instructions and Orazi backgrounds for intertitles are in the digital cutting room at http://make-filmhistory.com.

You Do It Now: **Shoot your own silent scene with two performers. Shoot it however you want, including techniques you learned or practiced earlier, but make sure that no dialogue is audible. Make sure you can see the actors talking. (You will need this footage for a dubbing exercise later). Then, write intertitles. As long or short as you want.**

PRODUCTION Make Film History
DIRECTOR
CAMERA
DATE   SCENE   TAKE
9

STUDIO FACTORY:
Sunrise (1927)

"Movies were seldom written. In 1927 they were yelled
into existence in conferences that kept going in saloons,
brothels, and all-night poker games. Movie sets roared
with arguments and organ music."

Ben Hecht

From roughly 1920 until the '50s, Hollywood studios assembled
movies the way car manufacturers cranked out product—they
built the movies, distributed and exhibited them. They controlled
every aspect of production, and the product itself. Like automobile
factory workers, studio workers filled slots in the production
line (and eventually organized unions to protect their interests).
Scripts turned into contracts and cost estimates for electricians,
carpenters, publicists, and after 1927, sound recordists. Directors,
actors, cinematographers and others who worked in movie factories
surrendered their individual talents to the collective effort
inherent in the American studio system.

If American studios viewed movies as mass-market products
created by craftsmen, filmmakers in Europe viewed them as artistic
endeavors, works created by artists. These different attitudes
produced far different results. In 1927, French filmmakers released
49 features and shorts. That same year, seven major American

The William Fox Studio (exterior) on North Western Avenue, Hollywood circa 1927.
Sunset Boulevard and Hollywood Boulevard are the next major cross-streets to the
north.

studios and several minors produced, marketed, and distributed
672. American movies were spreading from Hollywood to theaters
across the world.

Major studios—Loews/MGM, Fox, Warner Bros, and a few others—
effectively monopolized the movie industry in America through a

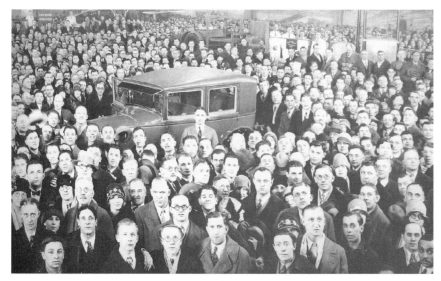

Ford Motor Company released the Model A for pubic sale on December 2, 1927. Ten million people—like these at a Chicago exposition—rushed to inspect the vehicle within the first 36 hours. Ford launched his new product, he stated, "to meet conditions as they will be during this coming prosperous period."

Sunrise opened that same week in Los Angeles. *The Los Angeles Times* reviewer offered praise that should have gratified William Fox. "Murnau has used the camera as would a painter," the reviewer wrote. But Fox's attention may have already moved elsewhere. Movies, like cars, were industrial products in 1927. They rolled off the factory floor almost as rapidly as cars did.

business plan described by financial analysts as "vertical integration." RKO became the fifth vertically integrated major in 1928. Other studios such as Universal, Columbia, and United Artists largely confined themselves to producing. Monogram, Mascot, Majestic, Chesterfield, and Tiffany—the "Poverty Row" studios—attempted both. Vertically integrated studios continued to dominate the industry until, in *United States v. Paramount Pictures* (1948), the Supreme Court effectively broke up the monopoly.

The Brown Derby Restaurant at twilight. Wilshire Boulevard March 28, 1928.

The view is westward down Wilshire Boulevard towards the Santa Monica Mountains. Model A Fords line the sidewalks. Before the Ambassador Hotel, a billboard advertises a William Fox Studios film, *Four Sons*. Proceed nine blocks to Western Avenue, turn right, and you reached the Fox Studio in a 9-minute ride by taxi.

Los Angeles had grown tenfold from 102,000 inhabitants in 1900 to 1,000,000 or more in the 1920s. One factory product transported you to another.

The "back story" of the studios that flourished in the '20s rang variations on a single theme: A hardscrabble, usually Jewish, immigrant became a merchant mogul of movies until his business slipped from his hands and entered a second and often a third life as a publicly-traded corporation.

The studio that William Fox built at North Western Avenue near Sunset Boulevard followed that "self-made mogul" path. In Fox's heyday, the late 1920s, wire services portrayed him as Horatio Alger. Fox rose, the AP reported, "in 27 years from a $17 a week position with a clothing company to control of one of the great organizations of the motion picture industry." Before his enterprise

F.W. Murnau c. 1927. Six feet nine inches of neurosis, Murnau infused his films with fretful intelligence.

William Fox promised him the run of the studio factory. "Mr. Murnau will have his own technical staff and cameraman and all the vast facilities of the Fox company at his command," Fox told guests at a banquet welcoming Murnau to America.

failed, Fox tried to burnish his films with what *Variety* described as "the new idea in the Fox establishment is to provide high-class screen product of distinction and break away from the hokum of flicker melodrama." For a few golden years, Fox attracted people of brilliance and ambition, people like F.W. Murnau, an icy German director who represented "art film" as Fox and other Hollywood moguls understood the concept.

Murnau had piloted a German fighter plane in World War One and had studied theater craft in Berlin with Max Reinhardt, a pioneer expressionist stage and film director. In 1926, while Murnau was shooting *Faust* for UFA, the preeminent German studio, Fox inveigled him to Hollywood to direct prestige movies. Best known then for *Nosferatu* (1922) and the subjective camera of *The Last Laugh* (1924), Murnau told a German publication in 1928, "I accepted the offer from Hollywood because I think one can always learn and because America gives me new opportunities to develop my artistic aims."

For both Fox and Murnau, *Sunrise: A Song of Two Humans* (1927) was that opportunity. Murnau's *Sunrise* annuls the distinction between American commerce and European art. It is a German expressionist movie shot on location at a California lake and inside Fox's studio 1.9 miles from Grauman's Egyptian Theatre on Hollywood Boulevard.

When Murnau arrived at 1401 North Western Avenue in Hollywood in 1926, he found a studio that occupied a ramshackle structure

Near midnight of the silent movie era. The set of *Sunrise* for shot 83A.

American film studios released 672 feature films in 1927, roughly 60 percent higher than their production in 1948, when the Supreme Court effectively terminated the vertically integrated studio system by ordering studios to choose between producing, distributing, or exhibiting movies. All 1927 features were silent, except for three using the Vitaphone disc system favored by Warner Bros. and three employing the Movietone system Murnau used for *Sunrise*.

F.W. Murnau (head above the slate) instructs George O'Brien and Janet Gaynor in shot 83A of the amusement park scene of *Sunrise*. Phillips Smalley looks on.

abutting trolley tracks. Model T Fords parked bumper to bumper along the sidewalk. A raised roof resembling a grain elevator (roof raised up to shine arc lamps down from the rafters) bore Fox's name. On the corner was a tire store, and across the street a billboard touting a sale at Innes Shoes. Nothing visible seemed connected to the movie business, yet everything was: Dorothy's

ruby red slippers in *The Wizard of Oz* (1939) were, it turned out, silk pumps manufactured by that self-same company, Innes. The streetcar in *Sunrise* transporting "the man" and "the wife" from the lake to the city suggests the Western-Franklin trolley that periodically passed the studio door, transformed by Murnau's imagination and mounted on the chassis of a Ford.

Murnau and party arrive in New York, July 1926. In the background, the elfin man in the checked cap with shaded eyes wearing a bowtie matching Murnau's was Carl Mayer, who wrote the *Sunrise* Script. In necktie and cap was Rochus Gliese, *Sunrise* set designer. Closing in on the Fox newsreel camera, Murnau seems to recall *The Big Swallow* of 1901. Murnau never made the voyage home. He perished in an auto accident on the Pacific Coast Highway in 1931.

There was something somnolescent and fairy tale-like about the silence that dropped over a set at Fox in 1927 as a take such as take 83A was about to begin. Grips in fedora hats squatted on platforms. Guards sank their hands into their pockets. Extras froze in the background. Light descended from the roof beams in a giant bell jar suffusing everything with the limitless glow of a dream made palpable and breathing. Take 83A would have required extraordinary discipline: bursts of breath punctuate other shots Murnau made of this "summertime" amusement park sequence. January 1927 was aberrantly cold for Los Angeles, and the William Fox studio was evidently unheated.

To identify director, shot, take, and cameraman for the editor, the slate man held aloft the slate (without clapper, the idea for clappers coming three years later, in 1930, when synchronizing voice and picture in talkies became a problem.) The waiter kept still. The extras hired for the afternoon to dance in the background stood with arms akimbo, motionless until Murnau gave the signal.

Sunrise titles identify nine actors, four writers, and two cameramen. Contemporary sources now name 51 individuals who worked on the film, but hundreds more passed obscurely in the background. (Even Murnau, turned extra, foxtrots in a crowd on a dance floor.) To appreciate the range of talents that collaborated on an American studio movie at that moment when silents were about to yield to talkies, consider just six people who contributed to *Sunrise*.

1. The writer. "You could never hear him walk. He would just appear..." British documentary filmmaker Paul Rotha wrote about scriptwriter Carl Mayer. Mayer completed the script for *Sunrise* in German, at home in Vienna, refusing to remain with Murnau in Hollywood. Mayer had previously scripted *The Last Laugh* (1924) and four other films for Murnau. Mayer's script for shot 83A of *Sunrise* consists of sentence fragments. Murnau made them images.

Carl Mayer's script for shot 83A		Murnau's execution

Close-up of the two:

Sitting at the table in foreground. In bliss—with half closed eyes While in the background. out of focus like. Slowly becomes indistinct And Now:

Visionary suggestions of ladders forming in the clouds Leading earthward. Little angels rustling down the ladders with many, many violins. Floating about the terrace. Pageant like above Ansass and Indre. Bowing melodiously. White out of the fantastic illusionary b.g. a beautiful meadow fades in, vision like. Fantastic flowers growing out of the verdure, in the gentle breeze. Blissful. Seconds.

Finally: vision like, approaching through all this fantastic b.g.

But suddenly, in solid form—standing in front of the table: the waiter! In perspiration In a great rush—to the two with pencil and pad.

TITLE: Will you please pay me—a new shift is coming on?

Carl Mayer's script for shot 83A		Murnau's execution

Ansass looks startled For seconds, staring at the waiter. As though waking from a dream. Now getting up from his seat. Almost timidly. In a half trance.

He reaches in his pocket. While the fantastic background. With angels and meadows Gradually disappear. Like soap bubbles—into nothing. And the whole background is now actual—real. People eating, drinking, laughing. Also dance orchestra playing with full verve. Ansass and Indre. (Close to camera) Ready to leave?

But! Alas! Is she unable to stand erect? Overcome with her great joy? She leans toward him—he supports her.

Perambulator shot of camera following them

Now they walk along like the happiest bridal couple. Through the terrace garden. Where guests at the tables look after them.

Amused at their supreme joy in each other. For seconds thus—the terrace garden. With the same activity. Then:

2 and 3. The cinematographers. Charles Rosher and Karl Struss shot *Sunrise.* Rosher was the senior, having recruited Struss to assist him on a Mary Pickford movie, *Sparrows* (1926). Charles Rosher shot the bulk of *Sunrise* with a silent Mitchell camera and Karl Struss, running the motor-powered Bell and Howell he owned, shot the remainder. Except for particularly challenging shots, neither could specify in later years exactly who shot what in *Sunrise.* Struss shot the Bell and Howell for the tracking shot

Cinematographer Karl Struss, marking footage in a note pad, and F.W. Murnau, in cap and bowtie, supervise the lighting men, the grips, and the operators cranking the camera to film Gaynor and O'Brien in a shot from a montage sequence of *Sunrise.* The grips on the left carry a black background on which a different shot, a bucolic exterior, is to be double exposed as one of several elements in an elaborate process shot.

that accompanies "The Man" on his liaison with "The Woman from the City." Requiring no cranking, the Bell and Howell was easier to shoot from a moving dolly. Rosher and Struss usually shot simultaneously, one shooting the European negative while the other shot the American. "We were both on the set at all times," Struss says.

Rosher, the slate shows, was primary cinematographer when shot 83A begins.

But who knows who shot what? The shot of "The Man" and "The Wife" at the table quickly dissolves into and out of a different shot, a soft-focus shot depicting five "angels" whirling hand-in-hand above the table. By multiple-exposure, other shots pour into the primary one. Several levels of footage blend until, like Prospero, the waiter dispels four of them.

A decade later an optical printer would have composited layers of shots like this. But no commercial optical printer existed in 1927. Using only their cameras, Rosher and Struss themselves fabricated the dissolves, double exposures, and multiple layer shots of *Sunrise.* They bi-packed (double-loaded) developed and unexposed film together to make composite images: shooting, counting footage, rewinding precisely, they served as their own special effects house. Struss and Rosher made real what Murnau envisioned.

Sunrise sometimes resembles European painting or "pictorialist" photos, a "high class" touch that must have pleased William Fox. This may be Struss' influence. Struss had worked as a New York pictorialist (photography as art) still photographer before he migrated to Hollywood. Consider these parallels, one a shot from *Sunrise* and one from elsewhere:

Sunrise frame enlargement (1927).

Jan Vermeer, *The Milk Maid* (c. 1658).

Sunrise frame enlargement (1927).

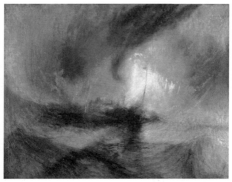

J.M.W. Turner, *Snow Storm—Steam Boat Off a Harbour's Mouth* (1842).

Sunrise frame enlargement (1927).

Karl Struss, *Brooklyn Bridge From Ferry Slip, Evening* (1912). Silver gelatin photograph.

Sunrise frame enlargement (1927).

Gustave Caillebotte, *Le Temps de pluie, Rue de Paris* (1877).

4. The Set Designer. Rochus Gliese sketched out sets and constructed miniatures for *Sunrise* in Berlin. He came with Murnau to Hollywood, but California evidently made little impression on him. At a California lake he constructed a plywood village set fit for Hansel and Gretel. A cross atop a steeple and a weather vane rooster atop another building seemed to state in plywood the emotional poles of the movie—fidelity versus transitory pleasure. A tree Gliese had transported to the lakeside landing slip dropped its leaves, and Gliese trucked in others, workers hand-pasting thousands twice when the first replacements withered. The work employed 300 laborers for two weeks.

Cottage in Tilsit, East Prussia, c. 1890.

Sunrise frame enlargement (1927); Village set, Lake Arrowhead, California.

From village to city, Gliese constructed an imaginary world that entraps the people in it. Floors of sets tilt upward, model trains arrive and depart in matte shots, a city constructed in false perspective (perambulated by midgets) dwarfs the people passing through it. Words blink or glow suggestively from the sets—"National," "Budd,"

"Panopticon" (a circular prison in which the inmates are unaware of being watched). Fox vice-president and general manager Winfield Sheehan recycled Gliese's city set. It doubled as Paris in *7th Heaven* (1927), which Frank Borzage was shooting at night at Fox while, during the day, Murnau was shooting *Sunrise*. Gliese's city set simulates New York in John Ford's *Four Sons* (1928).

Rochus Gliese, Pre-production sketch for *Sunrise* frame enlargement (1927). *Sunrise* (1925).

Rochus Gliese, Pre-production sketch for *Sunrise* frame enlargement (1927). *Sunrise* (1925).

Rochus Gliese, Pre-production sketch for *Sunrise* (1925).

Sunrise frame enlargement (1927).

Sunrise frame enlargement (1927).

5. An Extra. The "waiter" in shot 83A worked anonymously, as did hundreds of grips, electricians, carpenters, and laborers from Ciudad Juárez. Divorced from his wife of 21 years, the father of one child, this extra was 51 years old. He had starred in movies since 1911 but by 1927 he lived by impersonating waiters and men with monocles. He was Phillips Smalley, a Hollywood ghost.

Phillips Smalley. *Sunrise* (1927).

Phillips Smalley with Janet Gaynor and George O'Brien. *Sunrise* (1927).

Though Smalley had directed 339 films before 1927, by the late 1920s his name almost always preceded the lugubrious phrase—"once a famous director." His wife and co-director had been Lois Weber, the "greatest woman director" according to 1920s press agents. Smalley and Weber rose and fell together in two decades from obscurity to acclaim and back to obscurity. They met making silents in New York in 1905. By 1915, they were a Hollywood glamour couple. The Smalleys directed and produced hundreds of movies together, but who did what remains unclear. The marriage floundered, and Smalley grew bitter and alcoholic. Weber divorced him in 1922. She

From 1911 until their divorce in 1922, Smalley and Lois Weber acted in, directed, or produced 117 movies together. In the film they made before their divorce, *Too Wise Wives*, a straying husband, played by Smalley, is attracted to his former flame. This conflict foreshadows the conflict of *Sunrise*. In late 1926, just before appearing as the dignified waiter in *Sunrise*, Smalley played one final time in a movie directed by his former wife, *Sensation Seekers*.

Phillips Smalley (right) and Lois Weber (far right) directing Anna Pavlova in *The Dumb Girl of Portici* (1916).

then lost her studio, while Smalley kept shambling through bit parts. For only one in three of the 101 roles Smalley took between 1929-1939 did he earn a screen credit. In 1939, Smalley died in a hospital five miles from the William Fox Studio on Western Avenue.

6. The mogul. In 1927, William Fox was snatching up theaters across America from his headquarters in Manhattan. Gilded by celebrity, Fox had little idea he was nearly at his end. Movies he simultaneously bankrolled at William Fox Studios in 1927 both won Academy Awards at the first Academy of Motion Picture Arts and Sciences

award ceremony in 1929. Janet Gaynor won best actress for *Sunrise* and for *7th Heaven*. Rosher and Struss won for their *Sunrise* cinematography. Academy members conferred on *Sunrise* an award for "Unique and Artistic Production," the only movie ever so honored.

Fox had entered the work world in 1890 as an 11-year-old cloth sponger and lining cutter in Manhattan's garment district. He spoke rarely and, from Manhattan, ran the studio factory by proxy through hirelings he treated as shop foremen. "The only reason the Fox Film Corporation has made progress is because the power as

William Fox Studio School Room December 10, 1926. William Fox Studio operated a company school for child actors working in Fox movies. In the center is Fox Star Olive Borden—"the Joy Girl"—wearing her signature flapper hat and furs. She starred for Fox in six films in 1926 and died destitute in 1947. In 1927, gossip columnists were linking Borden romantically with "The Man" of *Sunrise*, George O'Brien.

North from the Hollywood Club, July 17, 1929.
"William Fox near death from crash," the AP reported on July 17, 1929. "Movie producer has brain hemhorrage and possibly fractured skull." The panorama shows sunset from Sunset Boulevard.

The Los Angeles Car Show of 1929 erupted in flames on March 5, 1929.

to what will or will not remain in a film has been entirely left with me," he was already writing to his west coast manager in 1918.

In 1929, Fox's moment as the operator of a Hollywood dream factory sputtered to an end. Gravely injured in a car crash, he lost his personal fortune when the stock market crashed three months later. The combined blows destroyed him. Fox lost control of his studio to investors in 1930. He filed for personal bankruptcy in 1936. That same year, Fox visited the Beverly Hills studio of Twentieth Century Fox, a company that had by then absorbed the studio that bore his name. No one recognized him. In 1939, he attempted to bribe a judge. The attempt earned him a jail sentence.When he died in 1952, Hollywood virtually ignored him.

A film and digital processing plant—Fox founded it in 1915—now churns out product at 1401 North Western Avenue, Hollywood. No billboard at that factory mentions that a factory of movies once stood there. But *Sunrise* lives.

EXERCISE TEN: STUDIO FACTORY

What this exercise teaches:

● **How to create variant trailers for different market segments**

● **How to think of a movie as a saleable product**

"Soon or late the movie as an art will have to emancipate itself from the movie as a vast, machinelike, unimaginative, imbecile industry...When that day comes the movies will split into two halves...There will be huge, banal, maudlin, idiotic movies for the mob, and no doubt the present movie magnates will continue to produce them. And there will be movies made by artists, and for people who can read and write."

H. L. Mencken, *The Chicago Sunday Tribune*, July 3, 1927

You Did It Then: **It's 1927. Lindbergh is flying solo to Paris. Movie mogul William Fox has snapped** up the Roxy for millions and he's about to invest a reported $100 million more in a chain of 300 theaters at the start of 1928. For America, for Fox, and the film business, this is the heart of the jazz age. Work with National Screen Service, the leading trailer production house, to create an integrated one-sheet (lobby poster) and trailer campaign that markets this poetic movie, *Sunrise*. Step by step instructions and the image sequence are in the *Make Film History* digital cutting room: http://makefilmhistory.com.

You Do It Now: **Hold a production meeting with others to discuss the nuts and bolts of the scene you will be shooting for Chapter 14 (Production Code). Prepare now for that scene from the perspective of each of these: writer, director, producer, actor, cinematographer, sound recordist, makeup artist, production assistant, and investor.**

ASPECT RATIO:
Abel Gance (1927)

"If it's not in frame, it doesn't exist."
"F.W. Murnau," *The Shadow of the Vampire*

Filmmakers use the term "aspect ratio" to express how relatively high and wide a film frame is. That proportion matters to filmmakers because it matters to people. The human eye sees a visual field roughly 60° inward (towards the nose), 100° outward (towards the ear), 60° up (towards the sky), and 75° down (towards the floor). But cameras can see more variably—interchangeable lenses modify their capacity to see extensively, sharply, or deeply. A fisheye lens, for instance, exaggerates distances, but it captures broad swathes of what's before it—up to 180°. A telephoto lenses see what's distant sharply but confines it to a narrow field of vision—30° or less. Differences like that tint how we feel about what we see on screen. Where an element appears within a frame expresses what it dominates, what dominates it, and what it is. Periphery and center, top, bottom, left, right, enclosed or flowing off the screen, are the elements of *mise-en-scène*. The frame itself, however, is your window. It determines what you see.

Consider 35 mm film stock, the industry standard. It derives from a single order for nitrocellulose film stock coated with a light-sensitive

Shadow of the Vampire (2000), dir. E. Elias Merhige.

Backed into the right foreground, John Malkovich playing director F.W. Murnau inveighs the actor he has cast as Nosferatu (Willem Defoe) to discipline his vampire impulses. The widescreen format creates an expanse that separates the characters. Facing different directions in foreground and background respectively, each exists in a solitude of his own making. The man and the actor (he really *is* a vampire) exchange words without exchanging glances. In effect, each soliloquizes himself as he appears to speak to the other.

The width to height aspect ratio of this shot—2.35:1—makes the psychic no man's land of this film immediately visible. Merhige shot *Shadow of the Vampire* with Super 35 mm negative film stocks that widen the standard 35 mm image by appropriating film stock margins normally reserved for analog sound tracks. Printing the Super 35 negative anamorphically—that is, by compressing the image horizontally to uncompress it during projection—Merhige completes the process of echoing, by widening it, the 1.33:1 world of Murnau's *Nosferatu* (1922).

The widescreen aspect ratio here establishes the cross-purposes of the characters.

The subjects seem perched in a ladder of light leading upward in this traditional Academy ratio (1.37:1) frame largely because the vertical dimension of the frame approaches the horizontal.

The central character seems crushed and dwarfed by the horizontal sign, balustrade, building, and, around them, the horizontal reach of the frame in this anamorphic widescreen (2.35:1) frame from *The Lives of Others* (2006). Aspect ratio conveys a point-of-view in each frame.

emulsion that Thomas Edison placed with George Eastman in 1892. Edison needed flexible film to run his peephole viewer, the Kinetoscope, then under development. The six ribbons of film Eastman sent measured fifty feet long and 1-9/16 inches (slightly wider than 35 mm) across. Edison employees perforated edges at even intervals to provide purchase for gears. Every fifth perforation inaugurated a new frame. With 5 mm outside each side of the picture frame sequestered for sprocket holes, a frame 24.89 mm wide and 18.67 mm tall became the motion picture standard, 1.33:1.

Although other early filmmakers invented competing products—for instance, the Lumières marketed a one-sprocket hole system and American Mutoscope's much wider 68 mm film slid without sprocket holes through camera and projector—the Edison aspect ratio prevailed. It emulated the human field of vision no better than competing shapes. But Edison headed up a major industrial conglomerate and could out-market and out-litigate the artisanal firms competing with him for camera and projector customers. Smaller film stocks intended for amateurs abounded—Pathé, for instance, sold an estimated 300,000 Pathé Baby 9.5 mm cameras

Aspect ratios measure rectangles but express values, too. The Fox Grandeur widescreen frame from *The Big Trail* expresses the sweep of the wagon train story. The narrower frame from *City Lights* fits the intimate, more personal scale of Chaplin's comedy.

Both *The Big Trail* (1930), above left, and *City Lights* (1931), above right, date from the transitional period of 1926-1932 when Hollywood was introducing sound tracks to movies. Studios then briefly experimented with wider and narrower non-standard aspect ratios. Different themes inspired different aspect ratios.

Technical as well as artistic concerns inspired the new aspect ratios. The *City Lights* frame is narrower (1.2:1) than the 35 mm standard because an optical sound track consumes space hitherto devoted to image in the silent film era. *The Big Trail* frame is far wider (70 mm) than the 35 mm standard for artistic reasons, but the Fox executives also required Raoul Walsh to simultaneously shoot a standard 35 mm version, anticipating that few theaters outside of Los Angeles and New York could exhibit the experimental Grandeur widescreen. Fox also created Spanish, French, and German versions using numerous different actors.

Widescreen Fox Grandeur failed when exhibitors resisted. The Movietone aspect ratio of *City Lights* disappeared when, in 1932, the Motion Picture Academy adjusted the 35 mm standard to accommodate a sound track, reducing the 35 mm image size standard to 22 mm by 16 mm, or 1.37:1.

and projectors starting in 1922-1923. But once Edison's association (The Motion Picture Patents Company) adopted 35 mm in 1909, 35 mm endured as the international standard until at least the early 1950s. To this day Kodak continues to manufacture 35 mm color negative, reversal, and intermediate film stocks (along with 65 mm film stocks for theatrical productions and 16 mm and Super 8 stocks for documentary and amateur use).

Numerous filmmakers had elongated the rectangle of film into a widescreen ribbon before the 1920s. A magician, Raoul Grimoin-Sanson, for instance, did three days' vigorous business at the Paris Exposition of 1900 exhibiting a 360° wrap-around movie of interlocking images revealing Brussels, London, Spain, Tunis, the Sahara, and elsewhere as seen from the perspective of a slowly rising balloon.

The Big Trail (1930). dir. Raoul Walsh.

Arthur Edeson shot the 70 mm Grandeur version (above and below left). Shooting from a tripod to Edeson's right, Lucien Andriot shot the 35 mm version (below right). In widescreen, the movie is a saga. In academy ratio, it is a romance.

Above, the pale region simulates what the camera lens captures. Within the camera, film gates crop the image into the standard rectangle of movie images.

No law of physics required movies to take the shape of rectangles. The curved surface of a camera lens bends light into a circle at the focal point, turning the image top to bottom and bottom to top, as the human eye does. Movies could have been round. The world appears round in a telescope. But circular film frames would necessitate radical changes in movie camera mechanics that audiences have not yet sought. So film gates in cameras simply lop circular images into rectangles by obscuring arcs of light peripheral to the target rectangle. Television engineers in the 1940s continued this practice, squeezing the circular image natural to the television tube into the 1.33:1 screen shape already familiar to film audiences.

Casablanca (1942), dir. Michael Curtiz.

Curtiz organizes this 1.33:1 film frame around the mouth of the piano player, actor Dooley Wilson. Wilson's mouth marks the point of dominant contrast created by the arches descending from above to a point midway between both vertical and horizontal edges. A backlight highlights Wilson's cheek.

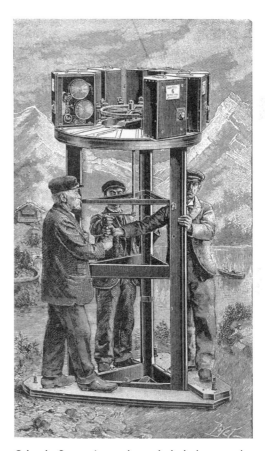

If this shot were cropped into the 2.35:1 aspect ratio of *Shadow of the Vampire*, as it is here, Curtiz's shot would lose a strong center. Dooley Wilson now sinks into the crowd, since he no longer marks the point where arches from above intersect the frieze of human faces. No darkness counterweights the lower left, so the shot looses balance, contrast, and depth.

Grimoin-Sanson's movie encircled viewers who gathered in the basket of a simulated balloon. Cameras fixed to ten points around the compass shot 70 mm footage from ascending and descending balloons. His screen was 10 yards high, 111 yards around. His aspect ratio was 11:1. Grimoin-Sanson's called this spectacle Cinéorama half a century before Cinerama Productions imitated the spectacle and borrowed back a variant of the name.

Gance's *Napoléon* triptych projected at its 3.99:1 aspect ratio.

But most important of the early non-standard widescreen films is 1920s French filmmaker Abel Gance's *Napoléon*. While American filmmakers in 1927 were slipping synchronous sound into movies, Abel Gance in Paris was conducting an experiment in "aspect ratio" that illustrates how pervasively the exterior shape of a movie influences how an audience receives it. Gance called his experiment with shape "Polyvision." In 1927 he moved the film screen outward towards the oblong shapes now in common use. Gance's Polyvision is less well remembered now than the Vitaphone sound track, but by the 1950s, widescreen formats deriving from Gance and others reshaped movies and transfused studios with a second life at a time when television broadcast networks seemed about to eclipse them.

In segments of *Napoléon*, Gance uses the film rectangle as an accordion (to use Gance's own metaphor) that expands and contracts according to the filmmaker's need to contrast or aggrandize images. *Napoléon*—or more exactly, that four-hour fragment of *Napoléon* Gance wrestled into loose narrative for his premiere—concludes with a widescreen segment that continues to influence film history. In a twenty-minute three-screen triptych conclusion, Napoléon, his soldiers, and an eagle advance into Italy. The segment prefigures the 146° widescreen of Cinerama by a quarter century and cinched Gance's reputation among producers as a genius director never to be trusted with a penny of your money. When the movie failed commercially, Gance regarded himself as

Napoleon (1927), dir. Abel Gance. "Polyvision" was Gance's term for the widescreen triptych he created for the climax of this first installation of *Napoléon*. Action plays on left, center, and right panels of the 4.0:1 screen, where images sometimes move in unison and sometimes counter point each other. Especially when double exposed shots occupy one or more panels, the rectangular screen seems to open and shut like an accordion. Gance never shot the successive five installations he contemplated, but the split screens of Michael Wadleigh's *Woodstock* (1970) recall Gance's innovation.

a *poète maudit*, that is, a poet accursed by the powerful. But in 1962, the Cinerama Corporation honored his achievement when it reopened the Paris theater near the Arc de Triumphe that it used for Cinerama movies, naming it "Empire Cinerama—Theatre Abel Gance." Gance lived to see *Napoléon* successfully revived in 1981. In the subsequent three decades, his film has risen to legendary status. "One of the most ambitious films ever made," composer Carl Davis called *Napoléon* before he conducted his original score

for a five and half hour revival version in 2012—in a 1931-era silent movie palace in Oakland, California.

Gance premiered *Napoléon* at a charity benefit attracting the elite to the Paris Opera House on April 7, 1927. A special purpose 40-foot-wide screen constructed in three sections behind a red velvet curtain displayed the triptych projected simultaneously by three projectors. *Napoléon* complete is six hours, more or less, of rapid cutting, subjective camera, thematic montage, tinting and toning. It is a handmade artist's movie—Gance cut it not with a Moviola but by squinting at footage he held aloft against a windowpane. As *The Jazz Singer* was mostly silent, *Napoléon* played mostly within the standard 35 mm rectangle. But what especially intrigued the invited crowd were those moments when Gance breaks out from the 35 mm rectangle and spills action across the three parallel screens. This was extremely widescreen footage, even by twenty-first century standards, approximately 3.99:1. Wrote one critic:

> **The curtains are parted without a sound, displaying side panels where the action unfolds with extraordinary scope and strength. The audience feels miraculously liberated. Reality and dreams no long appear through a tiny casement; a whole wall grows transparent like crystal and opens up another universe. The spectators suddenly become a crowd watching a crowd. The onrush of this magical world causes an emotional shock of rare intensity. This is one of those inventions which one knows to be absolutely essential immediately when one first contemplates them.**

The Return (2003) dir. Andrei Zvyagintsev. A caryatid emanating darkness that rises from her shoulders to fill the room, the woman in black centers this widescreen (1.85:1) shot. Illumination from an unseen source within the chamber on the right creates more shadow than light, and the resultant shadows raking across the walls and floor accentuate the mysterious starkness. We behold her from eye level as the solitary woman looks inward, regarding herself as we do. We see the whole room and, except for the woman, there is no one in it. Composed and lit this way, the widescreen rectangle inspires thoughts and feelings about mystery and solitude that pervade *The Return*.

But imagine if a broadcaster, as simulated (above right), were to crop the shot between right and left vertical edges of a 1.33:1 academy ratio film frame. The mysterious woman becomes a dreamy housewife sitting on a bed in an under-electrified bedroom.

How you use the dimensions of your film frame determines, in part, what viewers see in it.

Eisenstein, Pudovokin, and other Soviet filmmakers met Gance in Paris in 1929 and, says film historian Kevin Brownlow, thanked him for teaching them the art of making movies. But *Napoléon* failed commercially and Gance never finished it. The April 1927 release was merely part one of the six-part epic he contemplated, and by October 1927, *Napoléon* was yesterday's revolution. Synchronous sound films were supplanting the silent movie. Projecting *Napoléon* as a widescreen extravaganza required equipment and training few exhibitors were willing or able to install.

Other widescreen formats introduced in the late 1920s such as 70 mm Fox Grandeur, 65 mm Vitascope, and 63.5 mm Natural Vision, competed for screens, but exhibitors, investing now in sound projection technology, resisted them. Sound, for a moment, trumped image. To release *Napoléon* in America in 1929, MGM disfigured the movie, eliminating the widescreen segments and concluding it, according to Brownlow, with a close-up of George Washington and the American flag. In 1928, Gance sold off the scenario for the second installment of *Napoléon* to a German actor/producer. In 1934, Gance re-edited the 1927 fragment into a dubbed sound version, cannibalizing the original negative. This, too, failed. Disconsolate, Gance then burned the negative for all triptych (three-screen) segments except the final one, according to Brownlow. In 1958, Gance explained to Brownlow his enduring faith in "Polyvision," his term for the widescreen process he employed in *Napoléon*. "The cinema on one screen," Gance said, "is a melody played on the piano with one hand. Polyvision will orchestrate it, will provide the range and power of a symphony...Polyvision is a sort of accordion." The Polyvision segments of *Napoléon* remained in pieces until restorers, led by Brownlow, began reassembling them. In 1971, Gance cut *Napoléon* footage yet again into *Bonaparte and the Revolution*, shooting new scenes, dubbing old ones, and constructing new montages.

Widescreen formats—1.62:1 or wider—introduced in the 1950s constituted the film industry's push back against the Cyclops eye of television. Films got wider because cathode tube screens were taking over living rooms. George Stevens shot *Shane* (1953) in standard 1.37:1 35 mm, for instance, but Paramount premiered the movie as faux widescreen 1.66:1. The studio trimmed off top and bottom of the image using aperture plates custom installed in first run projectors and projecting the soft-matted (i.e., cropped in the projector) image with wide-angle lenses to further elongate the movie. Stevens detested the aspect ratio change: "It's fine if you want a system that shows a boa constrictor to better advantage than a man."

These various experiments with shape teach something critically important for contemporary filmmakers, particularly as film stocks and video formats evolve beyond the one-size-fits-all 35 mm standard of the classic Hollywood period. Like the shape of a face or the scent of a gardenia, the shape of an image can and does evoke emotion. The aspect ratio a filmmaker selects establishes a point of view, or at least invokes it. A shot resembles a set of nesting babushka dolls. The largest doll—enclosing all the rest—is the aspect ratio. See for yourself by experimenting with one of Gance's triptychs in the exercise below.

EXERCISE ELEVEN: ASPECT RATIO

What this exercise teaches:

● **How to crop movie shots**

● **How to combine multiple shots as "pictures in pictures"**

● **How the size and aspect ratio of a shot influences what it "means"**

You are an Abel Gance booking agent responding to an exhibitor in Provence unequipped to project *Napoléon*.

You Did It Then: Create new triptych shots for a "new version" of Napoléon combining standard 35 mm shots that Gance used elsewhere in the movie. Then take apart a widescreen triptych from *Napoléon*, convert it back into the three 35 mm shots it originally was. Then manipulate the shots other ways, too. Step-by-step instructions and the files you need are in the digital cutting room at http://makefilmhistory.com.

You Do It Now: Crop one of the still photographs you created for Chapter 5 (Mise-en-Scène). Create a new aspect ratio. Describe how it changes the feel of the shot.

PRODUCTION Make Film History
DIRECTOR _____
CAMERA _____
DATE   SCENE   TAKE
11

SYNCHRONOUS SOUND:
The Jazz Singer (1927)

"Can you feel the air?"
**Theodore Case, film sound pioneer, speaking in 1924
into his improved #5 microphone**

Sound did not enter movies at the end of the silent era. It was always there. There *was* no silent era. Filmmakers sought to use sound from the very beginning. Some used live musicians to convey to actors the mood of a scene. Others used it to signal the audience. Producers in the 1890s already accompanied movie prints with music scores, providing cues and leitmotifs for specific characters. As early as 1884, William Dickson tried synchronizing sound track (fiddle) recorded on the phonograph with picture track (men waltzing) for display in the peephole of the Edison kinescope. A pianist played as the Lumières projected their first movies in the Grand Café in 1895. A metronome or a piano paced actors in Georges Méliès movies. Entirely silent films were always as rare as solitude itself.

What audiences heard varied from venue to venue. A piano player, or an organist, or eventually a symphony orchestra might play. A tenor/composer from Pittsburgh, Joseph Carl Breil, composed an early film score for Adolph Zukor's Famous Players imported production of *Queen Elisabeth* (1912). Breil conducted the orchestra

Opening night for *The Jazz Singer* (1927), October 7, 1927.
The New York Times reviewer described the moment, "When the film came to an end, Mr. Jolson himself expressed his sincere appreciation of the Vitaphoned film, declaring that he was so happy that he could not stop the tears."

Sun-Up (1925), dir. Edmund Goulding.

In this production still (above left), Conrad Nagel clings to Pauline Starke while musicians evoke the mood of this silent movie scene playing harmonium and violin.

In a different production still (above right) showing the film as shot, the musicians have vanished. But in the theater others musicians played similar music for the audience.

Jean-Paul Sartre remembers in *The Words* about the silent movie theaters of his childhood, "I liked the incurable muteness of my heroes. But no, they weren't mute, since they knew how to make themselves understood. We communicated by means of music; it was the sound of their inner life."

for *Cabiria* when it played Chicago in 1914. D.W. Griffith commissioned him to score *The Birth of a Nation*. (*Intolerance* financially crippled Griffith because he saddled the movie with a costly road show symphony orchestra, not because it did poor business.)

By the mid-1920s, half of America's movie theaters interpreted film action with an organ. The rest used a piano or ensembles of two players or more. But virtually every theater used something. Music publishers sold boilerplate themes (Chase #3, Lovers #7) for movies. In 1927, the Rialto Theater on Manhattan's 42nd Street owned 20,000 musical themes for live musicians plus an organ that imitated instruments and twittered like birds. So the "talkie"

This cue sheet for a silent romantic comedy of 1926 provides 18 minutes of musical themes for the 70-minute film. Cues drawn from popular standards and music specifically composed to play behind films start at no specific film frame but, instead, begin when the conductor perceives onscreen the action the cue sheet describes. When "George leaves room-Doll still swinging," the music compiler instructs, play Steele's *The Players' Promenade*, "slowly, ala Burlesque...Keep in time with doll. A racket roll may be effectively used here and in previous number. A racket roll and thud on timpany as doll finally falls."

Gilbert Roland with Norma Talmadge.   **Raymond Griffith with Betty Compson.**   **Rudolph Valentino with Vilma Bánky.**

revolution of 1927 did not introduce sound into movies. It gave filmmakers, instead, a means to deploy sound precisely. Warner Bros., the studio that introduced synchronous features first, regarded recorded scores originally as a way to save on payments to live musicians.

Stars with limousine faces and streetcar voices often floundered in the synchronous sound era. In silents, Norma Talmadge epitomized glamour, but in talkies she spoke Brooklynese. Raymond Griffith was a silk top hat, a tuxedo, and a comic grin, but childhood disease left him unable to speak above an inaudible whisper. Vilma Bánky, ravished by Rudolph Valentino in *Son of the Sheik* (1926), spoke in a pleasant soprano, but her Hungarian accent in

This is Heaven (1929) rendered her virtually incomprehensible to American audiences. Silent stars often saw sound as the end of movies. Cowboy Tom Mix, for instance, soldiered on in nine movies and a serial during the sound era, but he lamented to director Raoul Walsh, "They ain't shootin' pictures any more. They're makin' phonograph records."

In the shorthand version, film history divided between silents and talkies in 1927 when Warner Bros. premiered *The Jazz Singer* on Broadway. But that compression distorts.

The Jazz Singer was a 15-reel silent film that included twenty minutes of Vitaphone sound-on-disc recorded music and two minutes of dialogue ad-libbed by singer Al Jolson. If perfectly synchronized, the recorded sounds and the projected imaged created the illusion of synchronous sound.

The Jazz Singer premiere was, indeed, as rich in pathos as, well, a silent era tearjerker. The day before the opening, Sam Warner, who led Warners Bros. into Vitaphone sound production, died unexpectedly in Los Angeles. Though the surviving Warners missed the opening, the show *did* indeed go on as scheduled, and the sound segments, recorded on separate 16-inch Vitaphone discs, *did* synchronize successfully. Viewers were entranced. "I for one realized that the end of silent drama is in sight," a reviewer wrote.

False, however, is the idea that no movie had ever offered recorded sound before *The Jazz Singer*. Edison (Kinetophone) and other producers had been jerry-rigging together phonographs and projectors since the first decade of the century, stymied only by their inability to synchronize sound reliably and their inability to amplify it adequately. In 1900, Clément-Maurice of the Phono-Cinema Theater was already projecting a fragmentary sound-on-cylinder and picture version of *Cyrano de Bergerac* at the Paris World's Fair. D.W. Griffith released *Dream Street* in 1921 with a song, brief crowd sounds, and a sound-on-disc prologue he himself orated. "I wonder if there isn't a Dream Street running through the heart and soul of every human being in the world," he mused.

By October 1927, American and foreign film producers had already released 500-600 vestigial sound movies. Fox had acquired rights in 1926 to sound-on-film technology developed by Theodore Case

"Talking Pictures," proclaims the International Theater of Niagara Falls, New York in October 1908, fully 19 years before *The Jazz Singer*. The films were likely E.E. Norton Cameraphone one-reelers. Beside the movie theater a 24-hour drug store sold Kodak films and glass plates. Between the movie theater and the drug store, in black from head to toe, stands a spectral, shadowy man, waiting, perhaps, for the streetcar to Buffalo or tomorrow.

and Earl Spoonable. Fox used it to record, for instance, Lindbergh's take-off on his trans-Atlantic solo to Paris from Long Island in May 20, 1927. In the film, viewers see the plane lumber forward, hear a voice shout, "Pull Up!" and see the spectators gathered at runway pushing towards the clouds as if to help Lindbergh's plane get aloft. Fox projected the footage at the Roxy Theatre that night and again the subsequent evening when Lindbergh landed. "More than 6,000 persons arose and cheered, drowning out the noise of the recording machine," a journalist reported.

Sound entered in stages into the movies. Warner Bros. used sound-on-disc technology developed by Vitagraph to release 45 synchronous sound short films during 1926 and 1927. In them, singers sing and vaudevillians deliver patter. Warner's *Don Juan* (1926) featured recorded sound effects and an orchestral score (but not dialogue). Fox released *Sunrise* with a sound track consisting of orchestral score and sound effects in September 1927 and re-released *7th Heaven* the same month, retooled with a sound track of music, sound effects, and non-synchronous voices.

Though not the first sound movie, *The Jazz Singer* was the first dramatic "talkie." And that *was* enough to make it monumental. Al Jolson's patter—"Wait a minute, wait a minute, you ain't heard nothing yet!"—inaugurated the sound movie era perhaps because, unlike music tracks surrounding action and characterizing it, Jolson's words seem to address the audience directly and emanate out of Jolson himself. He was "there," present in the movie, peering out, talking, and acknowledging you. The spoken words *were* Jolson.

After Jolson's even more commercially successful talkie of 1928, *The Singing Fool* (1928), a backstage tearjerker, silent movie production in America waned. Studios converted silents mid-production into talkies. Stand-ins spoke for actors who would not or could not—"The Woman From the City" in *Sunrise*, Margaret Livingston, became the voice of Louise Brooks in *The Canary Murder Case* (1929). Even then, audiences noticed the imperfect dubbing. "It is quite obvious that Louise Brooks... does not speak her lines. Why the producers should have permitted them to be uttered as they are is a mystery far deeper than the story of this picture," a reporter observed.

Of several rival sound-on-disc and sound-on-film recording systems, the Vitaphone sound-on-disc system seemed at first the most effective. A vacuum tube amplified the signal and produced

The Jazz Singer (1927), dir. Alan Crosland.

"It seemed almost unreal, not as if Jolson were there in person, but that his spirit was singing the words," a news service writer reported the day after the premiere. A "real toad," to use Marianne Moore's metaphor, had suddenly made real the imaginary garden of the silent film.

sound audible to large audiences. But the Vitaphone system was cumbersome. Discs that were worn, scratched, or shattered failed to synchronize with the film, which itself could tear. A projector accessorized with a turntable to play sixteen-inch shellac discs approached the size of a rhinoceros. Projectionists needed one hand to run the adjustable speed projector and the other to tend the phonograph.

From this dual purpose 35 mm Kalee projector of 1933 came Vitaphone sound-on-disc movies like *Lucky Star* (above) and sound-on-film optical movies.

Sound-on-disc recordings played outward from center to periphery. Rising to 40, a counter around the exterior was to record "times played."

Sound-on-film systems operated differently. Inside the sound-on-film camera, an oxide bulb responding to changes in electricity inscribed a sound track on the film negative. The track was either of variable density (Fox Movietone) or variable width (RCA Photophone). Variable density tracks represented loud and soft by means of horizontal lines of varying opacity. By 1930 Fox Movietone and RCA Photophone sound-on-film systems supplanted the Vitaphone sound-on-disc system. Today, film prints for theatrical projection continue to utilize the variable width sound emulation method, now radically improved. Dolby SR Stereo, Dolby Digital,

Sony Dynamic Digital Sound and scores of other innovations continue to evolve sound-on-film technology.

With a sputter of voices, movies then awoke. Audiences at home and abroad responded to talkies in whatever language studios cast them. During the winter of 1929, approximately a dozen Paris theaters exhibited sound movies. By June of 1930, about fifty did. Producers shot simultaneous domestic and foreign versions of their films. Hal Roach Studios exported English, Spanish, French, German, and Italian language versions of Laurel and Hardy's *Pardon Us* (1931). Technicians learned how to dub music under dialogue tracks by double-exposing sound tracks. Sound work could be as monkish as calligraphy—technicians preparing optical sound tracks for duplication employed small fluff brushes to sweep away dirt specks that created noise. Rouben Mamoulian may have pioneered the practice of editing sound on parallel tracks of 35 mm film when he shot *Applause* (1929). A four-track dubbing system standard developed in the 1930s—one track for dialogue and three for music and effects.

Naysayers mourned what they deemed the universal language of the silent movie. Australian film censor W. Creswell O'Reilly deplored "the slang and the atrocious accent, the vulgarity, the noise, and the preoccupation with the sordid that are so prevalent [in the American 'talkie'] and lamented "the loss of 'the eloquent and vital silence' and 'the mystery and beauty' of the silent film." But studios woke up jubilant. Before the stock market

"You—you're not supposed to come in here," stammered Emerson Slipe, the tone expert. "Why, Emerson!" pouted Roxie. "Not stay close to my tiger man when I'm not busy?" The purple eyes filled with tears. "You wouldn't say no, honey?"

By 1929, the movie sound engineer was becoming a romantic hero in popular fiction, as in this short story in *Photoplay* from July 1929.

Wrote recording pioneer David Sarnoff on June 16, 1928: "I could see we were going to need many sound effect records which we could dub or re-record in these productions, therefore we started to make 'effect' records...

We have in our library of 'effect' records automobiles, tractors, sounds of the rolling sea, army tanks, a Chinese Orchestra, crowds cheering... which can be embodied into sound pictures."

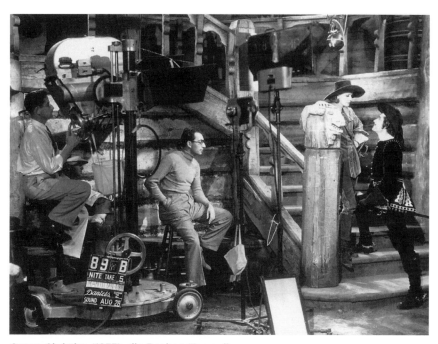

Queen Christina (1933), dir. Rouben Mamoulian. Mamoulian (center), a theatrical director, arrived in Hollywood when talkies supplanted silents. Here he directs Greta Garbo and John Gilbert for their last time together. Gilbert floundered in the synchronous sound era.

crashed, Warner Bros. estimated 1929 after-tax net earnings of $16,500,000—equivalent to $212,000,000 in 2012. *The Pittsburgh Press* financial columnist pronounced, "This will represent a new high record in profits for any amusement company and is extraordinary evidence of the revolution that sound films have brought about in the industry."

Those who resisted sound had a point. Synchronous sound *did* at first suppress motion, diffuse lighting, and straightjacket actors. Sequestered briefly into soundproof booths to muffle their grind and clatter, cameras moved less. Until Mitchell introduced the first

effectively blimped (sound suppressed) camera in 1932, directors shooting outside the booth sometimes resorted to hanging horse blankets on cameras to muffle them. Sound-on-film *did*, temporarily, dim expressive lighting. Editors now needed multiple cameras, shooting simultaneously from different angles, to cover even simple two-person dialogue—when a film stock carried both sound track and picture track, the tracks were essentially unseverable. But to light for multiple cameras shooting from different

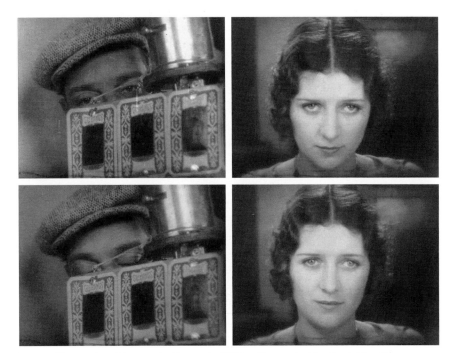

Buster Keaton lost his way in the early 1930s. Above, in his silent *The Cameraman* (1927), Keaton creates an electric moment out of crosscut close ups. Keaton loves an attractive stranger. She feels the same. Fourteen seconds flicker magically.

Above, in Keaton's first talkie, *Free and Easy* (1930), Keaton attempts a similar moment. But a thirty-seven second take of interminable "serious talking" dispels his magic.

Elmer: Will you do me a favor?

Elvira: Why, surely, Elmer. What is it?

Elmer: Well, I've got a lot of serious talking to do and you've got a lot of serious listening to do. What's the matter?

Elvira: I was listening.

Elmer: Oh. Well. I'll tell you. You know, a fellow reaches my age there's a lot of serious problems come up. For instance, taking a girl away from her mother. Oh, before I take a girl away from her mother, I...

Mother: [off screen]: Elvira!

Elvira: I'm coming, Mother!

places was, necessarily, to light for many of them imperfectly. Flat even lighting temporarily replaced the pencils of light that underscored action in late silent movies. How actors move—blocking—changed, too. The leading man in *Lights of New York* (1928) bruited his lines directly into the microphone secreted in the flowerpot. He had to remain audible.

So sound gave and it took. In part, sound put actors on a leash—Fred Astaire had to dance in sync to taps he had previously

recorded in order to render tap sounds audibly. But it also freed actors to utter in their own voices lines that express who they are. Sound is Garbo in *Grand Hotel* (1932), eyes downcast at a door jamb, murmuring, "I want to be alone."

Most directors had adjusted to sound by the early 1930s. A tracking shot at the start of Rouben Mamoulian's sound film, *Dr. Jekyll and Mr. Hyde* (1931), glides portentously. A montage of (albeit imperfectly mixed) sound tracks in Ernst Lubitsch's

Monte Carlo (1930) turns a train compartment carrying Jeanette Macdonald into a love song to the cosmos. But numerous silent filmmakers struggled, especially comedians. Chaplin resisted sound. Dialogue he wrote for *City Lights* (1931) he never used. He abandoned a draft of what would have been an anti-colonial talkie in 1932. Chaplin's lawyer fired letters at a producer who, in 1937, planned to slip the Little Tramp a voice by dubbing one into two-reel silent Chaplin movies.

Contemporary filmmaker can use sound more ways and more easily than the first generation could. Filmmakers today distinguish two kinds of sound—wild and synchronous. Wild sound (sound not recorded to coordinate simultaneously with the picture track) includes sound effects, voice-over or narration, room noise, and pre-recorded music tracks. Wild sound enters a movie by invitation only. Filmmakers insert it into a sound track to expand, explain, reveal, or contradict what the picture track suggests. Wild sound can weave an invisible net around a nondescript shot, turning prosaic footage into memorable imagery by vesting it in a context. Interpreted by wild sound, shots take on meanings or new meanings as the ear contextualizes what the eye perceives.

Once you've used wild sound to interpret a film frame, you perceive how it builds meaning in movies. Dancers, for instance, will seem to sway in time to music inserted in the sound track because the eye and ear crave connections and contrive to find them. Above, an actual voice-over and an imaginary one both appear beneath

"I can't be held to that promise...but something told me I would be...I had tempted fate, and fate had accepted. So I was in the desert now, a desert without end. I started a tour with Henry, civil defense in southern England, Henry and I sleeping side by side like figures on tombs. In the new reinforced shelter at Bigwell-on-Sea, the chief warden kissed me. I allowed him to, but felt nothing. I'm beginning to believe in you, God, and maybe that's how you work."

"If I take five cups of sugar and dump it all over the top of that dreadful sponge cake, would anyone in his right mind know that I bought it from a girl named Hortense in the supermarket? These shoes are killing my toes. I feel like a munchkin in this lipstick. I should go back to work. I wonder if I could pitch a 4-week multi-channel buy to the tire manufacturers' association. Let's see. 4 insertions into *Automotive Weekly* split 10 ways would run them each..."

a single frame from Neil Jordan's adaptation of Graham Greene's novel, *The End of the Affair* (1999). With voice-over, street sounds, music track, and sound effects, wild sounds all, cinematographer Roger Pratt's shot might represent a vast range of thoughts, depending on the circumstances of the character ruminating. Which is the fake?

In a comedy, the lines on the right above might seem credibly linked to that image. But in *The End of the Affair*, the character pictured above experiences what seems a miraculous response to a prayer. The voice-over Jordan actually uses in *The End of the Affair* is above on the left.

Film scholars—and since the 1960s filmmakers who learn from them at film schools—distinguish sounds somewhat differently. *Non-diegetic sound*, they say, is sound audible to viewers but inaudible to those "within" the movie. *Diegetic sound*, on the other hand, is sound originating from "inside" the film's cosmos, sound a normal character would or could normally hear. The wild/sync distinction identifies where a sound originates. The diegetic/non-diegetic distinction identifies the "mind" that hears it. Behind those cavalry soldiers inching ponies down a precipice might be coyotes actually howling when the shot was made (synchronous sound) or coyote howl sound files purchased from an audio library (wild sound). The howling might constitute diegetic sound (the company is passing through coyote-infested hills) or non-diegetic (a shell-shocked member of the company is delusional).

Synchronous sound intensifies action. Wild sound characterizes it. Diegetic sound flows out of the screen. Non-diegetic sound settles on it. Silent filmmakers could make none of these distinctions.

Signs (2002), dir. M. Night Shyamalan.
Crows shrieking and dogs invisibly howling in the cornfields are the wild sounds. A three-note motif—da, da, da!—structures the score. "I think God did it," is the dialogue. Each level of sound potentiates the other.

EXERCISE TWELVE: SYNCHRONOUS SOUND

What this exercise teaches:

● **How to synchronize a sound track with a picture track**

● **How to filter sound tracks to modify their acoustical properties**

● **How synchronous sound makes silent movies seem more "real"**

"Violin by WKL Dickson with Kineto" was an obscure broken wax cylinder at the Edison National Historical Site in West Orange, New Jersey, until a Library of Congress curator obtained it in 1998. Once repaired and re-recorded, it became, after a century, audible again. What it was became clear again when sound editor Walter Murch synchronized the cylinder's sound to the William Dickson film of men dancing in 1894. A century late, Dickson's experiment ultimately succeeded.

You Did It Then: Try synchronizing the picture track of *The Jazz Singer* to the sound track recorded on a Vitaphone disc and you'll see why, in part, exhibitors and filmmakers gravitated to the rival sound-on-film systems. Trim off the "academy leader" from a pair of shots from *The Jazz Singer* stripped of their sound track. Then synchronize the "Vitaphone" recording of synchronized dialogue track to Jolson's lips as he delivers the lines, "Wait a minute, wait a minute, you ain't heard nothing yet." Adjust volume and "fix" the skipping Vitaphone 33 rpm record. Then degrade the fidelity of a contemporary version of "Toot, Toot, Tootsie" down to Vitaphone quality by introducing noise and clipping. Step-by-step instructions and the files you can use are in the digital cutting room at http://makefilmhistory. com.

You Do It Now: Return to the silent movie you shot for Chapter Nine (Intertitles). Now, using the original actors or new ones, dub the dialogue back into the movie.

PRODUCTION **Make Film History**
DIRECTOR _____
CAMERA _____
DATE   SCENE   TAKE
12

THEMATIC MONTAGE, SOVIET STYLE:
Dziga Vertov (1929)

"In all reality, I write my films in the editing room."
Director, writer, editor Henry Jaglom

When you edit a film, you can cut at three levels. Cutting to continuity establishes a sequence of events and answers the question, "What happens next?" Classical cutting conveys the context of an action and answers the question, "What matters here?" But making a montage does something different. Montage juxtaposes shot against shot to convey theme or tone, offering in one image something that echoes, or violates, or otherwise sheds light on another image. Creating a montage, you are summoning feeling.

Montage begins as labor and ends as dance, sometimes inspiring mystical thoughts in otherwise practical minded editors. During the my-manifesto-is-more-correct-than-yours polemic wars of the Soviet 1920s, montage-making attracted theory, disputation, and crackpot diagrams the way alchemy once did. Everyone had a theory about montage, and some still make sense today.

In 1920s, film editors certainly thought about and wrote in practical minded ways about tools to turn montage-making faster and easier. Non-destructive digital editing now simplifies the

Man With A Movie Camera (1928), dir. Dziga Vertov.

Man With a Movie Camera (1929), dir. Dziga Vertov.

In *Man with a Movie Camera*, Dziga Vertov depicts his editor, Yelizaveta Svilova, assembling *Man with a Movie Camera*. Svilova's cutting, choosing, and splicing serve as an organizing leitmotif of the movie.

process, but editing was then an unrelentingly exacting activity and remained so even as better tools made cutting and recutting easier. The earliest editors sat at tables cutting film with a scissors over a light well. They simulated motion by advancing work prints by hand, cutting and splicing, and then transporting them to a projection booth to inspect their handiwork. The work was laborious, and editors in 1920s always looked for easier and faster tools for cutting and joining.

Editing evolved when, in 1924, Iwan Serruier sold his invention, a Moviola editing machine, to editors at Douglas Fairbanks Studios. The Moviola made cutting less laborious, and the invention spread among Hollywood studios. The original model sat on an editing table and advanced film with a hand crank. Later models stood on wheels and resembled Dorothy's Tin Man. Editors stood before them, advancing the film by depressing a foot pedal and marking

Moviola c. 1960.

Walter Murch, cutting *Cold Mountain* (2003), was still standing at his digital editing screen as he stood for years cutting movies on the Moviola. In 2005, Michael Kahn was still cutting *Munich* on a Moviola. But Moviolas were by then history.

The machines evolve but the process remains essentially the same. The editor's eye watches and the editor's psyche cuts. Though never visible, the editor is always in the frame. Editors cut:

● To join shots where joining them excites feeling
● To advance the narrative
● To move the viewer's eye where it ought to go
● To maintain the right/left orientation of action on screen

Elmore Leonard, a novelist, explains what, in his view, gives prose wings: "I try to leave out the parts that people skip." Most editors follow that procedure. The process is intuitive. It is nothing like thumping a bass drum for a marching band. It is jazz—part plan, part improvisation.

frames for cutting with grease pencils. Films passed in incremental stages from rushes to movies. Editors cut and recut using transparent tape and eventually conformed edited work-print with negative. Labs then created exposure-corrected "answer" prints— composite prints including all picture tracks, sound tracks, and optical effects.

By the early 1970s, most 35 mm and 16 mm editors had migrated to flatbed-editing machines such as the Steenbeck. Most contemporary editors now cut using non-linear digital editing systems that began supplanting flatbeds in the 1990s. Consumer editing software that gravitated to desktop computers thereafter—such as the software you may be using as you work your way through *Make Film History*—enables you, too, to work that way.

But most of the ferment about montage in the 1920s did not derive from incremental improvements in editing equipment. It derived from claims, particularly Soviet claims, that montage, instead of contributing to film art, *is* film art.

In this regard, Vertov was a quintessential 1920s avant-gardist. The avant-gardist's tape measure read in units of "new." Avant-garde manifestos called for new thoughts and new languages to liberate the present from the past. In Russia, poets were concocting "zaum," an allegedly universal language of the birds, the stars, and the gods. James Joyce in 1929 recorded a fragment of *Finnegans Wake*, his dream opus celebrating Everyman in language of Joyce's own invention. "Make it new," Ezra Pound instructed poets in 1934. The montage of *Man With a Movie Camera* expresses all these ideas.

Man With a Movie Camera.

Of the Soviet directors, none claimed more far-reaching consequences for montage-making than Dziga Vertov. Starting with himself, Vertov looked to film editing to "improve and transform" the human "from a bumbling citizen through the poetry of the machine to the perfect electric man." Vertov threw himself into revolutionary filmmaking while the czarist regime crumbled. Much as MGM studio head Louis B. Mayer designated July 4th as his birthday to express his political convictions, Vertov changed his birth name, David Kaufman, to Dziga Vertov ("Spinning Top") to express his revolutionary fervor.

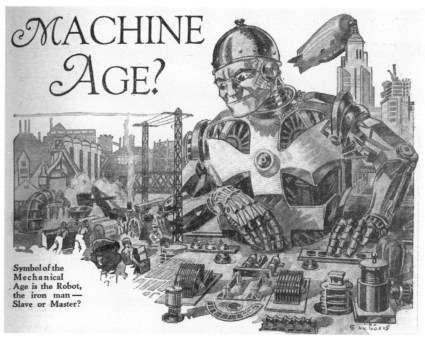

"Is Man Doomed by the Machine Age?' *Modern Mechanix* asked in March 1931. "With thousands of men unemployed, many of them because machines have forced them out of their jobs, the old cry that man has created a Machine Age which will destroy him has been taken up again. Which is the true picture—is the Machine a destructive monster, or a means to leisure and wealth? Is our civilization doomed to destruction because of our dependence on machines?"

To the magazine's question, Dziga Vertov's answer in *Man With a Movie Camera* was a resounding "No."

Eisenstein and other Soviet directors created montages to punctuate otherwise essentially narrative movies. In *Man With a Movie Camera*, Vertov created a film that was, in effect, one vast and seamless montage. One recurring montage element is the "man with a movie camera" who cranks out footage, some of which we view. Two cameramen actually shot this film. One—Mikhail Kaufman, Vertov's brother—moves in the world he is recording— cranking from the back of truck, double-exposed into a beer glass, wherever. Another cameraman records him recording.

Using "Film Truth" and "Film Eye," Dziga Vertov's *Man With a Movie Camera* (1929) purports to show a new humanity emerging in a Soviet city, an amalgam of Moscow, Odessa, and Kiev. "Film-Truth" was the image on the film. "Film Eye" was the vision of the editor. In montage, Vertov states, film truth and film eye combine.

A documentary film about a documentary film, *Man With a Movie Camera* (1929) is poetry disguised as Marxist analysis. In it, Vertov depicts the daily life of a composite Soviet city. He infuses this subject with a conviction that the world includes the mind surveying it. The film depicts not only the city but, with equal fervor, the camera and editor depicting it.

The movie begins and ends with a movie—itself—playing on the screen of a theater. A preliminary intertitle points out the absence of intertitles in favor of the absolute language of images. Other intertitles declare the film's absolute break from literature, theater, actor, and script, and they identify the director, the editor, and the cameraman.

Of the teeming people populating this vast montage, just one is a performer—a magician who conjures mice from empty saucers. Modern life itself, Vertov seems to say, is everyman performing. Part home movie, part ingenious work of art, filmed by Vertov's brother and edited by his wife, *Man With a Movie Camera* excited praise from European avant-gardists, who likened it to Walter Ruttmann's *Berlin: Symphony of a Metropolis* (1927).

Vertov maintained that the new Soviet man required a new kind of movie. His vast montage—containing countless slow motion shots, time-lapse shots, double exposures, tilt shots—expressed the consciousness of revolution made visible, Vertov believed. Soviet film executives nevertheless denounced the movie, objecting to Vertov's failure to observe socialist realist conventions and, above all, to the razzle-dazzle editing. Vast montages were not the future they foresaw for Soviet movies. In 1929, the Soviet Cinema Trust turned its attention instead to the first Russian language talkie. Their plan

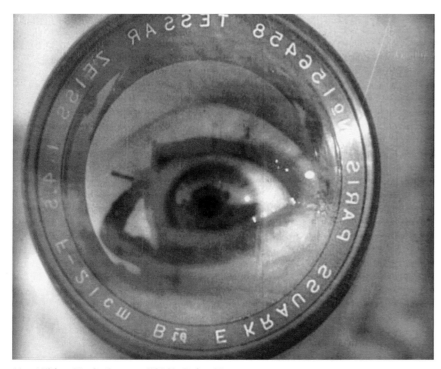

Man With a Movie Camera (1929). Dziga Vertov.

Part communist, part cabalist, Vertov held a semi-mystical belief in the camera's capacity to evolve humans "from a bumbling citizen through the poetry of the machine to the perfect electric man."

The movie camera, Vertov argued, perceives truths invisible to the human eye. Debrie Parvo 35 mm silent movie cameras recurrently appear in the film as cyborg-like extensions of the operator cranking them. Within the circle of the camera lens, man, machine, and the attentive eye, as above, conjoin in the all-knowing, all-seeing movie. The cameras serve as both (invisible recording) subject and (visible non-recording) object of the movie.

The camera is a witness and montage creates a spell, Vertov seems to argue in *Man With a Movie Camera.*

was to open 20 theaters built to exhibit talkies, one to specialize in

features showcasing the five-year industrial program of 1928-1933.

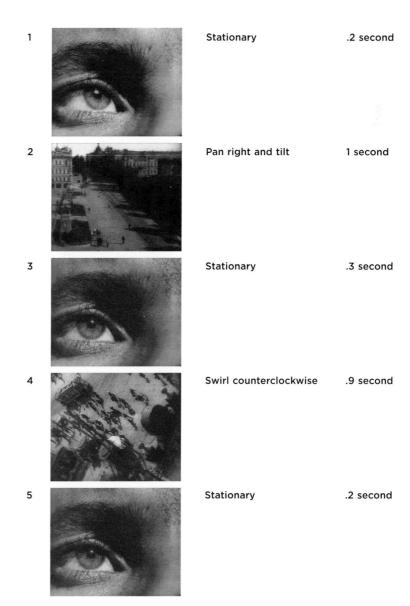

1		Stationary	.2 second
2		Pan right and tilt	1 second
3		Stationary	.3 second
4		Swirl counterclockwise	.9 second
5		Stationary	.2 second

The five-shot fragment above—two seconds from *Man With a Movie Camera*—demonstrates above how Vertov's montage operates. From a pit between the parallel tracks, Vertov's camera first records the approach and passage of an onrushing trolley. Then for two frames (shot one) an eye starts to blink. Abruptly, shot two commences. Transported from the pit, we see now *through* the blinking eye. Above the city for ten frames (shot two), panning and tilting down right, we see... what? Our search aborts. The eye makes another blink (shot three), as incomplete as the first. We look down now (shot four) at the street, whirling like a record on a spindle. Not this, not that, the world is passing to and through our eyes. Birds see this way. Then the eye turns right, passing in shot five to another object.

In a movie playing one hour seven minutes, that five-shot action consumes two seconds—400 beats of a hummingbird wing. Almost everywhere, *Man With a Movie Camera* sprints. On average, Vertov and Svilova cut every 2.3 seconds. Shots in 1929 generally changed far more slowly. The first two shots of Ernst Lubitsch's *Love Parade* (1929), combined, run 40 seconds, for instance. But Lubitsch was in Hollywood making fantasy. Vertov created montage like that five shot sequence to lift the cloth covering the cage of reality so the birds inside could see.

Seven decades after its first life, *Man With a Movie Camera* now lives in a second life on the Internet. People from around the world are creating a continuously changing montage with footage they upload to a website that recreates, in contemporary terms, Dziga Vertov's universe. Vertov's film plays as it is, but the new film changes daily. The goal is to create a movie made by everybody.

Kuleshov, Eisenstein, Pudovokin, and Dziga Vertov all saw montage as the natural expression of the Marxist idea that history is class conflict. They differed on details. But when Stalin turned against it in 1934, thematic montage disappeared from Soviet movies. Soviet filmmakers then watched as the inexplicable happened. In the west, where movies were entertainment, not philosophy, montage flourished. In Hollywood of the '20s and '30s, montage served primarily to rush moments of pure feeling or dream or nightmare through otherwise narrative films, shrinking space and fast-forwarding time. Stripped of its Marxist nomenclature, Dziga Vertov's montage survived as a method, in Hollywood films, to represent magic and reify dreams.

European avant-gardists exiled to Hollywood were especially productive and evocative montage makers. While Vertov in the USSR was reduced to cranking out works such as *In Memory of Sergo Ordzhonikidzhe, Ardent Fighter for the Cause of the Working Class, for the Cause of Communism, Fearless Leninist-Bolshevik, Friend and Comrade-in-Arms of Stalin the Great* (1938), Slavko Vorkapich, a Serbian in Hollywood, created self-contained montages for roughly 50 Hollywood studio productions, especially during the 1930s. Vorkapich's montages are those familiar two-minute movies tucked inside movies of the '30s—Jimmy

Stewart, for instance, in *Mr. Smith Goes to Washington* (1939), entering Washington for the first time. With optical effects, especially double exposure and dissolve, they convey the rush of time and the play of a mind making connections. So Soviet montage flowed west, seeping from the montage eyeball of *Man With a Movie Camera* (1929) to the montage eyeball of *Un Chien Andalou* (1929) to the montage eyeball *of Crimes Without Passion* (1934) to the montage eyeball of *Spellbound* (1945) to the corporate eyeball of CBS television (1951). Hollywood is the great muddy river absorbing everything.

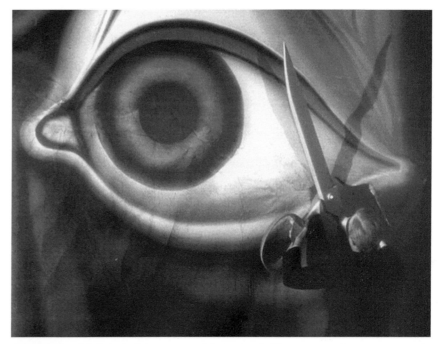

Producer David O. Selznick truncated Salvador Dalí's montage for a sequence in Hitchcock's *Spellbound* (1945), but its debt to earlier montage movies, including the eyeball imagery of Luis Buñuel and Dalí's own *Un Chien Andalou* (1929) remains obvious. Even abbreviated, Dali's montage represents dream material, as montages frequently did in Hollywood studio films.

Montage in the Soviet Union began as an expression of Marx, but in the west montage drew more often on the dream analysis of Sigmund Freud. G.W. Pabst's *Secrets of A Soul* (1926) first represented an actual dream analyzed by Freud for "psychoanalysis." Two Freudian analysts advised the production. Freud himself reviled movies. In 1925, he turned down a $100,000 offer from Samuel Goldwyn to collaborate in Hollywood on a love film about Antony and Cleopatra.

EXERCISE THIRTEEN: THEMATIC MONTAGE

What this exercise teaches:

- **How to construct and pace a montage**
- **How to accelerate, retard, and reverse motions**
- **How to rotate film clips horizontally and vertically**
- **How to create special effect visual distortions**
- **How to assert theme and variation in montage using similarity and repetition**

"I am the machine that reveals the world to you as only I alone am able to see it."

Dziga Vertov

You Did It Then: Editors necessarily leave their fingerprints on the negative—it goes with seeing life as footage to cut. Channeling Vertov's editor (and wife) Yelizaveta Svilova, assemble shots of a contemporary streetcar, pedestrians, and traffic into a thematic montage that expresses your own sense of reality. Add effects as freely Vertov and Svilova did. Step-by-step instructions, shots, and a sound track you can use are in the digital cutting room at http://makefilmhistory.com.

PRODUCTION Make Film History
DIRECTOR _____
CAMERA _____
DATE | SCENE | TAKE
13

PRODUCTION CODE HOLLYWOOD:
Scarface (1932)

"O, bind him, bind him! let him not come near me."
Shakespeare, *Comedy of Errors*, Act 4, Scene 4

If you were writing films scripts after 1934, you could not punctuate a sentence without considering the Motion Picture Producers and Distributors of America (MPPDA) Code of 1934. The code summarized "best practices" the studio heads agreed to clap on themselves. Under this system, code administrators vetted all scripts that major studios intended to film and all movies they expected to release. Their original goal was to fend off state, local, or federal censors anxious in the 1930s to subdue studio films with the chloroform of censorship. Implementing the code, filmmakers avoided censorship of others by themselves fitting the movies they made with handcuffs—and a book of common prayer—until another generation of studio heads terminated the code in 1968.

What induced the moguls to join in a system that restricted them was the struggle censors, studio heads, and MPPDA administrators waged over producer Howard Hughes' right to release *Scarface* (1932). The film was the third of three major '30s-era movies depicting gangsters as confident, alpha males. The protagonist of *Scarface* gleefully annihilates rival gangsters while, passionately,

"Let me lie down, Tony. I'm all hollow inside."

In Howard Hawk's *Scarface* (1932), "x" marks the spot (as above right) where each of 25 murders transpires. Before he fires, Tony Camonte (above left) whistles habitually *sotto voce*, "Chi me frena in tal momento? (Who restrains me at such a moment? Who disrupts the course of anger...") from the opera, *Lucia di Lamamoor*.

Hughes released *Scarface* in 1932, when the MPPDA was still whee-
dling but not ordering studios to modify scripts to placate local
boards of censorship. Persuasion usually sufficed. In 1931, a telegram induced Hughes to alter the ending he originally intended
for *Scarface*. That ending violated the moguls' agreement to
punish wrongdoers and hold police harmless in the movies they
released, one code administrator complained to another in the
telegram. Particularly outrageous was the protagonist's obvious
"resemblance to well-known gangster [Al Capone] who so far has
succeeded in defeating the law at every turn." The telegram read,
in part, as follows:

> Camonte's heroic battle against the police when spurred
> on by proud sister unquestionably tends to glorify gang-
> ster...This glorification is emphasized by his final gesture
> of bravado when he deliberately walks out into police
> gun fire, a lone man braving the world and braver than
> the world...In final scenes Camonte should be shown
> as cringing coward...There should be some evidence
> before the conclusion that Camonte is fundamentally a
> yellow dog.

Code administrators then objected to Hughes, and he revised the
script. A bullet kills Camonte's sister. Stuttering and trembling, the
gangster surrenders in the revised script. Parroting the telegram,
the sheriff sneers, "You squeal like a yellow rat." When he evades
the sheriff's handcuffs, the gangster rushes out the door, only to
crumple outside near the gutter, killed by a fusillade of policemen's bullets he hadn't thought to anticipate. When the camera

"In this business, there's only one law you gotta follow to keep outta trouble. Do it
first, do it yourself, and keep on doin' it."
Tony Camonte's statement in the original *Scarface* of the code he lived by explains,
in essence, why the moguls agreed to handcuff their writers and producers with the
MPPDA Code of 1934. If they didn't do it, someone else—local censorship boards,
religious denominations, and government bureaucrats—would.

he loves his sister. Boards of censorship abhorred this storyline—
it reeked of corruption—and banned the movie. To mollify them,
Hughes modified his script, particularly the ending. In the alternative endings of *Scarface*, one catches a glimmer of the censor
passing through the screen to rearrange camera angles, eliminate
dialogue, and redefine the conflict of the movie.

Al Capone c. 1925

Paul Muni as Tony Camonte, *Scarface* (1932).

rises one last time to the travel agency sign that has served to express throughout the film the gangster's aspirations—"The world is yours"—the movie judges him.

But Hughes sensed that censors would find that ending still insufficiently condemnatory. So he reshot it. He truncated dialogue and altered camera angles. Cut is the declaration that the sister shares the gangster's soul. In a new close-up—underlining her revulsion—she perishes while despising her brother as a coward. Hughes then appended to this ending still another ending. The gangster fades out while the sheriff frog marches him away. The camera serving as *his* eyes now, the gangster reappears before a judge for sentencing. "You are ruthless, immoral, and vicious," declares the judge, condemning the gangster to death. At the movie's new

end, the gangster hangs ignominiously off screen as policemen, like three Greek fates, cut the gallows cords. Hughes perceived that the reshot ending was anticlimactic and in March 1932 begged code chief administrator Will Hays to relent:

> **I gave up 'Queer People' to cooperate and I cut up 'The Cock of the Air' until it wasn't any good in order to cooperate. I think if you don't let me show this with the original ending, I am discriminated against. What I want to do is use the last two hundred feet of it—I will use the last version in everything else if I can use the last two hundred feet. I want to use when the girl comes into the room to the end, the way the original had it. Nobody ever told me this picture was contrary to the Code, that was never suggested.**

Even with the "justice-is-served" ending, the New York Board of Censors rejected the movie in April 1932. Capone entered prison in May, and the New York censors then passed the movie.

By The United Press

CHICAGO, May 3—Al Capone sulked in his county jail cell today, cursing those who sought to see him before he starts tonight for Leavenworth penitentiary to begin serving the 11 years he must spend behind bars for income tax evasion.

"Go to hell, you lousy rats," the "Scarface" bellowed when newspapermen approached his cell. "Want to take me for a ride some more, eh? Well, I'm not talking—see! Get to hell out of here."

The 265-pound gangster trembled with rage. His face went a sickly purple. He shook his fist. While the man who once ruled the

Chicago gangs with machine gun and bomb, making this his capital of crime whence he drew millions in revenue from liquor, vice and gambling, stormed in his cell, arrangements were made for sending him to the Federal penitentiary at Leavenworth, Kan.

He will go with some 16 other Federal prisoners, narcotics dealers, auto thieves and the like, on a Chicago, Burlington & Quincy train. He will be taken from the jail directly to the Union Station.

Capone will be handcuffed like the others. Guarding him will be United States Marshal Henry C. W. Laubenheimer and three of the

brawniest deputy marshals in the Chicago office. Each weighs 200 pounds or over.

Time of the train's departure was not announced. The officials feared disorder at the station, or a possible attempt to liberate Capone.

The scar-faced gangster saw only sister and his aged mother spent a considerable time talking with him in low tones. Capone managed a crooked smile when they came in.

His wife, May Capone; a married sister and his aged mother spent a considerable time talking with him in low tones. Capone managed a crooked smile when they came in.

Scarface electrified many viewers, most of whom regarded the film as reality cast as myth—"Scarface" was what newspapers began dubbing real-life gangster Al Capone.

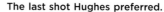

Complying with the code could mean rewriting scenes whole cloth or just changing their pitch to muffle their overtones. Compare these two treatments of Cesca's warning to Tony.

The last shot Hughes preferred.

The last shot Hughes created to placate censorship he anticipated.

In the ending Hughes shot and ultimately released, the gangster and his sister recognize their essential unity:

Cesca: Tony, they're coming. The police. They're after you. They're going to get you, Tony.

Tony: Why didn't you shoot, Cesca? Why didn't you shoot?

Cesca: I don't know. Maybe because you're me, and I'm you. It's always been that way!

In the ending Hughes shot to placate censors, the sister, now across the room from her brother, issues a functional warning:

Cesca: The police!

By then, however, Hughes had reverted to the ending he originally shot and released the film in two versions. Where no board of censors existed to ban it, the original played. Where a board of censors suffered it to run, the second played. The hearings were lengthy and expensive. They incited politicians and moralists. Hughes' ordeal inclined other studio executives to conclude that persuasion no longer sufficed to ward off censors. To preserve their business, they would have to restrain themselves.

Before studio executives bound themselves with the MPPDA code of 1934, American movie censorship had passed through numerous stages. The first official-sounding American board of film censorship—the National Board of Censorship—formed in New York in 1909 as a confederation of exhibitors, distributors, and even a social welfare organization organized to *combat* censorship, not practice it. But in 1915 the U.S. Supreme Court ruled unanimously in *Mutual Film Corporation v. Industrial Commission of Ohio* that movies were purely commercial activity, not art protected as free speech.

The Federation of Women's Clubs debated female suffrage in 1914—most delegates supported it—and considered resolutions to "improve" the nation's morals. "The federation ought to take a stand on the question of dress that has a sex appeal," a speaker told the delegates.

Evan Chesterman, Chairman of the Virginia Board of Censors, reported to the governor in 1928: "Business steadily increases. Never before in the history of censorship has the volume of business been so great."

Will H. Hays, January 14, 1922.

"It is frankly admitted that the Postmaster General's services would be helpful to the industry in connection with hostile censorship legislation. Mr. Hays hopes to accomplish a more comprehensive scheme of voluntary censorship," *The New York Times* reported on January 15, 1922.

By 1916, the National Board of Censorship evolved into the National Board of Review of Motion Pictures, an unofficial but influential censor. Censorship boards with similar missions proliferated. Wary moguls first convened an industry advocacy group in 1922, the Motion Picture Producers and Distributors of America (MPPDA), recruiting Postmaster General Will H. Hays to head the organization. Hays was to intercede with local censors and, generally, to add a genteel presence to their numbers. Hays was responsible for advising the studio chiefs but not censoring them.

By 1927, Hays was circulating a list of "Don'ts and Be Carefuls." The document enumerated plots to avoid and subjects requiring "special care" so that "vulgarity and suggestiveness may be eliminated and that good taste may be emphasized." The major studios agreed to make no movies involving drug trafficking, sex perversion, white slavery (forced prostitution), "miscegenation," "excessive or lustful kissing," picturing in an unfavorable light another country's religion, history, institutions and prominent people.

But the studios could flout the list with impunity. Worse, the "Don'ts" and "Be Carefuls" provided them little protection from censorship boards. Of 572 movies studios submitted to state and local censorship boards in 1928, less than 10% passed without complaint. And when numerous studios filed for bankruptcy during the early 1930s, survivors essentially rushed to do the "Don'ts." In those Depression-era times—so-called "Pre-Code Hollywood"—studios trolled for audiences with macho gangsters and semi-topless chorus girls. But moralists excoriated those movies. A letter to a 1932 New Zealand newspaper delivered this oft-repeated indictment of the Pre-Code films of Hollywood: "If a scene in a picture is detrimental to public morals the censor's tarbush should smother it on sight."

In this time of anxiety, the moguls now feared for the survival of their studios. The Catholic Legion of Decency threatened to warn off Catholic patrons. New Dealers contemplated a federal bureau to elevate the moral tone of movies. Social scientists piled on, confirming with graphs that movies disturbed children's sleep and impaired their judgment. The Irish Free State in 1934 limited

Paramount Studios released *Murder at the Vanities* on May 18, 1934.
Two months later, as the MPPA prepared to institute the mandatory seal-of-approval system, the AP reported that Patrick Cardinal Hayes was hearten to see "the widespread awakening throughout the country to the evil character and shocking debasement of many motion pictures."

onscreen kisses to three seconds. Other nations did likewise. Studio executives commissioned a Catholic layman and a Jesuit priest in 1930 to devise a code of best practices. A consensus was forming: you could cure a bad movie with a scissors.

Wire service stories convey the atmosphere in America on Sunday, July 15, 1934, when the moguls instituted their equivalent of a

Clara Bow in *Call Her Savage* (1932).

"He swaggered from a neighborhood theater last night into the raking fire of government guns," the AP story led.

"The gospel of indecency is being preached from the screen," stated a minister at a mass rally.

Movies, mayhem, and sermonizing clergy inspired the MPAA approval seal system.

censorship system. Studios were paying five million dollars in annual fees to local censorship boards to trim and sometimes mutilate their movies. Buster Keaton was filing for bankruptcy. Lupe Velez was filing for divorce from her "violent, cursing, furniture wrecking husband" Johnny Weissmuller, "Tarzan." A lawyer in New York feared "the movement for film reform might lead to 'prohibition of production and exhibition of motion picture films similar to liquor production.'" Drugged, suicidal, and delirious, a temporarily notorious female Hollywood extra testifying as prime witness in a front-page "Hollywood morals" case was found wandering night streets. One Sunday later, FBI agents in Chicago gunned down the gangster John Dilllinger as he exited a movie theater where he had viewed, naturally, a gangster movie, *Manhattan Melodrama* (1934).

Everywhere beset, the major studios agreed that theaters they controlled would exhibit no film lacking an MPAA approval seal. Since the major studios owned and operated 70% of the first run movie houses in America, this handshake among moguls determined what could appear in American films. Studio heads served as MPAA directors and adjudicated appeals. Studios submitted scripts to Joseph Breen, chief administrator of the Production Code Administration (PCA). From 1934-1968, Breen and his assistants or successors approved scripts and pre-release films. Like camels in a long caravan, movies drifted slowly through the eye of Breen's needle.

Details changed over successive iterations, but the theme of the code descended from three general principles stated in the code as follows:

> • **No picture shall be produced which will lower the moral standards of those who see it. Hence, the sympathy of the audience shall never be thrown to the side of crime, wrongdoing, evil or sin.**
>
> • **Correct standards of life, subject only to the requirements of drama and entertainment, shall be presented.**
>
> • **Law, natural or human, shall not be ridiculed, nor shall sympathy be created for its violation.**

The principles were vague, but specific Don'ts sprang from them like thorns.

Memos to producers from Breen, his associates or successors, applied the general principles of the code to the words and sentences of scripts. Critiquing the script for *Psycho* (1960), code administrator John Vizzard wrote Paramount executives in 1959. "It was necessary to reject it [*Psycho*] under the code for the following reasons. 1) In the opening sequence the love making on the bed is entirely too passionate. Both the man and the woman are only partially dressed, and are rolling around on the bed locked in extremely lustful intimacies, including, among other things, a quite blatant open-mouth kiss."

Breen and his delegates niggled, but their memos expressed the ideas informing the code. Natural law is "written in the hearts of all mankind." We live in bodies but survive as souls. Wrongdoing corrupts both. Moviemakers should not depict wrong activities, except to condemn them. When treating acts of love or violence, suggesting works better than showing. These ideas are the hackwork of a pair of zealots, but they are also Shakespeare's.

Breen's edits and objections infuriated writers, but they may have helped studios survive the cataclysmic years of the 1930s depression. The code didn't stymie imaginative writing. It often induced a kind of poetry in scripts. It helped create the American studio-era movie style—that allusive restraint with which stars like Cary Grant performed before cameras that came in for close-ups but, like the scripts themselves, went no further. For all it took, the code could sometimes give. Screenwriters in the code era resorted to

A clause in the code—"The treatment of bedrooms must be governed by good taste and delicacy"—in practice meant that no male character could enter a bed where a female character awaited him. But in code-compliant humor, one male and one female cuckoo clock marionette could break away from their track and scurry away together through a clockwork portal to end *The Awful Truth* (1937).

Trouble in Paradise (1932) dir. Ernst Lubitsch. The famous "touch" of Ernst Lubitsch consists largely of suggestive evasions such as slowly closing doors to express the sexual congress within. Lubitsch's allusive style owes at least something to the code that, as tea infuses water, pervades American movies of this era.

synecdoche (part for whole) and metonymy (associated thing) to suggest. The code was a source of restraint, and restraint imbues these movies of the classical studio period with an inner life. That life defies analysis because you sense that more is being said than is being said and you can not exactly pin down where it comes from or what it is. Inside a stone you hear a heart beat.

In 1952, the Supreme Court revised its 1915 opinion on movies, ruling that movies *do* qualify for first amendment free speech protections. Breen resigned from the MPAA in 1954. Administrators who succeeded him annotated scripts with a lighter pencil. By 1959, a movie treating almost anything could earn a seal, provided its villains felt "moral conflict." The MPAA retired the code

Writing with one eye on the code sometimes turned how people normally talk into language that burnished the actors who delivered it.

Director (and horseracing fan) Howard Hawks maintained that *he* wrote the dialogue for this scene cut into *The Big Sleep* (1946), and maybe he did. Producers at Warner Bros. cut it into the movie after all other work on the production was complete in order to showcase Lauren Bacall, their young new star, as an impudent, flirtatious wit.

In the scene that this scene replaced, Bacall had murmured when Bogart kissed, "I like that. I'd like more." Hawk's substitute dialogue—Shakespeare might have called it a trope—gave sparkle to what Bacall had originally straightforwardly stated.

Hawk's dialogue is below.

Vivian: Well, speaking of horses, I like to play them myself. But I like to see them work out a little first, see if they're front runners or come from behind, find out what their whole card is, what makes them run.

Marlowe: Find out mine?

Vivian: I think so.

Marlowe: Go ahead.

Vivian: I'd say you don't like to be rated. You'd like to get out in front, open up a lead, take a little breather in the backstretch and then come home free.

Marlowe: You don't like to be rated yourself.

Vivian: I haven't met anyone yet who could do it. Any suggestions?

Marlowe: Well, I can't tell till I've seen you over distance of ground. You've got a touch of class, but, uh, I don't know how far you can go.

Vivian: A lot depends on who's on the saddle.

Joseph Breen (right) and British producer Harold Huth screen a 1946 British film. "Joe Breen to Cue Brit Pix on U.S. Production Code," *Variety* pattered July 10, 1946.

November 1, 1968, and replaced it with an early version of the G/PG/R system now in force. MPAA seals still appear at the end of movies, but they indicate merely that someone has classified the film, not judged it.

The day the code expired, detectives in Hollywood reported the murder of Ramon Novarro, once a glamorous icon of 1920s films. A script dramatizing wire service reports of the murder would have violated the code. No one noticed the singular conjunction—the star expired when the code did. But movie plots no longer turned on coincidence. Like the silents and Novarro, the code was dead.

Ramon Novarro, c. 1925

HOLLYWOOD, Calif. (UPI) — Ramón Novarro, matinee idol of silent and early sound movies, was found beaten to death in his Hollywood Hills home yesterday. The star of the first "Ben Hur" was 69 years old.

Forty years ago, Novarro was a dark-haired, dashing leading man who wooed Hollywood's glamor girls on the screen and off.

NOVARRO, a life-long bachelor, was another in the mold of Rudolph Valentino as one of the flickering screen's great Latin lovers. He successfully made the transition from silent movies to talkies.

Hollywood Chief of Detectives Robert A. Houghton said the actor's pajama-clad body was discovered at approximately 8:30 a.m. by his male secretary, Ed Weber. Officers said Novarro's glasses were broken and furniture disarranged, indicating a struggle.

Houghton said Novarro apparently had suffered massive head injuries.

Police Lt. Gerald Lauritzen said "there was blood all over the place." So much in fact that we couldn't tell immediately whether an instrument had been used."

Wire service story, November 1, 1968

EXERCISE FOURTEEN: PRODUCTION CODE

This exercise teaches:

● **How to dub, that is, create A(utomated) D(ialogue) R(eplacement) dialogue**

● **How to think like a MPPA code administrator**

● **How to preserve your vision armed with stealth, cunning, and imagination**

"The vilest kind of sin is a common indulgence hereabouts and the men and women who engage in this sort of business are the men and women who decided what the film fare of this nation is to be."

Joseph Breen, Motion Picture Association of America Code Administrator, 1932 letter to Rev. Wilfrid Parsons, S.J.

You Did It Then: Channeling the mindset of a Production Code of America administrator, screen these scenes from *I Cover the Waterfront* (1933), marking down whatever might violate the MPPA production. Then "re-edit" the scene by excising shots or dubbing new dialogue or both, conforming the movie to MPPA guidelines. Step-by-step instructions and the scenes from *I Cover the Waterfront* are in the digital cutting room at http://makefilmhistory.com.

You Do It Now: Shoot a scene that is in clear violation of the MPAA code. Go as wild as you want. Give the scene to someone to else to censor. Respond to your censor's findings, trying to see if you can preserve the essence of the scene—or not. Then screen the censored and uncensored versions, comparing them.

STORYBOARD:
Webb Smith (1933)

Webb Smith, a story developer at the Walt Disney Studios, introduced storyboarding into movies in the early 1930s as a practical way to previsualize story ideas as images. The practice spread from animation to live productions during the 1930s and continues today because storyboarding helps filmmakers tweak plots out of stories. A story is what happens. "Mrs. Morton died later than her husband did," is a story. A plot structures a story.

He first deceas'd; she for a little tried
To live without him, liked it not, and died.

is how poet Sir Henry Wotton (1568-1639) plotted that story. The commonplace becomes unforgettable when an artist structures it. The story tells. The plot intrigues. Plot is story arranged to waken feelings. Animators resemble versifiers like Henry Wotton. Disney and his gagman were naturally interested in devising labor-saving ways to previsualize camera angles and *mise-en-scène* because animators, while thinking like poets, must labor like industrial workers. Previsualizing a camera's path through a movie can be confusing. Storyboarding enables moviemakers to foresee a clear route.

Most early filmmakers saw little need to previsualize movies—most were industrialists who built empires out of flanges and widgets,

not plot points. Edison had first envisioned the phonograph as a better pen for secretaries. In 1924, Auguste Lumière still thought of himself as the progenitor of the autochrome color photography process and contributed research to *Colloidal Chemistry, Theoretical and Applied*. Lumière *actualités* were light on plot, turning, when they turned at all, as slowly as grind stones in grist mills. The moviemakers who joined together in 1908 as the Motion Picture Patents Company—Edison, Biograph, Vitagraph, Essanay, Selig, Lubin, American Star, and American Pathé—regarded their common enterprise as manufacturing, not plot construction. "The play has not been the thing in the moving-picture world," a *New York Times* reporter noted in 1913.

The reporter was asserting the indisputable. William Selig entered the movie business in 1900 making industrial promotionals for Armour Meats. Siegmund Lubin had operated a Philadelphia optician shop. Georges Méliès charged by the meter, hawking movies like dry goods. He did work out scenes in pre-shooting drawings, but his brother Gaston, sent to Manhattan to copyright and distribute his brother's fantasies, eschewed preplanning, shooting a yacht race documentary and turning eventually to formulaic westerns. As members of the Edison trust saw it, sprocket holes needed

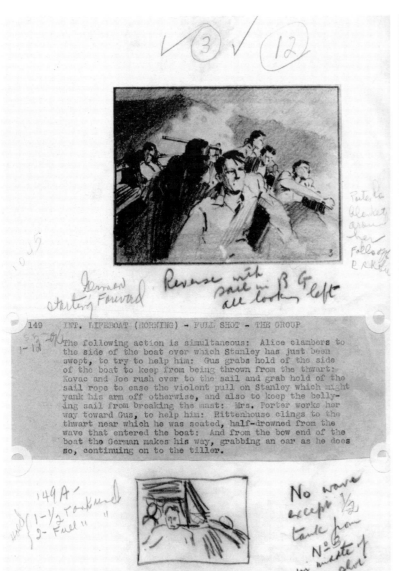

149 INT. LIFEBOAT (MORNING) - FULL SHOT - THE GROUP

The following action is simultaneous: Alice clambers to
the side of the boat over which Stanley has just been
swept, to try to help him: Gus grabs hold of the side
of the boat to keep from being thrown from the thwart:
Kovac and Joe rush over to the sail and grab hold of the
sail rope to ease the violent pull on Stanley which might
yank his arm off otherwise, and also to keep the belly-
ing sail from breaking the mast: Mrs. Porter works her
way toward Gus, to help him: Rittenhouse clings to the
thwart near which he was seated, half-drowned from the
wave that entered the boat: And from the bow end of the
boat the German makes his way, grabbing an oar as he does
so, continuing on to the tiller.

Shot 149 as Hitchcock ultimately filmed it in *Lifeboat*. The three principals remain in positions envisioned in the sketch, but all others were excised from the shot as actually filmed. The action is a turning point in the film: the German prisoner is assuming command of the lifeboat. The actual shot thus renders this transformation more simply than the sketch did.

Shot 149 storyboard for *Lifeboat* (1944), dir. Alfred Hitchcock. John Steinbeck wrote the story and Jo Swerling wrote the script. Hitchcock himself storyboarded virtually every shot to envision the optimum point of view for every action. Ostensibly adrift, the lifeboat was merely a collection of boat components in a single tank at Twentieth-Century Fox. Hitchcock's drawing above renders complex action into a single image for a shot in an action sequence.

Above, Disney Story Department staff c. 1933-1934 pose for a shot before the storyboard. Preliminary images for *The Grasshopper and the Ants* (1934) line up in four rows each holding nine paper sheets, each displaying a pencil-drawn sketch. Walt Disney leans forward at the center of the image.

In the early 1930s a Disney cartoon began life as a "good story." In the storyboard, a Disney innovation, written scenarios turned visible as multi-level characters and backgrounds. Disney defined "a good story" in a memo to Disney employees as "not merely a bunch of situations thrown together in any form, just to allow an opportunity for action. A good story should contain a lesson or have a moral—or it should definitely tell something interesting which leads up to a climax that will have a punch and impress an audience." In 1933, Disney ran a story-writing contest for all studio employees, except directors or story department staff. Submission deadline was February 1, 1934. Accepted ideas qualified for the $50 prize.

The "burglar" was Stuart Blackton, one of the principals of Vitagraph. Al Smith, his partner, proceeded to crank the camera when the woman intruded. This is the antithesis of the storyboarded movie.

patent protection but plots could take care of themselves. A janitor's wife who wandered on to the set wielding a broom became an accidental hero of Vitagraph's first movie, *The Burglar on the Roof* (1897). The janitor's wife took the actor (Stuart Blackton) for a criminal when she saw an actress restraining him and she launched into whacking him. Audiences perceived no problem with the unanticipated woman. Those movies were wonderful at first to those who saw them first because motion itself was their story.

But in the long run, movies need *action*, not things just moving. Action is activity undertaken for a purpose. Movies that audiences care about tell stories. Stories describe what happens when a protagonist—someone who wants something crucial—strives for what he wants. As the world resists or accedes to his desire, the protagonist's actions create a story. His countless masks disguise a single face, but we recognize him by his strivings and longings. We experience his desires our own, even if we do not seek for ourselves what he does. In *Bicycle Thieves* (1948*)*, Antonio Ricci searches for a stolen bicycle. In *The French Connection* (1971), Jimmy Doyle pursues drug dealers. In *10* (1979*)*, George Webber pursues a dream girl. In *Moonstruck* (1987*)*, Loretta Castorini searches for renewal and love. In *Black Swan* (2010), Nina Sayers searches for perfection as a ballerina.

In 1863, Gustav Freytag described a story's stages as exposition, rising action, climax, falling action, and resolution. Movie plot gurus like Syd Field now more often describe it as a structure of three acts—a setup that leads a protagonist to undertake achieving a goal, a confrontation where the protagonist struggles (and fails) to achieve it, and a resolution where, with increasing desperation, the protagonist succeeds or fails. However you think of it, the protagonist's struggle creates the stages of a story, and the stages of the story drive the structure of the plot. Expressed as images, plot is what appears on storyboards.

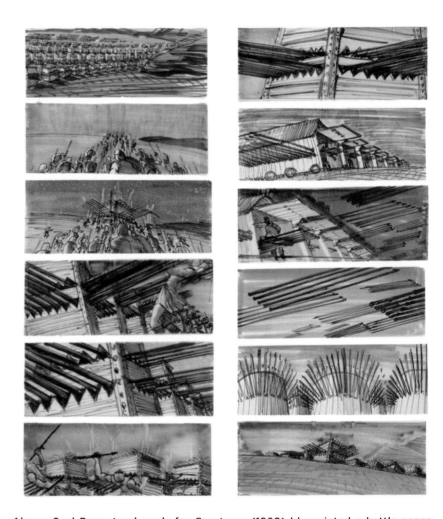

Above, Saul Bass storyboards for *Spartacus* (1960) blueprinted a battle scene. Multiple shots of small groups and props were to contain production costs. Ultimately, producers covered the action with a master shot—a single long shot showing the entire action from start to finish.

During the pre-storyboard silent era, photoplay writers and, different people, title card writers created movie stories. Some photoplay writers were freelancers mailing in supposedly original scenarios. In 1913 Vitagraph was receiving roughly 500 over-the-transom scripts per week, rejecting almost all. Others were professionals, primarily women—for instance, Maibelle Heikes Justice, who cranked out 45 scripts or stories for Selig, Metro, Lubin, Essany and others from 1913-1925. By the 1920s, most studios employed photoplay writers, not freelancers, if only to forestall the numerous plagiarism charges that frequently followed rejected freelance submissions.

But most silent photoplays were works of convention without need for storyboarding. Douglas Fairbanks gibed about silent movie plots in a 1918 magazine article: "Villains always must have a riding crop and a pair of chamois gloves; the riding crop is to drop in front of the heroine, so that he can apologize and thus start an acquaintance, and the gloves are used to strike the hero with, when the hero springs forward to protest against the acquaintanceship. For the remaining five thousand feet, the hero strives to get back at the villain for that glove trick—and that is the plot!"

Title card writers created dialogue. From 1918-1930, Joseph Farnham wrote titles for 91 movies and won the first and only Best Writing, Title Writing Academy Award.

Storyboarding entered movies at Disney's Los Angeles studio because Disney animators needed to preplan shot sequences more meticulously than producers of live action. 1930s animation was famously laborious. At Disney, an animator hand-drew key frames on transparent sheets of cellulose acetate. Others created in-between motions and background cels. The process was perplexingly intricate. Storyboarding blueprinted the process.

Webb Smith was puzzling over shot sequences for *The Three Little Pigs*, Disney's first Technicolor movie, when he stumbled into the movie storyboard era. "I'd drop in Webb's office and he'd have the sequence sketched out on sheets of paper," Walt Disney remembered. "They'd be scattered all over the room, on desk, on the floor, every place. It got too tough to follow them; we decided to pin all the sketches on the wall in sequence. That was the first storyboard." Smith tacked forty sketches of pigs and a wolf up on a bulletin board in the Story Department. Today, with hard drives, assistant directors and storyboard artists follow where Webb Smith's thumbtacks led. Transformative ideas are inevitably simple.

Once introduced at Disney's Hyperion Avenue studio, storyboarding spread over the Hollywood Hills to the world beyond. By 1939, most Hollywood movies migrated from screenplay to visual world, entirely or in part, within the frames of storyboard sketches. Production designer William Cameron Menzies, for instance, storyboarded every shot of *Gone With the Wind*. While some resist the practice, many contemporary filmmakers perpetuate Menzies' method. Editor Thelma Schoonmaker relied on storyboards to sequence footage for action scenes in Martin Scorsese's *Raging Bull* (1980). Scorsese shot the final fight scene for ten days. He

The Rake Taking Possession of his Estate.

The Rake's Levée.

The Rake at the Rose Tavern.

The Rake Arrested: Going to Court.

The Rake Marrying an Old Woman.

The Rake at the Gaming House.

The Rake in Prison.

The Rake in Bedlam.

Not that storyboarding actually started at Disney. For centuries illustrators have narrated secular and sacred stories in sequences of drawings, paintings, and sketches. British engraver William Hogarth depicts above in *The Rake's Progress* (1734) the downfall of a young man. Not *quite* a storyboard—it omits numerous shots, *The Rake's Progress* could be described as a collection of "key frames." Animators imported this practice to the movie studio.

Left, *Three Little Pigs* (1933). Right, *Three Little Wolves* (1936).

Animators creating *Three Little Pigs* tucked into background cels of this first storyboarded Disney cartoon "images" tacked to walls in the manner of, well, the storyboards they tacked up in their offices. They repeated the effect in *Three Little Wolves*. Like an animator at a Disney story conference, the Big Bad Wolf holds forth before the wall of images.

meant to duplicate how Hitchcock, two decades earlier, had sequenced shower scene shots in *Psycho*. When Schoonmaker cut the footage, she followed the storyboard—36 drawings—that Scorsese had previously created to enable her to find the scene in hours of footage.

Storyboards serve four purposes in contemporary filmmaking. Pitchers use key frame sketches to convey to investors and producers the concept of a movie. (Try saying, "It's *Westworld* set on Mars, only this time the Yul Brenner character is a human.") Set designers work up production illustrations to hammer out features of a set or a location. Ad agencies paste images on small boards to map out ideas for clients. Most importantly, storyboard artists—or assistant directors, or directors, or even editors working with unplotted footage—work up a plot on storyboards.

William Cameron Menzies storyboards for *Gone With the Wind*

Combined with sound and dialogue tracks, storyboards become "animatics"—that is, simple movies made from storyboards that filmmakers use to test the flow and pace of movies in development. They are "photomatics" when they sequence photos, not drawings. Animatics and photomatics simulate motion on the screen when a digital "camera" (now usually a "Ken Burns" computer-based effect) pans and zooms within them. When you complete the filmmaking exercise accompanying this chapter, you'll make one, too, because in animatics you can inspect the structure of your story in miniature. Combined with overhead schematic diagrams depicting where on a set or location cameras, actors, props, and lights are to be configured, editorial storyboards establish the camera angles, motions, lighting sources in which the exposition, rising action, climax, falling action, and closure of a movie plays. Every work of art is a coil of energy. In moviemaking, storyboard is the box holding Jack in.

Scene xxx. Shot 14. C.U.

Action: Judge listens to Thomas's summation.

Dialogue: Major Thomas: "Soliders, at war...

FX:

Scene xxx. Shot 15. Track to judges & back.

Action: Major Thomas' concludes summation.

Dialogue: Major Thomas: "are not to be judged...

FX:

Scene xxx. Shot 16A. High Angle L.S.

Action: Major Thomas returns to defense table.

Dialogue: None.

FX: Dissolve to 16B. (Same as 16A, w. no humans).

Scene xxx. Shot 16B. High Angle L.S.

Action: None.

Dialogue: None.

FX: Humans (but nothing else) fade out.

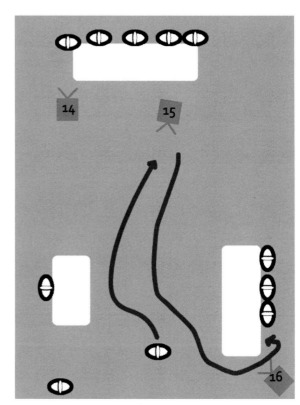

In *Breaker Morant* (1980), director Bruce Beresford concludes a military court room scene by juxtaposing shots representing action seen from the point of view of the participants with a high angle shot in two parts representing the court room as a noose might view it. Not Beresford's actual storyboard, these images derived from shots in the film nevertheless suggest how storyboarding could blueprint a sequence expressing, in reverse angles, the tense climax of the story.

Breaker Morant overhead diagram (simulated) of camera placements for shots 14, 15, 16a and 16b. Script, storyboard and overhead schematic together map out the story.

EXERCISE FIFTEEN: STORYBOARD

What this exercise teaches:

- **How to create an animatic**
- **How to create a photomatic**
- **How to insert subtitles into a movie**
- **How to sequence shots using a storyboard**

"I go inside their heads, try to understand what they are thinking, and put it on paper. I always try to make the drawings theirs, not mine...It's like they're making a movie in front of me. They tell me the shots. I do fast and loose drawings on a clipboard with a Sharpie pen—one to three drawings to a sheet of regular bond paper. I try to establish the scale, trap the angle, ID the character, get the action."
J. Todd Anderson, on storyboarding for Joel and Ethan Coen

"People often ask me if I make storyboards. The idea appalls me! I look at it my own way, I speak for myself, but it's out of the question that I would make a storyboard for a film I make because the storyboard, while similar to a comic book, is in my view light years away from what you need to make a movie."
Patrice Leconte, director, May 27, 2007 *Actua BD*

You Did It Then: **As Webb Smith did first at Disney, sequence these sketches into narrative storyboard order. After you allocate to each the time it requires, print them out and view them. Then adjust your sequence if necessary, add subtitles for dialogue, and adjust color. Using zooms and pans, create an animatic. Repeat the process with live action stills, creating a photomatic. Step-by-step instructions and the files you'll need are in the digital cutting room at http://makefilm history.com.**

You Do It Now: **Storyboard the scene for which you held the production meeting in the Chapter 10 (Studio) exercise.**

PRODUCTION Make Film History
DIRECTOR
CAMERA
DATE   SCENE   TAKE
15

16

SCORE:
Max Steiner (1939)

"You saw it?"
"Not saw, heard... heard."
Graham Greene, script for *The Third Man*

Studio musical directors in the 1930s "scored to cue"—that is, they synchronized music segments to begin or end at frames showing action of prime significance. Audiences rarely "hear" scores composed to cue because the music seems to come from nowhere and settle over everything. "So often one's efforts are scarcely noticed, not because the music is unworthy, nor that the picture may be more or less successful, but because it is frequently taken for granted," composer Bernard Herrmann wrote in 1960 to a fan who had praised his score for *Psycho*. Composing for film obliged composers to think not in movements but in four-bar phrases. But little can say much. Score can expresses characters' wishes and desires, even unspoken ones. It contains no words but divulges secrets.

Musicians accompanied silents years before composers scored to cue. French composer Camille Saint-Saëns had already composed an original score for a one-reel, nine-shot film in 1908—*L'Assassinat du Duc de Guise*. Nickelodeon pianists banged out "Love's Old Sweet Song" to explain onscreen smooches. They led audience

Excerpt from Max Steiner's score for *Gone With the Wind*.

sing-a-longs. Drummers "kidded"—punctuated—onscreen action with snare drum rolls. Behind-screen actors voiced lines for onscreen characters. Projectors were noisy, and exhibitors hired piano players to drown out the clatter. Phonographs in lobbies scratched out standard tunes and, by 1909, phonograph-movie systems such as Léon Gaumont's Chronophone and E.E. Norton's Cameraphone attempted—and failed—to synchronize, amplify, and realistically record sound for movies. Gear-driven phonograph and hand-cranked projector failed to mix.

During the movie palace era of the 1920s, professional musicians guided film viewers through the standard program—overture, news-reel, scenic, musical acts or sing-along, two-reel comedy, spoken prologue, and finally feature film. Movie palaces served effectively as concert halls—a 60-piece symphonic orchestra accompa-nied movies at the 4,717 seats Stanley Theater in Philadelphia, for instance. "Photoplayer" machines cast sound effects and music out of a contraption that combined a player piano with an organ, drums, whistles, and sundry implements imitating thunder, gunshots, and birds. Under the baton of "musical directors," musicians performed barebones arrangements of classical stan-dards. Composers like Ernö Rapée turned out reusable "themes" for theater chain music libraries and wrote "cues" for individual movies. Sheet music versions of the theme song Rapée and Lew Pollack composed for *7th Heaven* (1927) sold vigorously.

Composers for silents—like Rapée—generally relished movie work,

Silent film accompanists would strike up familiar musical phrases to summon familiar feelings. In early talkie cartoons, sound cues continued this practice. Van Buren Studios may have first inserted this cue into a sound movie—*Laundry Blues*, a 1930 Photophone sound animated movie. *Laundry Blues*—like numerous works of the 1930s—traffics in caricature. This pentatonic (five note scale) phrase triggers racist ideas about Asians. A Jewish customer requests his laundry with a ticket that reads, in Hebrew, "Kosher."

but others disguised their identities. J.S. Zamecnik, the composer of the score for *Wings* and some 2,000 other pieces for Sam Fox Music in Cleveland, would sign pieces sometimes as Lionel Baxter, R.L. (Robert) Creighton, Arturo de Castro, "Josh and Ted," J. (Jane) Hathaway, Kathryn Hawthorne, Roberta Hudson, Ioane Kawelo, Dorothy Lee, J. Edgar Lowell, Jules Reynard, F. (Frederick) Van Norman, Hal Vinton, and Grant Wellesley. All were Zamecnik, who had studied symphonic composition with Dvořák in Prague and, as highbrows sometimes did, might have felt that movie work tainted him. Or Sam Fox—who hid his own identity in the first name he first gave his company, "Sandbox Music Publishing"—may have required the disguises to puff the size of the creative staff he employed. Or Zamecnik may have been an ironist. "William Wilson," a doppelgänger in a story by Edgar Allen Poe, was another Zamecnik "collaborator."

Among the most distinguished American movie composers of the 1930s were Jewish émigrés from Europe who fled Germany

Charles Previn—great uncle of contemporary film music composer André Previn—directed, composed, arranged, or conducted 225 films at Universal in the 1930s and '40s. He conducts here on Stage 10 at Universal, built in 1929 as a soundstage.

to survive. Max Steiner, Franz Waxman, and Erich Korngold wrote the classical music derived from European romantic symphonies that pervades Hollywood sound tracks of the 1930s. Alfred Newman, Bernard Herrmann, David Raksin, Charles Previn, all born in America, and Dimtri Tiomkin from Russia continued in this vein. Surrounded by parking lots purple with jacaranda trees, they wrote lyric, dense orchestral cues throbbing like symphonies by Brahms, Rachmaninoff, Schumann, Strauss, Mendelssohn, and Tchaikovsky.

Bride of Frankenstein (1935), dir. James Whale.

The composers' circumstances drift through their scores like notes in a bottle. Franz Waxman struggled to see through an eye injured in childhood. In Waxman's score for *Bride of Frankenstein,* "Satan in Music" (trumpets playing the dissonant diminished fifth chord) telegraphs how the bride's unblinking eyes assess the world she suddenly perceives. But Waxman settled happily into the Hollywood Hills behind a dense green hedge along Mulholland Drive.

Strangers in a land of palmettos, these composers evolved a shared sound. David Raksin transmits an anecdote from Erich Korngold's son:

One day Steiner said to him [Erich Korngold], 'Tell me something, Korngold. We've both been at Warner's for

Erich Korngold and family. c. 1938.
With meticulous intensity, Korngold composed "operas without singing" alone in a silent room...so long as his wife remained there with him in the room. He pitched cues to complement the register of an actor's voice.

ten years now, and in that time your music has gotten progressively worse and worse and mine has been getting better and better. Why do you suppose that is?' And without missing a beat my father answered, 'I tell you *vy dat iss*, Steiner, *dat iss* because you are stealing from me and I am stealing from you.'

Max Steiner in the throes of composing for *Gone With the Wind* illustrates the compulsive energy driving almost all of these

Max Steiner composing, c. 1946.
Steiner needed no eraser on that pencil. While he added a note, he clenched a stogie. On the tie on his chest, cutlasses with handles like G clefs ran in diagonal rows. On the curtains were sentry cowboys.

composers. In 1939, Steiner was 51. He was working and smoking, shuttling up and down Santa Monica Boulevard. He composed in his office in Culver City and raced home to Beverly Hills where he lived with a piano and the third of his four wives. (His second wife divorced him in 1933. He was a workaholic. He refused to pay his debts or talk to her, wire services reported.) As a child in Vienna, Steiner had studied musical composition with Brahms and Mahler and had been working as conductor for Broadway impresario Florenz Ziegfeld when, in 1929, he migrated to Hollywood. He came to help convert Ziegfeld's *Rio Rita* (1929) into an RKO talkie for the European market. For RKO's David O. Selznick in 1932, Steiner created a demo score of original music to play behind a scene in *Symphony of Six Million* (1932)—the first original score for a talkie. In October, 1939, Steiner spent twenty hours a day composing cues for *Gone With the Wind* while also composing the score for *Four Wives* and incidental music for *Intermezzo*. The Germans and Russians were then dividing up Poland. Steiner had scored 250 movies by the time he came to score his last one in 1953.

A four-stage process for scoring developed in Hollywood during the '30s. The composer roughed out "melody is character" scoring first. He worked up a musical leitmotif—a phrase or two—capable of expressing the emotional world of a film or the thoughts and wishes of a character. Other composers ascribed the leitmotif procedure to Max Steiner. Steiner attributed it to opera composer Richard Wagner. Composers, second, progressed to "scoring to catch cues," cues being frames deemed by the film's director to show action of prime significance. A music editor physically marked those points by punching holes in work print frames and then "spotted" the picture with a grease pencil marking diagonal "streamers" across frames preceding the cue. The markings served to prepare the conductor to anticipate imminent cues. The composer, third, would then develop his musical ideas, refining ideas as he worked them into actual cues. The composer or a colleague, fourth, conducted the score.

Max Steiner recording a film score c. 1939. A click track audible in metronymic earphones helped synchronize the music to the streamers and cues passing across images projected on the soundstage screen.

Scoring is usually underscoring—orchestral music establishing mood at moments of dramatic inflection. "I Had a Farm in Africa," John Barry's theme for the beginning of *Out of Africa* (1985), for instance, is 65 bars that evoke rural Africa and the sensibility of the protagonist, novelist Karen Blixen. ("I start with a tingle," she told a *Paris Review* interviewer in 1956, "a kind of feeling of the story I will write. Then come the characters, and they take over, they make the story.") Score is also sometimes music created

Film music composers continue to score-to-cue, digital tools now replacing manual methods.
In *The End of the Affair* (1999), composer Michael Nyman cues a half-minute violin solo, four hypnagogic notes, to underline three actions of primary importance.

Cue 1 [Theme starts]
Sipping a drink in his lover's husband's study and hearing a footfall downstairs, Bendrix recognizes, instantly, from the sound of the tread, that Sarah is entering.

Cue 2 [Theme crescendo]
Raising her eyes to Bendrix as her husband approaches, Sarah recognizes Bendrix. "You?" she says.

Cue 3 [Theme fades]
Bendrix sits alone in his distant flat, tapping away at his typewriter, and his voice-over begins.

to mimic or underline specific actions—"mickey mousing." King Kong ascends the Empire State Building and, even as he pauses, in Max Steiner's score—bam, bam, bam, and bam—Steiner mickey mouses his ascent in the sound track. In Alfred Newman's sound cues for *Rain* (1932), kettledrums thump out passion—the passion a missionary unwillingly and irresistibly feels for a prostitute.

Thirties composers used score to make audible the invisible. Bernard Herrmann repeats a faint phrase played by a theremin in *All that Money Can Buy* (1941) to identify the soul of a man imprisoned by the devil in a moth. Franz Waxman employs an electronic organ and two synthesizers as cues for a sinister presence in *Rebecca* (1940). The sixteen-second fanfare Steiner created in 1937 to identify Warner Bros. pictures typifies the sound. Trumpets launch the theme—Dat!

Dat! Daah!—and hand it off to violins and harps to conclude it. This is music for trumpet, strings, and angels wearing fedoras.

Steiner's most familiar music is his score for *Gone With the Wind* (1939). *Gone With the Wind* consumed 190 minutes of scored-to-cue music, most of it original music by Steiner or folk tunes adapted by him, some by Heinz Roemheld and Adolph Deutsch. Themes that Franz Waxman composed for *His Brother's Wife* (1936) ended up in *Gone With the Wind*. But Steiner himself wrote most of the score, fighting off sleep with Benzedrine during a three-week blur of activity in late 1939. Scarlett O'Hara primping for the barbecue is violins, flutes, and xylophone do-si-doing like flowers in a Disney *Silly Symphony*. The famous Tara theme was a hand-me-down. Steiner recycled it from music he composed to

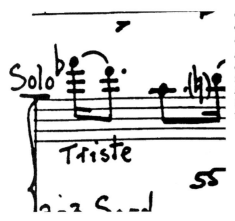

Cello solo, *Johnny Belinda* (1948), composer Max Steiner.

"I happened to have a talent of being able to take a phrase and get tears out of your eyes, cellist Eleanor Aller Slatkin. remembers in *The Hollywood Sound* (1995). "Max Steiner, after he heard me play, wrote more cello solos than anybody else in this town."

Dark Victory (1939), dir. Edmund Goulding. "Give them champagne and be gay. Be very, very gay. I must go in now."

In *Dark Victory* (1939), an ultra "weepie," the Bette Davis character slips into her final sleep while Steiner's strings, sopranos, and a harp throb together. "My theory is that the music should be felt rather than heard," Steiner said.

Steiner excelled at writing to catch the cues. In his score for *The Informer* (1935), Steiner sets thumping percussion and harp strings to make something portentous of Gypo trudging home and striking a match against a lamppost.

play beneath credits of *Crime School* (1938). Steiner used it again in *They Made Me A Criminal* (1939) before finally, nipping and tucking it, he settled it around Tara.

In the end, the score expressed more of Steiner than of Tara. Two months before the premier, Producer David O. Selznick, who wanted "little original music and a score based on the great music of the world, and of the South in particular" was still insisting "two or three musicians could be gotten in to play the themes for me before we go into the expense of arrangements." Fretting that Steiner could not compose fast enough, Selznick surreptitiously hired Franz Waxman to compose an "insurance" score. A month before the premier, Selznick was still considering replacing Steiner with Herbert Stothart. A week later, Selznick, ever chimerical, praised the score and urged Steiner to "go mad with the *schmaltz* in the last three reels." Steiner did. Academy voters nominated

Steiner's score for Best Original Score of 1939. (Herbert Stothart won that year for *The Wizard of Oz*.)

Other Hollywood composers composed slightly differently, following action less exactly than Steiner did. Waxman (*Bride of Frankenstein,* 1935) and Korngold (*Robin Hood,* 1938), for instance, played through specific cues in order to create sound that parallels, without exactly matching, onscreen action. But all rapped batons and, with coronets and violins, raised dreams from invisible sources.

"When a great moment knocks on the door of your life, its sound is often no louder than the beating of your heart and it is very easy to miss it," novelist Boris Pasternak reputedly wrote in a letter to Olga Ivinskaya, his inspiration for *Dr. Zhivago*. In his score for David Lean's film of *Dr. Zhivago* (1965), Maurice Jarre seems to transmute Pasternak's thought into melody. Jarre and countless other composers learned to do that from Max Steiner.

EXERCISE SIXTEEN: SCORE

What this exercise teaches:
- **How to synchronize shots to music using beat marks**
- **How to insert, pin, and float background scores to digital movies**
- **How to add sound effects**
- **How to duck sound tracks (reduce volume in one to make another more audible)**
- **How to select a score appropriate for your project**
- **How to judge when silence is better than music**

Letter from Audrey Hepburn to Henry Mancini c. 1961

Dear Henry,

I have just seen our picture—*Breakfast at Tiffany's*—this time with your score.

A movie without a score is a little bit like an airplane without fuel. However beautifully the job is done, we are still on the ground and in a world of reality. Your music has lifted us all up and sent us soaring. Everything we cannot say with words or show with action you have expressed for us.

Lots of love
Audrey

You Did It Then: Warner Bros. released *Santa Fe Trail* (1940) with a Max Steiner score in an experimental "Vitasound" sound track that directed bursts of monophonic sound to supplementary left and right speakers during emotionally charged scenes.

Reinsert Steiner's score into a scene of *Santa Fe Trail* (1940) from which it has been extracted. Repeat the process with other scores extracted from other 1940s movies. Consider what each score did contribute or would contribute to the scene. Step-by-step instructions and the files you'll need are in the digital cutting room at http://makefilmhistory.com.

You Do It Now: Create a score for the silent film you shot for Chapter Nine (Intertitles) and dubbed for Chapter Twelve (Synch Sound). Feel free to collaborate with any composers or musicians you know... it's encouraged.

ENDINGS:
Casablanca (1942)

"I could have done more."
Oskar Schindler, *Schindler's List*

Screenwriters who can readily list the stages of a movie nevertheless struggle to end one. Good endings surprise and delight and feel inevitable, but writers can rarely write them to order. Good endings, like prints emerging in a darkroom, appear to writers when the chemicals call them. E.L. Doctorow, a novelist, once explained how intuition guides him to endings—"It's like driving a car at night: you never see further than your headlights, but you can make the whole trip than way." Other writers get there differently. But all agree that a protagonist defines himself as he struggles. At root, "protagonist" means first combatant, first pleader, first actor. A writer may fashion a protagonist as gangster, mother, sheriff, dancer, elephant, but however the protagonist begins, through struggle he or she evolves into someone different. In an ending that satisfies, the protagonist has evolved from who he was and becomes at last who he *is*.

To get to the end, screenwriters can:

● Follow a formula (*When Harry Met Sally*)

● Write backwards to and from an ending (*Lolita*)

● Follow where a character seems to wish to go (*8½*)

● Market test an ending (*Fatal Attraction*)

Who wrote the dialogue Bogart and Bergman deliver at the end of *Casablanca* (1942) remains unclear. Twins Philip (left) and Julius Epstein (right) wrote major portions of the movie, but so did seven others. Screenwriting is part craft and part enigma. Screenwriters express themselves through characters as, in ancient Greek tragedy, actors spoke through masks.

To set the stage for an ending, screenwriters generally agree, it takes three acts. In the first act, something challenges or frightens or perplexes the protagonist, who then sets about restoring his world. During the second act, when each step takes him further from himself, the protagonist acknowledges that he is lost. He struggles harder, only to transform misfortune into catastrophe. During the third act, the protagonist engages whatever opposes him in momentous combat. When the battle ends, the movie ends, and the protagonist considers where struggle has led. All paths in a movie lead here—to the ending where, for eternity or an instant, the protagonist stays the flow of change. Viewers feel joy or relief or grief, depending on how the protagonist fares. In a tragedy, the protagonist loses. In a comedy, the protagonist prevails. Hairdresser, shoe salesman, mother of seven, in essence the protagonist is a warrior.

Good endings often intimate what is to follow after the movie ends. Like rests in music, these endings appear to make temporary pauses in action that promises to flow onward. When a character whose fate most concerns us achieves at last what we desire for him—which is not necessarily victory, but rather self-knowledge and steady bearings in the world—a movie ends strongly.

Picture these endings that suggest what will happen if the story were to continue off-screen. In *The Third Man* (1949), the protagonist strides down a cemetery lane and passes in silence the woman he loves. The ending intimates that he never sees her again. (The mind's eyes make league with the movie and follows the man into shadows.) In *La Strada* (1954), the camera ascends from the drunken, solitary protagonist. He gazes upward in darkness from the damp sand of a beach while Nino Rota's throbbing music plays. The ending suggests that this flesh-bound man has sensed, at last, what brutality has wrought. In *Bicycle Thieves* (1948), father and son walk as if pilgrims away from the camera. Implicit in their retreat is the certainty that these wounded souls now accept each other's failings. At the end of *The Lives of Others* (2006), the former surveillance man discovers that the author he surveilled has dedicated his novel to him. "This is for me," the

Big Night (1996), dirs. Campbell Scott, Stanley Tucci.
Brothers breakfasting together in silence end *Big Night*. From their gestures and postures and the omelet they share, the viewer believes that they will survive their catastrophe and cook together again.

surveillance man says, and we feel that this drab and lonely man will experience redemption.

An artful storyteller can make any ending seem inevitable. In David Lynch's *The Straight Story* (1999), an infirm elderly man makes his way to his equally infirm brother... on a lawnmower. In Michael Powell and Emeric Pressburger's *I Know Where I'm Going* (1945), the protagonist comes to embrace, in a land-poor Scottish naval officer, the opposite of what she thought she wanted. Love wins over status.

Finding the right ending is frequently an agonizing process. "I was terribly worried about the ending of the picture [*Gone With the Wind*]," David O. Selznick wrote his story editor three months before *Gone With The Wind* (1939) opened. "We found it impossible to get into script form even the hint that Scarlett might get Rhett back... We tried two or three ways, and even shot one...but it didn't work." King Vidor shot alternative endings for *The Crowd* (1928). Fellini concludes *8½* (1963) with footage he had shot as a trailer: The dream people of his self-reflexive movie about the irresolution of a film director pass in a circle until, responding to the director's shouts through a megaphone, they fade away.

Preview screening—in effect, enrolling a sample audience as co-writer—can suggest what audiences want. Preview screening is a Hollywood tradition. Harold Lloyd analyzed *Speedy* (1928) by marking down where preview audiences laughed. Frank Oz reversed the ending of *Little Shop of Horrors* (1986) when test

Sunset Boulevard (1950), dir. Billy Wilder.

Norma Desmond, the crazed silent movie star, inhabits forever her false self at the end of *Sunset Boulevard* (1950). "You see, this is my life. It always will be. There's nothing else. Just us and the cameras, and those wonderful people out there in the dark... All right, Mr. DeMille. I'm ready for my close-up."

audiences detested what he proposed—that the protagonist feeds his love to a man-eating plant, which then eats him, too. In the film Oz released, the protagonist annihilates the plant and marries his love, as preview audiences requested. We do not want our cards fairly shuffled, preview audiences repeatedly say. The deck must be stacked in our favor because we want to feel that, notwithstanding the dealer's fair deal, another hand, invisibly dealing an ace, loves us.

But no formula unfailingly works. Frank Capra describes his search for a satisfying ending for *Meet John Doe* (1941). "Riskin and I had written ourselves into a corner. We knew we were loaded with entertainment; we had a startling opening and a powerful development that rose inexorably to a spectacular climactic wow. But—we had no acceptable SOLUTION to our story. The first two acts were solid; the third act was a wet sock."

"You guys can't find an ending to your story because you got no story in the *first* place," was what script doctor Jules Furthman offered. Capra shot four endings and had already released alternative prints with alternative endings when an anonymous letter signed "John Doe" urged him to rescue the protagonist with the ordinary people John Doe had, however falsely, inspired. Embracing this suggestion, Capra shot his fifth ending. Editors spliced it into the movie. Audiences loved it.

A team of writers, similarly, struggled to end *Casablanca*. High school teacher Murray Burnett and co-author Joan Alison wrote a script in 1940 for a play, *Everyone Comes to Rick's*. Characters in the unproduced play act much as they do in *Casablanca*, but their motives are different. In the play, Rick Blaine is a burnt-out lawyer who once practiced law in Paris and now runs a café for émigrés in Casablanca. He says he believes in nothing. But when his former lover, Lois, arrives with resistance leader Victor Laszlo, Rick helps

Lois and Laszlo flee. This Rick commits an apparently pointless act of self-destructive heroism on behalf of a woman he now professes to despise. The German captain controlling Casablanca arrests Rick for his act of heroism, consigning Rick to virtually certain death.

A few weeks after America entered World War Two, Warner Bros. producer Hall Wallis bought the property and renamed it *Casablanca*. Shooting was scheduled to begin mid-May, 1942. Writers Wally Kline and Aeneas MacKenzie began reworking the play and managed to turn out some pages of dialogue. Unsatisfied, Wallis turned the job over to Julius and Philip Epstein.

The Epsteins submitted their draft in March, 1942. In this version, Rick has become a man with a mysterious past. As in the original play, Lois—now named Ilsa—continues to flee with Laszlo, and Rick still acts as a self-destructive hero for no reason anyone could name. The draft needed more work. Writer Howard Koch joined the Epsteins and they labored to endow the resistance leader with more substance. Four weeks before shooting, yet another writer, Casey Robinson, came aboard and created a back-story romance between Ilsa and Rick. By the time shooting began on May 25, nine writers, including Wallis himself, had invested themselves in this script, which was largely finished—except for the ending.

As Emily Dickinson once mused in a poem, each life converges to some center. The nine writers could hear what Rick said but they could not hear his heart. A satisfying ending for *Casablanca* therefore eluded all of them. In every version of the script, Rick continued sending Ilsa away on the airplane, but no one could motivate his action. Rick was giving up Ilsa because, presumably, he was in despair and had come to the end of palliatives. In this May 11 draft, he expressed nothing more than self-contempt.

RICK:

I'm not the Rick you knew in Paris. I'm not a man you can love any more. I serve drinks. I run a crooked gambling table. Every morning I lock myself in a room and drink myself dizzy. That's all I'll be doing every day and night for the rest of my life—

ILSA:

Then I'll do it with you.

RICK:

No, I've got it down to a science now. I don't need any help doing it. I don't want you around. (pointing to Laszlo) You go with him. He wants you. I'm all finished. You belong to a fighter, not a saloon-keeper—

ILSA:

(tearfully) If you think you can talk me out of—

CUT TO:

248. CLOSE SHOT RENAULT

RENAULT:

I beg your pardon, Madame. I do not like to interfere in this matter—but the choice is not yours. Rick will spend the rest of his natural life in a concentration camp.

Close, but still one degree off center, the compass needle quivered and continued to search for the pole. On July 1, six weeks after shooting began, the writers were still rewriting. No document establishes which of them wrote the lines that director Michel Curtiz shot on July 17. But those lines point true north. In matching felt hats on a rain-misted tarmac, Rick and Ilsa say their farewells. Lights glow from the passenger windows of a distant two-engine plane.

ILSA:

"You're saying this only to make me go."

RICK:

"I'm saying it because it's true. Inside of us we both know you belong with Victor. You're part of his work, the thing that keeps him going. If that plane leaves the ground and you're not with him, you'll regret it."

ILSA:

"No."

RICK:

"Maybe not today, maybe not tomorrow, but soon, and for the rest of your life."

ILSA:

"But what about us?"

RICK:

"We'll always have Paris. We didn't have it—we'd lost it—until you came to Casablanca. We got it back last night."

ILSA:

"And I said that I would never leave you."

RICK:

"And you never will. But I've got a job to do, too. Where I'm going you can't follow—what I've got to do, you can't be any part of. Ilsa, I'm no good at being noble, but it doesn't take much to see that the problems of three little people don't amount to a hill of beans in this crazy world. Someday you will understand that. Now now. Here's looking at you, kid."

A single plot thread remained to tie. French Captain Louis Renault needed to respond when, once Ilsa departs, Rick shoots German Major Strasser. Renault might plausibly arrest Rick, shoot him, or summon the Third Reich to incarcerate him. The writers puzzled. Renault's response would establish the significance of Rick's act. It would convey if Rick had begun to change the world or merely his heart. Julius and Philip Epstein settled the matter when, according to Julius, driving down Sunset Boulevard, "We turned to each other and yelled, 'Round up the usual suspects!'" Rick, they determined, had begun to change the world. Rick escapes arrest. Renault throws his lot in with Rick, and the two stride off together towards darkness as strains of "La Marseillaise" play.

"Operation Torch," November 8, 1942.
Reality follows where Rick leads. No American troops battled in French North Africa during the months Warner Bros. shot *Casablanca*, but American and British troops landed in darkness in Casablanca, Oran, and Algiers on November 8, 1942. Warner Bros. rushed *Casablanca* to a premiere in New York two weeks later.

This ending defines love as selflessness. After loving Ilsa inscrutably through numerous drafts, Rick now loves as mythic heroes have always loved—in sacrifice and duty and service. Love turns into righteousness, duty trumps personal loss, thought gives way to action. The protagonist may die or lose what he ardently desires, but he acts to save the world. Rick begins as a cynic and ends as a soldier of righteousness. The ending inspires viewers to find their greater selves.

Warner Bros. executives expected *Casablanca* to last no longer than a cocktail napkin at Romanoff's. But it has never stopped playing, especially in the darkroom of memory where movies develop continuously, largely because the ending calls viewers to transcend themselves. "yes and his heart was going like mad and yes I said yes I will Yes," is how James Joyce's novel, *Ulysses* ends. A well-ended movie brings viewers to that point of assent.

Producer Hal Wallis called Bogart back into the studio a few weeks after shooting concluded to loop one of a pair of lines of dialogue over the last shot. One line Wallis was considering was, "Louis, I might have known you'd mix your patriotism with a little larceny." Wallis ultimately rejected that line. The other line brings harmony to former adversaries. "Our expenses? Louis, I think this is the beginning of a beautiful friendship."

In revival theaters, viewers still smile and chant those words.

EXERCISE SEVENTEEN: ENDINGS

What this exercise teaches:

- **How a protagonist whispers to her writer what others hear only at the end**

- **How to offer a character what he or she is still missing**

- **How to "seal the deal" with an audience in a memorable word, a look, or a gesture**

- **How to make an ending that bookends the beginning**

On August 7, 1942, producer Hal Wallis dictated this memo to Owen Marks, who was editing *Casablanca*:

INTEROFFICE COMMUNICATION

There are also to be two wild lines made by Bogart. Mike is trying to get Bogart today, but if he does not succeed, will you get Bogart in within the next couple of days.

The two lines to be shot with Bogart, in the event that Mike does not get them, are:

RICK:

Louis, I might have known you'd mix your patriotism with a little larceny.

(Alternative line)

RICK:

Louis, I think this is the beginning of a beautiful friendship.

****

HAL WALLIS

***You Did It Then*: "No passion in the world is equal to the passion to alter someone else's draft," H.G. Wells reputedly said. Over selected stills from the ending of *Casablanca*, re-write the dialogue to get Rick, not Victor, on that plane with Ilsa. Step-by-step instructions and the files you'll need are in the digital cutting room at http://makefilmhistory.com.**

TECHNICOLOR:
Michael Powell (1947)

"One is starved for Technicolor up there."
"The Conductor" speaking of Heaven in Powell and
Pressburger's *A Matter of Life and Death* (1946)

Color in movies declares what black and white suggests. Black and white films induce the mist of fantasy. From the black and white movies that predominated in the '40s it is easy to picture Britain as steam engines drawing into rain-lashed stations, men in flat caps throwing darts in pubs while a gauze of black and white settles over the countryside. "We watch so many old movies our memories come in monochrome," novelist and screenwriter Angela Carter wrote in *Wise Children*. But color in movies is an irrepressible expression of vitality—the id of movies. Color in movies is a dancer with no veil.

The earliest filmmakers developed numerous techniques to work color into orthochromatic film stock. Blind to red and dark orange and sensitive only to blue and green, orthochromatic stocks create monochromatic movies. But to meet a demand for color, women laboring at workbenches in the first years of the twentieth century were routinely hand-finishing movies by brushing, stenciling, tinting or toning aniline dyes into release print frames. Pathé created an assembly line for tinting near Paris.

Black Narcissus (1947), dir. Powell & Pressburger, cinematography by Jack Cardiff.
The glade is plaster bamboos set in a studio in England six miles from Windsor Castle. The "moonlight" is a bank of electric lamps flooding down 800-foot-candles of light before a Technicolor camera shooting at f2.8. In a color print, the eye would see it as dreamy and erotic, but would there be a word for the color of that dress? Plum? Maroon? Ruby? Beneath the flotsam of words flows the river of feeling that is color in movies. (See http://makefilmhistory.com for color plates.)

Jean Simmons acted simultaneously in two films in 1946. At Denham Studios she played Ophelia in Laurence Olivier's black and white *Hamlet* (above left). Four miles away at Pinewood Studios, she played Kanchi in Michael Powell's Technicolor *Black Narcissus* (above right). Her two roles convey the antithetical qualities of monochrome and color movies.

Filmmakers had originally tinted frames to stymie those who, without right, would duplicate their films. "This film is sold subject to the restriction that it shall not be used for printing other films from it," Edison was still thundering in 1903. Pirates simply bleached away the tints. Filmmakers then tinted to inspire feeling. Edison Manufacturing had already in 1895 hand-tinted a Kinetoscope of Annabelle Moore, a teen-age dancer whirling in a skirt. A craze developed for pinks, reds, and yellows applied by stencilists on dancers. Pastel and evanescent, the dancers resembled peonies in the process of dropping petals. Edison employees shot and hand colored these fantasies in New Jersey, and the Lumières shot some in Paris. Loïe Fuller famously performed in several. Aniline dyes daubed on these dancers at the workbench turn them into apparitions.

The hand-coloring process was arduous but profitable. Méliès, for instance, charged double for hand-colored prints of *A Trip to the*

Annabelle's Serpentine Dance (1895). William Heise filmed this movie for the Edison Manufacturing Company. Tinting gives it emotion. On the left, tint applied globally gives the space the look of molten blue glass. A second layer of color applied by hand turns the dancer into a jinni. The same frames, untinted on the right, render the dancer abstractly. (See www.makefilmhistory.com for color plates).

Moon. By 1920 viewers expected coloring, and almost everyone making movies did it, relying on six principal methods to use separately or in combination.

First, exposed film stock could be *tinted* (soaked in dye to transform the entire image into shades of the dye selected.) Amber or orange stood for daytime interior. Blue became the night. Red was

Darren Aronofsky sought a similar effect in *Black Swan* (2010). But Aronofsky's task was different. CGI effects give actress Natalie Portman wings. *Black Swan* began on super 16mm film stock and HDTV files. It evolved to a 35 mm anamorphic 35mm film print through a digital intermediate filmmakers used to adjust grain, sharpness, and color. *Black Swan* certainly required no hand tinting.

Convention deemed day sepia and night blue, but fantasy otherwise ruled in color toned silent movies like *Mark of Zorro* (1920).

These variant treatments of a frame from *Casablanca* simulate what tinting and toning, respectively, contributed to the emotional range of monochromatic movies. Top left is the frame as Warner Bros. released it. Center simulates the light hand of tinting on the image. Top right simulates the heavier hand of toning. (See http://makefilmhistory. com for color plates.)

fire or fury or passion. Purple was the time between times. Green was mystery. This method was relatively easy, requiring only that each release print be assembled individually, filmmakers splicing together segments of the film differentially dyed. Second, exposed film could be *toned* (by chemically replacing the silver compounds still present in the emulsion with salts of different metals). Toning imbues some, but not all, of the image with a new color.

Third, the exposed film stock could be *hand-colored* (highlighting detail on exposed film frame by frame by drawing or painting free-hand on segments of each image). Hand-coloring required the eyesight of a watchmaker and the patience of a glacier. Fourth, exposed film could be manually *stencil colored* (highlighting detail on exposed films frames by drawing or painting within a stencil cut from another print). Stencil coloring required a taste for lace making and tatting. Fifth, exposed film could be machine *stencil colored* (the Handschiegl color process that layered dyes onto a

positive print in a multiple exposure process). Sixth, by 1929, prints could be released in Kodak Sonochrome, a stock pre-tinted in 17 colors to avoid disrupting sound reproduction where splices join tinted scenes together.

Albeit haltingly, moviemakers shot color film before Technicolor. George Albert Smith's Kinemacolor, an additive (first one color, then another) process created softly pastel frames by using alternating red and cyan filters in both cameras and projectors. From 1908-1914, producer Charles Urban shot 262 Kinemacolor feature and travel films and exhibited them in theaters he opened in London, Paris, and New York. He terminated Kinemacolor operations in 1914 when he lost a patent dispute at the onset of World War One. (Urban sold the Kinemacolor studio in Hollywood and his plan to film Thomas Dixon's *The Clansman* in 1913 to D.W. Griffith, who converted Urban's project into *The Birth of a Nation*.) Kinemacolor registered colors imperfectly and stuttered unavoidably. Projecting successive red and green versions of an image degraded them. But the method created images—paddle wheel steamers plying the Nile and Gurkha horsemen racing on parade grounds in Delhi—that trace the colors of a century ago as a faintly remembered dream.

There were other Technicolor forerunners. In 1913, Kodak introduced Kodachrome, first as a two-color subtractive (absorb and reflect) system. Starting with a dual lens camera shooting orthochromatic negative, a series of transformations evolved. From color filters, separation positives, bleaches, tanning agents, double-coated duplicate negatives, green/blue dye bath, and red dye baths, a positive with colors as delicate as jellyfish emerged. Several scenes in Vitagraph's *The Light In the Dark* (1922) employed this two-color Kodachrome process.

The partners who ran Prizma, primarily a small travelogue producer, invented additive and then subtractive color film systems that

Shooting Kinemacolor from an African river shore in 1909 was Urban cameraman Joseph DeFrenes.

Charles Urban (with hat, cane, and pith helmet) in Delhi, India, in 1911, with Kinemacolor cameramen DeFrenes and Albuin Mariner.

created "scenes that would make any man wonder at the earth upon which he lives have been reproduced with realistic effect," a *New York Times* reporter noted in 1918.

Everything changed, however, when Herbert Kalmus, Daniel Comstock and others, operating as the Technicolor Motion Picture Corporation, developed Technicolor, first in 1916 as a two-color (red and green) additive process similar to Kinemacolor, then in 1922, more transformatively, as "Process 2," a subtractive process. Inside the "Process 2" camera, a prism split an image into two.

One instance of the image passed through a red filter to expose a frame of black and white negative. The other passed identically to the negative through a green filter. Prints focused softly and scratched easily—emulsion coated both sides of the filmstrips, ripped frequently, and spliced awkwardly. A single production could occupy half Technicolor's inventory of Process 2 cameras. (There were eleven available in 1926, and Douglas Fairbanks used four in 1926 for color sequences in *The Black Pirate*.) The process rendered color selectively. During a comic scene in *Irene* (1926) concocted by First National to be shot in two-color Technicolor, Colleen Moore, playing a dressmaker's model, mounts a turntable so that a couturier might swath her in a blue dress. But two-color Technicolor, rendering blue unpredictably, failed in this instance. "Everything possible was tried to make the dress appear as blue but there was nothing anyone could do about it. Audiences had to settle for a pale green," director Mervyn LeRoy, then a lab technician, remembered.

In 1928, Technicolor improved the process, supplanting the cemented bi-level release print with a "Process 3" single-level release print. "Process 4," introduced in 1932, completed the Technicolor migration. Prisms in Process 4 cameras split light into one-quarter/three-quarter components to expose three strips of black and white film while they advanced in tandem through separate film gates. Recombined in a complicated dye-transfer printing process, a positive that began as separate negatives for green, blue, and red versions of a frame emerged as full spectrum Technicolor.

Jack Cardiff, cinematographer of *Black Narcissus* (left), and fellow British cinematographer Gregory Unsworth at a Process 4 Technicolor camera.

The Toll of the Sea (1922), dir. Chester M. Franklin. The first two-color Technicolor feature movie.

Technicolor produced it, Anna May Wong starred in it, and the ad campaign described it as "the first picture in perfect natural colors."

Process 4 was the cumbersome but classic "three-strip color process" Technicolor of the 1930s and 40s. A voluminous sound-suppressing cover—the "enchanted cottage" director Michael Powell called it—enveloped the three-strip color process camera. Operating the dials on the camera resembled maintaining the course of a submarine. The Technicolor Corporation manufactured just 36 Process 4 cameras, leasing them to studios accompanied by an obligatory technician and an obligatory contract for film processing. By 1939, studios shot one movie in ten in color.

Black Narcissus, director Michael Powell. Cinematographer Jack Cardiff.

The frame above from *Black Narcissus,* where Sister Clodagh on the right (Deborah Kerr), attempts to dissuade Sister Ruth (Kathleen Byron) from fleeing, shows (at www.makefilmhistory.com) how color communicates. The page edges of Ruth's Bible in Clodagh's hands are a plum color identical to the color of her dress. But the color of Ruth's dress signals her flight from religious vocation and the madness that will kill her. In Ruth's psyche, Technicolor

conveys, a nun is already a harlot. In black and white, this characterization would be indiscernible. Black and white movies veil the world; Technicolor movies ripple the world open.

Technicolor footage in 1946 was, by Technicolor corporate policy, sharp and brilliant. It could be difficult, in 1946, to use Technicolor subtly. One incident conveys the Technicolor mindset then. On the last day of actress Deborah Kerr's scheduled work on the set of *Black Narcissus,* the color consultant assigned to the film by Technicolor UK Ltd. telephoned cinematographer Jack Cardiff with appalling news. According to the consultant, the previous day's work was completely ruined. The problem was pearlescence— a glow that muted colors and softened focus. Pearlescence had paled rushes of a shot of Deborah Kerr. The news mortified Cardiff. The shot is below.

As the Technicolor consultant saw it, soft focus and pearly color rendered this shot worthless. As Cardiff and Powell saw it, it was perfect, spreading the nun's anxiety in fields of white and tan from the walls to the edge of the world.

Black Narcissus (1946), Jack Cardiff cinematographer.

Black Narcissus, Jack Cardiff, cinematographer.

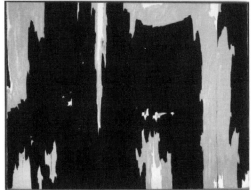

Clyfford Still, *D-1, 1957*. Albright-Knox Museum. Oil on canvas.

Girl with a Pearl Earring (c. 1665), Johannes Vermeer [oil on canvas].

To visually disperse the nun's anxiety and sink it into the wind, Cardiff had exposed the footage with a weak (#2) fog filter. Technicians rushed the footage to the Pinewood Studio set where Cardiff and director Michael Powell sat down to contemplate the wreckage. "The moment I saw it on the screen, I knew it was good," Cardiff remembers. Powell exulted, "Wonderful, Jack. This is just what I wanted." Powell turned to the Technicolor rep and said, "It's about time you learned something about art in movies."

Cardiff says that Technicolor UK selected him from other young cinematographers at Denham Studios to learn Technicolor camerawork in 1936 and teach it to other cinematographers because he expressed admiration for how painters like Rembrandt and Pieter de Hooch used color as shorthand for feeling.

"Vermeer was the sort of painter I had in mind on *Black Narcissus*. Because the light had to be clear and as simple as possible," Jack Cardiff says in *Painting With Light*.

Set in the Himalayas, *Black Narcissus* was shot entirely on an interior soundstage and exterior lot at Pinewood Studios and in a British exotic plant garden. Machines created wind. On an exterior lot, scenery flats pitched at obtuse angles simulated distant mountainous peaks. Cardiff's cinematography created a world that a storybook prince might see inside an emerald. The shot remained in the movie as Cardiff exposed it.

Technicolor constituted the film industry color standard until the late 1940s. Federal courts then ruled against the Technicolor Corporation in 1947, deeming its business practices monopolistic.

In 1950, Kodak began marketing Eastmancolor, a single-stripe color film stock suitable for ordinary cameras. Studios then abandoned the three-strip Technicolor camera. Technicolor continued to operate, gradually withdrawing its cameras and focusing instead on producing single-strip color negatives and prints for other manufacturers and studios. The last feature film in America made with a three-strip Technicolor camera was *Foxfire* (1955). Technicolor closed its Hollywood dye-transfer facility in 1974. But for ravishing color, will anything surpass a newly struck dye-transfer release print of a three-strip Technicolor movie?

Contemporary color film stocks render green, blue and red effectively on three layers of emulsion. In this blue-toned shot from *Chungking Express* (1994) above, a young detective looks east through a hotel window as dawn breaks in Hong Kong. Director Kar Wai Wong shot Agfa XT color 35 mm motion picture film, now discontinued.

EXERCISE EIGHTEEN: TECHNICOLOR

What this exercise teaches:

- **How to transition seamlessly from gray scale to color images**

- **How to time shots by setting exposure, brightness, contrast, and saturation levels**

- **How color makes the "climate" of a Technicolor movie**

- **How Technicolor differed from earlier color systems such as tinting**

"Technicolor has demonstrated through the years its complete and absolute integrity and pride of craftsmanship about every single print that comes out of its laboratories in Hollywood and in England..."

David O. Selznick September 23, 1949

You Did It Then: Strike a virtual answer print (a timed, color-corrected provisional print) of shots from a scene of *Black Narcissus*. Where necessary, time the shots to normalize exposure levels. Evoke from the film stock the look that's right for this film. Strike a gray scale print, too. Step-by-step instructions and the files you can use are in the digital cutting room at http://makefilmhistory.com.

You Do It Now: Play with the color of one of your *Make Film History* movies. Modify brightness, contrast, saturation, red, green, and blue gain, and anything else you can control. Experiment. See how much you can change.

PRODUCTION **Make Film History**
DIRECTOR _____
CAMERA _____
DATE   SCENE   TAKE
18

VOICE-OVER:
Portrait of Jennie (1948)

"You talkin' to me? You talkin' to me? You talkin' to me? Then who the hell else are you talking... you talking to me? Well I'm the only one here."

"Travis Bickle," *Taxi Driver* (1976)

To understand voice-over, first understand what it is not. Voice-over is not narration. Unlike voice-over, narration speaks authoritatively. Narration is the voice of certainty. Narration entered movies in '30s documentaries when producers replaced written intertitles of the "silent" era with narrators who, in effect, spoke them. Narrators remain "outside" the movie they narrate, explaining, commenting, contextualizing, pulling the curtain open when act one begins but never acting in it.

Masculine and godlike, narration of 1930s demanded credulity. Narrators might offer bombast. "The Indian road is like no other in the world. It traverses not only India but the very sands of time," says the *veddy* British narrator of *A Road in India* (1938). They might deliver dactylic couplets—"This is the night mail crossing the Border, Bringing the cheque and the postal order," John Grierson recites in *Night Mail* (1936). But most of all, narrators offered authority.

Jennie stares off into space as Joseph Cotten, playing painter Eben Adams, greets dawn from the steps of the New York Public Library.

Introducing the turning point of *Portrait of Jennie* (1948), this shot expresses in shadow and light the note of recognition implicit in their first conversation when the child Jennie says to Adams before she offers him her name:

"I don't have to go home yet. Nobody's ready for me. Anyway, you're with me."

"I'm with you," is what voice-over whispers to viewer.

The March of Time narrator Westbrook Van Voorhis typifies the portentous, authoritative 1930s manner. Van Voorhis certainly invited parody—the "News On The March" newsreel in *Citizen Kane* (1941) imitates his drumbeat style perfectly. "Famed in American legend is the origin of the Kane fortune... How, to boarding house keeper Mary Kane was left the supposedly worthless deed to an abandoned mine shaft: the Colorado Lode." But Van Voorhis' kettledrum diction and his repeated refrain, "Times Marches On..." seemed to authenticate *The March of Time* news and news reenactment series he narrated from 1935 to 1952. That is the purpose of narrators—to confirm, to reassure, to authenticate. *Someone knows*, the voice of the narrator says.

Murder (1930), dir. Alfred Hitchcock. "Funny that S.O.S. coming on top of that other... Save her soul... Save her..."

Westbook Van Voorhis.

Voice-over suggests the opposite. Unlike narration, voice-over is tentative, personal, inward. Alfred Hitchcock introduced voice-over to movies in *Murder* (1930). A member of a murder trial jury stares at his face in a mirror while he shaves. He cogitates on testimony he has heard, and, while he thinks them, viewers hear his thoughts. Hitchcock directed *Murder* the first year he shot talkies. The sound track balances poorly. But Hitchcock's original instance of voice-over points the way for all voice-overs.

Voice-over directs our attention not to action outside but to what a character, inside, makes of that action. As long as the process of mixing sound tracks in the early 1930s taxed the limits of movie sound recording technology, directors made little use of voice-over. In the first years of synchronous sound, even dubbing was daunting. In Hitchcock's *Blackmail* (1929), a British actress delivered lines into an off-camera microphone while a Czech actress mimed them for the camera. Preston Sturges used voice-over segues in *The Power and the Glory* (1932) to sequence scenes of the life of a railroad tycoon. Publicists hyped the technique as "narratage."

Voice-over became common in the post-war period. A new zeitgeist may, in part, be responsible. Thirties screenwriters with an ear pressed to radio speakers to overhear what Stalin was saying to Hitler may have been little inclined to hang on the unspoken thoughts of imagined individual people. The gangster movie, the backstage musical, the western—prevailing genres of the '30s—required action, not nuanced self-reflection.

But by the late 1940s and early 1950s, the frame of reference of Hollywood writers had significantly evolved. Freud had largely supplanted Marx. Psychoanalyst Otto Fenichel had been an impecunious refugee when, in 1938, he fled Prague and first deployed an army cot as an analytic couch in Los Angeles. By 1950, psychoanalysts in Los Angeles were so numerous and prosperous that they established rival institutes. Judy Garland and Marilyn Monroe were then consulting the psychoanalyst that director King Vidor had helped bring to America, Ernst Simmel. Analyst Ralph Greenson treated Tony Curtis, Frank Sinatra, and Vivien Leigh. A psychiatrist character figures in 51 American movies from 1945-1952. Movies of the late '40s and '50s increasingly looked inward. Voice-over expresses this change.

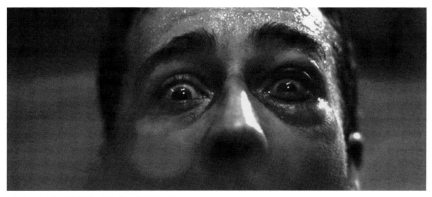

Fight Club (1999), dir. David Fincher.
Voice-over is the still small voice that an audience but no character hears, except for the one who is speaking it. It is the narrator of *Fight Club* (1999) telling us about his demonic alter ego, "People are always asking me if I know Tyler Durden."

The character delivering voice-over remains in his movie while he steps outside of it. The character seems to be speaking to you but is conversing with himself. Voice-over resembles a Möbius strip—you never quite know for sure which side of the screen you are on when you hear it. Words head outward towards the audience and, without ever turning, end back where they started, inside the film.

A speech at the end of *Blade Runner* (1982) conveys the introspective sound of voice-over:

> **I don't know why he saved my life. Maybe in those last moments he loved life more than he ever had before. Not just his life, anybody's life, my life. All he'd wanted were the same answers the rest of us want. Where did I come from? Where am I going? How long have I got? All I could do was sit there and watch him die.**

Viewers enter *Rebecca* (1940) on a voice-over similarly mysterious and inward:

> Last night, I dreamt I went to Manderley again. It seemed to me I stood by the iron gate leading to the drive, and for a while I could not enter... for the way was barred to me. Then, like all dreamers, I was possessed of a sudden with supernatural powers... and passed like a spirit through the barrier before me.

Human feeling is the essential subject of first person voice-over. "Do the machines in the factory ever need rest, does a ship ever feel tired, or is it only people who are so weary at night?" a voice asks when *The Naked City* (1948) begins. A common feature of films in the late '40s and early '50s, voice-overs continue to infuse the subjective into movies. *Annie Hall* (1977) lacked shape, editor Ralph Rosenblum maintains, until a narrative emerged in the first-person voice-over Allen created as he spieled into a microphone while a rough cut ran in a screening room. In *The Diving Bell and the Butterfly* (2007), a protagonist incapacitated by a stroke and able to move nothing but an eyelid explains and affirms himself solely by speaking in voice-over.

The Prize Winner of Defiance Ohio (2005), dir. Jane Anderson.

On the left, the protagonist—played by Julianne Moore—is a jingle writer who has now died. The script derives from a memoir by Terry Ryan, above right, who is the real life daughter of the jingle writer character. The mother no longer there and the woman who remembers her meet in this final shot of the movie. The protagonist begins her final voice-over:

Oh, my goodness. I believe this was the very last thing I ever wrote.

Every time I pass a church
I stop to make a visit
So when I'm carried in feet first
God won't say, 'Who is it?'

Voice-over answers the question, "Who is it?"

The heyday of voice-over was the last of the 1940s and first of the 1950s. Philosopher Jean-Paul Sartre sounded the note in a speech he delivered in 1945: "We must begin from the subjective." The wish to see *into* another heart pervaded the zeitgeist. In *Lady In the Lake* (1947), for instance, the camera shows nothing but what the private eye protagonist sees. We glimpse the protagonist's

hands and feet from time to time but see him fully only, when in reflection, he glimpses himself in a mirror.

Voice-over joins two related ideas of the post-war '40s and '50s. The first held that what is outside human personal experience is meaningless. "The benign indifference of the universe," the

Dark Passage (1947), dir. Delmer Daves.
Warner Bros. gave Humphrey Bogart similar treatment in *Dark Passage* (1947). Before a plastic surgeon grafts him a new face, Bogart's character remains invisible to viewers. He delivers dialogue and unburdens himself in voice-over. "Brother, you never drove a cab. You have no idea how lonely it gets," the cab driver tells the face we cannot see.

protagonist calls the world outside in Albert Camus' *The Stranger*. The companion thought held that, out of nothing but ourselves, humans spin webs of meaning. Taken together, these assertions constitute "personalism," or the idea that human personhood is the ultimate source of meaning and reality.

"God help you if you use voice-over in your work, my friends. God help you," the screenwriter/guru Robert McKee character warns

a seminar room of aspiring screenwriters in *Adaptation* (2002). Voice-over is not superglue, McKee meant. It cannot adhere otherwise unrelated story elements. Voice-over can *indeed* signify, as McKee argues, that writers have had to resort to telling what they should have shown. Editors, for instance, did trim Victor Fleming's *Joan of Arc* (1948) down from 148 to 100 minutes and called back Ingrid Bergman to voice-over the missing minutes, hoping to resuscitate a movie that viewers were rejecting.

But "rules" for making movies resemble Somerset Maugham's rules for writing novels—"There are three rules for writing novels. Unfortunately, no one knows what they are." Ironically, voice-over is what organizes *Adaptation*, where an actor playing McKee decries it. The movie begins in voice-over. It ends there when the screenwriter protagonist exits in his car from inside an underground garage and drives down a Los Angeles street, imagining himself, in voice-over, as star of his own movie. "I wonder who is going to play me? Someone not too fat. I like that Gérard Depardieu, but can he not do that French accent? Anyway, it's done. And that's something. So. Kaufman drives off from his encounter with Amelia, filled for the first time with hope. I like this. This is good."

Portrait of Jennie (1948) demonstrates what both narration and voice-over contribute to a movie. A painter (Joseph Cotten) falls in love with a girl (Jennifer Jones) who seems to be a spirit returning from the past. The painter alone can see the girl, who grows and changes as he falls in love with her. He eventually paints her. "Is it really of me, Eben?" she asks. After he signs the painting, Jennie vanishes. The inconsolable painter searches for her wherever she may be. When he at last encounters her in a gale at the light-house where she perished years before, he disappears into eternity with her.

Producer David O. Selznick worried *Portrait of Jennie* through countless incarnations. The project overwhelmed him—his first marriage was disintegrating, and his studio teetered on insol-vency. "This whole *Portrait of Jennie* venture was doomed to be one of the most awful experiences any studio ever had," he wrote an associate.

Selznick's scriptwriters worked up a spiritualist potpourri—images of Manhattan seen from God's eye, allusions to Euripides, Keats, Browning and, sometimes, dialogue given to Jennifer Jones that only a character in a Harlequin Romance could successfully deliver—"There is no life, my darling, until you've loved and been loved—and then there is no death."

Both narration and voice-over both play a role in *Portrait of Jennie*. If voice-over keeps the story moving, narration sets it in motion. *Portrait of Jennie* begins with an assured voice delivering narration (written by Ben Hecht) over a matte painting depicting Manhattan as a cloud would behold it:

> **Since the beginning, man has looked into the awesome reaches of infinity and asked the eternal questions, 'What is time? What is space? What is life? What is death?'**

"I know we were meant for each other. The strands of our lives are woven together, and neither the world nor time can tear them apart," Jennifer Jones (Jennie) tells Joseph Cotten (Eben Adams) in *Portrait of Jennie* (1948).

In Robert Nathan's first-person novel, the source of the movie, that prose seems less purple. Nathan slips the thought into Eben's head, not Jennie's. David O. Selznick hired and fired four writers in the process of adapting Nathan's supernatural romance. Hyperactive, chain-smoking Selznick wrote numerous lines himself. Selznick cast Jennifer Jones as Jennie and married her in 1949.

Through a hundred civilizations, philosophers and scien-tists have come with answers. But the bewilderment remains. For each human soul must find the secret in its own faith. The tender and haunting legend of *The Portrait of Jennie* is based on the two ingredients of faith— truth and hope. There is such a portrait that hung in the Metropolitan Museum in New York. And there was such

The film begins (above) with a matte painting of Manhattan over which live action shots of clouds are superimposed. *Portrait of Jennie* won Oscars for Selznick's special effects team, led by Clarence Slifer.

"I know now that Spinney didn't see Jennie, but all I knew then was that she kept a watchful eye on me as though I were a patient that needed watching. I was happy when I realized that it was Saturday, and I could scarcely wait to find out what Jennie was going to present to me at Hammerstein's," states this Joseph Cotten voice-over from *Portrait of Jennie* (1948).

The protagonist delivering this voice-over is a painter with no gift for painting who finds himself as he encounters "Jennie," a visitor from eternity invisible to all except the artist.

Cast as the artist reaching from life to immortality, David O. Selznick's friend Joseph Cotten plays a role that, in retrospect, seems premonitory. When Selznick anticipated his imminent death from heart attack in 1965, the dying producer issued written instructions to his son on the conduct of his funeral. "I suppose a few words will have to be said; I would like them spoken by a good voice, so if Joseph Cotten is in the country I want him to say them," Selznick wrote.

Cotten maintains that, before he lost his voice in a 1981 stroke, his voice had failed just once—the instant his mother died in Virginia. He was then working in a radio station in distant California, speaking into a microphone.

a girl named Jennie who sat for it. So much is true. For the rest, science tells us that nothing ever dies but only changes, that time itself does not pass but curves around us, and that the past and the future are together at our side forever. Out of the shadows of knowledge and out of a painting that hung on a museum wall comes our story, the truth of which lies not on our screen but in your heart. And now, *Portrait of Jennie*.

The words of the Hecht's narration proceed as imperturbably as bricks in a row. But the voice-overs swivel like compass needles to return the movie to the point where the writers wish it to go. What keeps the story moving—what *is* the story—is voice-over.

In the film as released, Cotten delivers ten voice-overs while his character wanders city streets alone. Closing and opening like eyelids, his voice-overs move what the viewer sees through the painter's consciousness. In earlier drafts of the script, other characters deliver voice-over. "Eben, Eben, how slowly the years go by—such tired dead years—if I could only turn them back to you. Yes, back to the days when you were poor—and cold—and friendless—your work unknown," muses the spinster art dealer (Ethel Barrymore) in one 1947 shooting draft. In another, Jennie calls to Eben from the lighthouse boulders in a voice tricked out with a Sonovox. Except for one, though, Selznick and his writers ultimately restricted voice-over to Eben, where it had been in Robert Nathan's first-person novel.

Only in the last shot does Jennie's voice seem to emerge from the painting. "O Eben is it really me?" the voice-over asks. " I think someday it will hang in a museum and people will come from all over the world to see it."

Voice-over leads inevitably to the spiritual. The spirit girl delivers the final voice-over.

EXERCISE NINETEEN: VOICE-OVER

What this exercise teaches:

- **How to detach audio from picture track**

- **How to tone voice-overs using speech enhancer, vocal transformer, and tremolo**

- **How to complement or counterpoint picture track action with voice-over**

Memo to scriptwriter Ben Hecht from producer David O. Selznick November 24, 1948:

DEAR BEN: VERY MANY THANKS IN ADVANCE FOR COMING TO THE RESCUE AGAIN ON A FOREWORD...THE AUDIENCE WAS ENCHANTED WITH THE WHOLE IDEA OF THE FOREWORD, AND IT SET THE MOOD BEAUTIFULLY FOR THE PICTURE...BUT IT SEEMED TO ME TO FAIL IN THE FOLLOWING PARTICULARS:... TOO ABSTRUCE AND HIGHFALUTIN' FOR COMPLETE AUDIENCE UNDERSTANDABILITY. IT NEEDS...A CERTAIN ARTISTIC TONE WITH THE OLD HEARST SUNDAY-SUPPLEMENT TYPE HOKEYPOKEY, PSEUDOSCIENTIFIC APPROACH... WARMEST REGARDS. MOST GRATEFULLY. DAVID

You Did It Then: **Change the emotional temperature of** *Portrait of Jennie* **by recording a voice-over track of your own voice over the sound track that sound engineer James G. Stewart created. In one new voice-over, "Eben" speaks. In another, "Jennie" does. You'll mix the voice-overs, ducking Jennie's "voice" over Eben's, and vice-versa. You'll adjust the original sound track to overweight the voice-overs. Step-by-step instructions and the files you can use are in the digital cutting room at http://makefilmhistory.com.**

You Do It Now: **Shoot a new scene based on the Storyboard and Studio exercises. It has to have a voice-over. Other than that, do what you want in the movie.**

PRODUCTION Make Film History
DIRECTOR
CAMERA
DATE   SCENE   TAKE
19

JUMP CUT:
Breathless (1960)

"The time is out of joint."
Hamlet, Act 1, Scene 5, line 188

Beginning roughly in 1910, "filmmaker" meant someone who simply produced movies. "Mr. Gaston Méliès, a leading film-maker in Paris," a New Zealand newspaper reported in 1912, "is making a tour of the South Pacific Islands and Australia, with a party of 15 to take moving pictures of island scenery and life." By the early 1960s, "filmmaker" was coming to mean something less executive and more visionary—an artist who creates not on canvas but in movies. A producer has ideas, executes contracts, and oversees the nuts and bolts of movies. A "filmmaker," on the other hand, creates cinema, has vision, and expresses an identity. "Auteur criticism," the Parisian idea that the identity of a single author, not a team, pervades a movie, was largely responsible for this change in tone.

The idea excited production on both sides of the Atlantic. In 1957, Françoise Giroud coined the term *La Nouvelle Vague* (The New Wave), referring to postwar writers and artists, but 1950s American independents like Morris Engel had already shown the way. "Our French New Wave would never have come into being, if it hadn't

Jean-Luc Godard allegedly remarked once, "I believe a film should have a beginning, a middle, and an end, but not necessarily in that order."

As filmmaker, his goal was to terminate the tradition of the "well-made movie."

Jean-Paul Belmondo plays the car thief who guns down a policeman in *Breathless*. Impulsive, predatory, criminal, roguishly charming, the character seems the quintessential anti-hero of numerous movies of the 1960s.

Little Fugitive (1953), dir. Ray Ashley, Morris Engel, and Ruth Orkin.

Making *Little Fugitive*, Engel followed a seven-year-old boy though Brooklyn and Coney Island with a silent, custom-built 35 mm camera. The movie only *looks* documentary: Academy of Motion Picture Arts and Sciences writer members nominated the screenplay written by Ashley, Engel and Orkin for a 1953 "Best Motion Picture Story" academy award. Engel's entire production team could have met in a station wagon. Shot on similar scale seven years later, Truffaut's *400 Blows* (1959) set off the French "New Wave."

Far left, Englel and Orkin confer with their "star," Richie Andrusco.

been for the young American Morris Engel who showed us the way to independent production with (this) fine movie," François Truffaut told a *New Yorker* interviewer, speaking of *Little Fugitive* (1953).

Film aficionados in Paris sought to create new films in new ways, even if doing so diverged from Hollywood practices. One tool for "making it new" was jump cutting, which American editors then regarded as a sign of editorial ineptitude. But when a French-Swiss filmmaker, Jean-Luc Godard, intentionally inserted jump cuts in *Breathless* (1960), he led movies of the 1960s to a thousand other visions of "the filmmaker" anxiously regarding his own anxious face.

What is a jump cut and when should filmmaker use one?

Consider the opposite of jump cutting, "cutting on action." Cutting on action means joining different shots showing a single action at that frame in each shot where the action has advanced identically. It binds together virtually every movie. Few viewers notice.

Picture the last frame of a long shot showing a dancer holding her hands aloft. In the next shot, a close shot, the dancer continues her gesture. The second shot begins on the frame in which the dancer deploys her hands precisely as she did at the end of the first shot.

The viewer's distance from the dancer changes, but the viewer ignores the difference. To human viewers, her dance appears to ripple from the first shot to the second. The viewer doesn't startle at the crack between the dancer's finish in a frame and her resumption in another. Shot elides to shot as noun cleaves to verb, affirming what sane humans generally sense—that time flows and the world is continuous.

Shot 1.

Shot 2.

These are match cut shots from *An American in Paris* (1951). The embrace flows without impediment to the second shot because essential actions in the second shot begin where they ended the first shot—heads, arms, and shoulders matching perfectly. Viewers ignore how the camera's point of view reverses and how the gentleman onlooker's right arm, slack in shot one, rises in shot two.

Vincente Minnelli shot that embrace "in Paris"—and joined those shots—not in Paris but in a Culver City, California studio. In 1954, François Truffaut denounced studio movies—"*le cinema du papa*"—and argued instead for "a cinema which is applying itself to show life such as one sees it on a fourth floor on Saint-Germain-des-Pres." Jean-Luc Godard shot the bedroom scene of *Breathless* precisely as Truffaut, five years before, had suggested—on the fourth floor of Hotel de Suede on Quai Saint-Michel in Paris. As Culver City is to Paris, match cuts are to jump cuts.

Cutting on action, or match cutting, is a moviemaking "best practice," as expected as driving a car on the right side of the road. Other editing conventions abound.

- "Hard cutting" joins thematically related but otherwise dissimilar shots to annul time or obliterate space. In *Lawrence of Arabia* (1962), for instance, Peter O'Toole blows on an orange tinged match flame in a ministry office in Britain. The flame seems to become, in a hard cut, the sun emerging from identically orange sand on the horizon of the Arabian Desert.

- "Split editing" joins shots, but staggers sound track and picture track transitions. In effect, the second shot begins as a sound from the unseen, so it anticipates or pervades the first as premonition or memory. In *The Pawnbroker* (1964), Rod Steiger, playing a Jewish proprietor of a Manhattan pawnshop, descends into wartime memories on split edits.

- "Cutting away" bridges the gap between two shots. It inserts a shot—often a reaction shot—between them.

Others did it earlier, but movie editors (usually women) of the nineteen teens standardized cutting on action. Many used kitchen scissors to sever frames of 35 mm negative pressed against light bulbs. In the shot she is about to cut, a film editor discerns a crime that, fortuitously, the camera shooting a movie has recorded in *The Evidence of the Film* (1913).

But cutting on action trumps all others. Cutting on action shows what continues when seen from a new perspective. It knits together the worldview of the modern world. The idea is that, notwithstanding how poorly we may comprehend it, "reality" is not inside us but rather is continuously "out there." The world doesn't end where we do. This is a habit of mind that distinguishes adult thought from infantile projection. It is why practical-minded inventors, not yogis or shamans, invented cameras. Editors may be practical people who scoff at theories, but they can't avoid expressing their intuition of how the world works when they cut a movie. Match cuts says the world is "out there" and continuous. Jump cuts say something different—that the world crackles discontinuously. The world is "out of joint," Hamlet puts it.

Jump cuts join shots of an action without matching them. The difference is crucial. Match cutting is cutting with a scalpel. Jump cutting is cutting with a switchblade.

Editors now recognize two kinds—temporal jump cuts and spatial jump cuts.

A temporal jump cut joins two shots of an action at slightly different stages. For instance, a gangster reaches towards his gun during a long shot. When the next shot starts—a medium shot—the gangster has already finished squeezing the trigger. Time has cracked. The missing footage prises apart the shots and time jumps out. This is a temporal jump cut.

A spatial jump cut joins two shots of an action from insubstantially different angles, or more precisely, from angles that differ by less than 30°. The gangster again reaches towards his gun during a long shot. When the next shot starts—this time also a long shot—the gangster fingers his gun. No stage of his action is missing. But from our new vantage point, the gangster seems suddenly situated differently *vis-à-vis* the frame he occupies. Space has cracked. The slightly different angle pries apart the shots and the gangster jumps out. This is a spatial jump cut.

Breathless begins with a theft and ends in ambiguity. The jump cuts are machine gun statements of Godard's lifelong preoccupations and ambivalences. In *Breathless*, a thief from the south of France, Michel Poiccard (Jean-Paul Belmondo), steals a car. He then kills the policeman who pursues him as he drives the car to Paris to collect both a debt he never collects and an American college girl in Paris (Jean Seberg) whom he supposes loves him but doesn't. The girl speaks execrable French and the thief apes Humphrey Bogart (who had died two years before Godard shot the movie). The pair crisscrosses Paris while she decides if she will flee with him to Italy—she won't—and the police close in. She eventually reports him to the police, who shoot him in the street as he flees. "*C'est vraiment dégueulasse,*" the dying gangster utters ambiguously to the American girl. He means, alternatively, I am disgusting or this gun shot wound feels nauseating or you are disgusting or the situation is disgusting or the world is disgusting, or in the Jean-Paul Sartre sense of the word then

This jump cut from *Breathless* joins images of Jean Seberg in different stages of a single motion. We do not see her cross the yards separating her from Belmondo. So when the second shot begins, she "snaps" toward him. Hitherto invisible, Belmondo is suddenly there. So is Seberg. The jump cut feels magical, a movie version of a quantum leap. It violates the golden rule of editors—"Thou shalt render no cut that destroys the illusion of continuous time/space." But it expresses the intuition pervading *Breathless*—that you just don't know what moves the inner life of another.

Standard practice would handle that action differently. It would insert a "cutaway" to bridge the missing frames. (Editing 101 teaches filmmakers to avoid the "snap" Godard's jump cut creates.) Inserting the middle shot (above) would restore conventional flow to the scene. It would move the viewer's eye from Seberg, to the man in sunglasses following her, back to Seberg and Belmondo. Cut this way, Seberg would pass to Belmondo as unremarkably as a pencil passing over paper. But Godard doesn't want to use her for unremarkable purposes. In the jump cut, she becomes an eraser. She nullifies space.

Godard says that he brought jump cuts into *Breathless* (1960) for nuts and bolts reasons. He needed to trim some boring minutes from scenes in a work print 30 minutes too long, he says. In one scene, Belmondo and Seberg drove too slowly through the streets of Paris so he snipped the tails of shots. When they spent too long in bed in another scene, he quickened them. When Seberg talks too long elsewhere at a café table, Godard cauterized with jump cuts. The jump cuts were unpremeditated sudden stabs. His editor, Cécile Decugis, affirms this. "Oh, that was Godard," she laughs.

According to Decugis, other French filmmakers whispered that the movie, were it released, would become "the year's worst film." "*Breathless* is a film destined to flop like a car that advances by backfiring," Godard scribbled in a notebook. "Let's hope it's never released. It will ruin your career," Jean-Paul Belmondo's agent advised him. Godard had reason to worry. He rushed through the shooting. He wrote out scenes with a fountain pen in a café on the morning he was to shoot them, doling to his actors, ventriloquist style, lines to deliver on screen seconds before they mouthed them. (Cinematographer Raoul Coutard shot *Breathless*

circulating through the cafes of Montparnasse, existence itself is nauseating. "*C'est*"—It is—refers to everything or nothing specific. The girl asks a policeman what the gangster said. The policeman explains nothing. "He said you are a *dégueulasse*." A hole in the world seems to open and Paris falls in.

without sound using a clattering Caméflex Éclair 35 mm camera. In its use of sound, *Breathless* emulates the dubbing of 1940s documentary.) When shooting stopped, Godard worked with his editor in a cutting room near Paris—jammed with film trim bins—to cut a movie that twitches everywhere with low-grade anxiety.

The jump cuts express his mindset. In 1959, while he was shooting *Breathless*, French film laboratories were under legal order to liquidate their nitrate film collections—"film that explodes"—or donate them to the Cinémathèque in Paris. Making *Breathless*, Godard seemed generally to have pictured himself as liquidator of the "well-made" movie. (His characters view several American studio movies, including *Whirlpool* by Otto Preminger, who discovered Seberg.) But his temperament shows most obviously in the jump cuts. They rap out an aesthetic: *Improvised is better than carefully constructed. The mind is fast but a gun is quicker. Ambiguous is better than clear. In a world of liars, the roguish thief is king.* Godard professed a love of American gangster movies—he dedicates *Breathless* to a by then merged out of existence American maker of low budget cowboy and gangster

As a roguish criminal in *Breathless*, Jean-Paul Belmondo careens through Paris while police close in. In Belmondo, Godard undoubtedly saw himself.

"I have a headache," Seberg says.

"We won't have sex. I just want to be with you," Belmondo says.

"That's not it, Michel," Seberg says.

Seberg had been looking outward but—jump cut—she is suddenly studying herself in a mirror. She touches her forehead as if to draw something out from in there. Jump cut again. Jump cuts shatter time like pebbles cracking windshields.

This series of jumping Sebergs in the convertible was the sequence that brought the jump cut into the movies.

movies, Monogram Pictures. Jump cutting is Godard's version of the gangster gospel Tony Camonte delivers in *Scarface* (1932): "Do it yourself, do it first, and keep on doing it."

After *Breathless*, the jump cut became a short-hand character denoting something like "anxious" or "work-in-progress" or "the impetuosity of youth." Fifty years of jump cuts have followed. In *Persona* (1966*)*, Bergman fuses jump cuts (and dissolves) into a face composited from characters, animated figures, and unrelated amorphous shapes. Lee Harvey Oswald jactitates down the street in jump cuts in *JFK* (1991). Scorsese jump cuts his way through *Mean Streets* (1973) and Steven Soderbergh jump cuts in *Erin Brockovich* (2000)*,* and jump cuts twitch now in movies such as *Moon* (2009).

But in origin, jump cuts are Paris as she was in 1960—Citroëns, walk-up flats, and gangster movies screening at 6:30, 8:30, and 10:30 P.M. at Henri Langlois's Cinémathèque Française on Rue d'Ulm. ("To love film is to love life," Langlois used to say, bear-hugging film fans in the lobby.) They are Monmartre at dawn rendered by Jean-Pierre Melville in *Bob le Flambeur* (1956). They are "la politque des auteurs," sound tracks by Bach and Brubeck, neo-Marxist manifestos, and Jean-Paul Belmondo, his lip curled beneath a Gauloise, smoke perpetually rising.

This imagery (the stuff of dorm room posters and lost youth) began with Godard jump cutting *Breathless*. Before then, youth had features but no face.

"What surprised me most was after the film was edited, because it wasn't at all like I'd imagined it. There was a panache in the way it was edited, that didn't match at all the way it was shot. The editing gave it a very different tone than the films we were used to seeing. And the story had a liveliness that 'classic films' just didn't have back then."
Raoul Coutard, cinematographer, *Breathless*

"We just went into the boulevards, like the Champs-Élysées and filmed Jean Seberg and Jean-Paul Belmondo," Coutard remembers. Above, a corner in Paris in 1959 as Belmondo regards it in *Breathless*. Below, the same corner now as a Google street view map renders it.

EXERCISE TWENTY: JUMP CUT

What this exercise teaches:

● **How to match cut**

● **How to cutaway**

● **How to jump cut**

● **How to cut at the top of the "content curve"**

"Wednesday, we shot in full sun with Geva 36. Everyone thinks it stinks. I find it extraordinary. It's the first time that we asked the film to give its all, making it do what it's not made for. It's as if the film itself is suffering from being used to the extreme limits of its possibilities. Even the film, you see, is getting breathless."

Jean-Luc Godard, letter to Pierre Braunberger describing his progress on *Breathless*, August 23, 1959.

You Did It Then: Reinvent the New Wave with Godard. Cut into a scene contemporary footage of a couple driving in a convertible. Assemble three cuts: first, cutting it on action, then "cutting out the boring parts" by jump cutting it, then cutting it randomly (à la Joe Hutshing cutting Oliver Stone's *JFK*). Step-by-step instructions and the files you can use are in the digital cutting room at http://makefilmhistory.com.

You Do It Now: Introduce a jump cut or two into your Voice-over movie from Chapter 19. See what difference it makes.

PRODUCTION Make Film History
DIRECTOR
CAMERA
DATE   SCENE   TAKE
20

MIXING SOUND:
Walter Murch (1979)

"It's very important that you understand that the sound track is an entity... that joins with the film that is at least as important as the film... And many people have been working on this sound track. The key person in the sound track, the director of the sound track of the entire movie, that's Walter Murch."

Francis Ford Coppola

"Music is the medium of the *human* soul in its most ecstatic condition of wonder and terror."

Alan Bloom

Characteristically pensive while listening to Coppola discuss the sound track of *Apocalypse Now*, Walter Murch was 32 years old on this evening of March 26, 1979, in San Francisco when, across the Pacific in Hanoi, Vietnam and China were spurning peace talks proposed to terminate a border war between them.

Shots show. Words mean. Sounds feel.

Contemporary sound editors fold sounds into movies, adjusting volume, changing pitch and tempo, reducing noise, equalizing low-, mid-, and high-frequency sounds, and otherwise transforming sound into the heartbeat of movies. These manipulations—called mixes—turn movie sound psychoactive. For instance, by narrowly compressing dynamic ranges—the difference between the loudest and softest sounds—recordists make TV ads sound louder than the shows they interrupt.

1930s sound engineers created sound tracks with tools far less finely calibrated than those contemporary sound engineers employ. Before RCA introduced four-track mixing consoles, engineers hand-mixed into a single track signals emanating from omni-directional microphones that poorly distinguished between signal and noise. They added Foley sounds—that is, the tap of feet walking and doors creaking and other ambient sound simulated after the event—while the rough cut film projected silently in a

Foley sounds—sound created in studio to emulate real world sound sources—identified *Gangbuster* (above) to listeners. The radio show dramatized FBI cases. Episodes began with the wail of gunfire, police sirens, prisoners treading in unison in chains, and a narrator shouting out, "Calling the police! Calling the G-Men! Calling all Americans to war on the underworld!" First broadcast in 1935/6 and running until 1957, this episode aired in August 1938.

preview theater. Once studios settled on the sound-on-film standard in 1931, engineers embedded sound tracks in 35 mm optical sound track negative.

Thirties recordists could wheedle, flatter, and dissimulate when circumstances required, especially when professional recording equipment was scarce. MGM, for instance, owned one cardioid (directional) microphone in 1935, imported from Germany to record

Jeanette MacDonald. When Nelson Eddy demanded an identical microphone, prop men contrived to enclose the omni directional condenser mic actually recording Eddy inside a fake they fabricated to placate him.

Without resort to subterfuge like that, sound engineers advanced recording technology throughout the '30s. Others claim earlier credit, but Edmund Hanson at Fox Films patented the boom microphone in 1930. In 1935, British inventor Alan Blumlein produced experimental short films that split sound into stereophonic tracks, but throughout the Depression and war years movie sound tracks remained monaural until *This Is Cinerama* (1952).

But even a primitive sound track enriched a movie, and in 1927 a wire service writer articulated the purpose of sound in movies. "I looked at a reel of the picture both ways," he wrote of the silent and talkie segments of *The Jazz Singer*. "Without the Vitaphone it was flat. The Vitaphone touch was like putting life into something already dead. It seemed almost unreal, not as if Jolson were there in person, but that his spirit was singing the words."

Monophonic sound tracks of the 1930s and surround sound tracks today speak a common language, but differently. Two swashbuckling films—*Mutiny on the Bounty* (1935) and *Master and Commander: The Far Side of the World* (2003) illustrate the difference. Douglas Shearer, MGM's sound wizard, placed all sounds for *Mutiny on the Bounty* into a single monaural track. Constructing the sound track for *Master and Commander: The Far Side of the*

Mutiny on the Bounty (1935), dir. Frank Lloyd.

Master and Commander: The Far Side of the World (2003), dir. Peter Weir.

While Princess Sophia Frederica (Marlene Dietrich) replies to a warning from a priest in Josef von Sternberg's *The Scarlet Empress* (1934), her costume upstages her. Swish-swish-swishing like brushes on a snare drum, the gown Dietrich wears gives this interview a faintly comic and certainly unintended tone. The sound engineer was Harry Mills, who first recorded a variable density Movietone sound track for Paramount in 1929 (*The Dance of Life*) and continued in the industry until 1961. *Singin' In the Rain* (1952) memorializes moments like this one.

World, contemporary digital sound designer Richard King worked differently. Behind dialogue tracks, King layered multiple tracks of non-human noises—throbbing ocean, creaking ship, cannon balls and the sound of wind rushing in the rigging (created by King by recording and sampling real wind rushing through a wood frame and barbecue grills and refrigerator grills on the back of a pickup truck racing through the Mohave Desert).

Richard King describes his sound design for *Master and Commander: The Far Side of the World* this way:

> Soon as sound stops serving the drama of the film, it's failed. Soon as it draws attention to itself, it's failed. What you want to do is put the audience in that situation. You're not hearing every little detail of what's going on, but you're hearing the force and the drama and the aggression of the storm. The film ultimately tells you what's needed.

The point is that sound enters movies by invitation only—someone has determined that *this* sound in *this* shot excites *this* thought that induces *this* feeling. Alfred Hitchcock's instructions to his Foley sound technicians for Reel 5 (the shower scene) of *Psycho* (1960) convey the selective nature of sound in well-made movies, even monophonic films like *Psycho*. Hitchcock instructed as follows:

> **We should hear some kind of movement in the room, such as putting a brush down or a hanger going up or some sound of whatever Janet might be doing in her undressing.**
>
> **Throughout the killing, there should be the shower noise and the blows of the knife. We should hear the water gurgling down the drain of the bathtub, especially when we go close on it. Naturally, as we pan off the bathroom into the living room and out to the house, the shower should recede.**
>
> **Tony's voice should have the bass taken out when he says, 'Oh, Mother, blood,' etc. When Tony runs out of the house after the 'Oh, Mother, blood,' we should hear the door slam and his running feet start down the steps.**

But Walter Murch's work on the mix for *Apocalypse Now* (1979) can best illustrate how mixed sound works in contemporary movies. On a fall day in San Francisco in 1978, Murch peered into the screen of his K.E.M. flatbed-editing machine with the alert, attentive senses of the amateur beekeeper that he is. Murch was scrolling backwards and forward for a sound. He had been laboring over *Apocalypse Now* for a year.

Apocalypse Now is a morally serious film—Coppola described it once as a "journey into the nature of man, and his relationship to

the Creation." In Vietnam during the Vietnam War, an American special operations captain (Captain Willard) must travel to a remote location to kill—"terminate with extreme prejudice"—the mentally disintegrating U.S. Army colonel (Colonel Kurtz) who rules there with monstrous viciousness over tribal people. No actual incident inspired the story. It is fiction begotten of fiction: The story roughly follows Joseph Conrad's novella, *Heart of Darkness*, but the production stalled, primarily because Coppola was unable to decide what Willard's trip to Kurtz was to signify. D.W. Griffith shot *The Birth of Nation* in 17 weeks, but Francis Ford Coppola spent 17 months shooting *Apocalypse*. He and writer John Milius incessantly tinkered with the script. Martin Sheen—Captain Willard—suffered a heart attack. Marlon Brando—Colonel Kurtz—rejected his lines.

Editing on the film was to consume three years. Murch sound-edited the entire film and picture-edited some of it. Just mixing the sound track—Murch's primary responsibility—was to take nine months. Murch and other editors would eventually trim it, but on this day in 1978, the unassembled footage ran 370 hours.

Because helicopter noise or instructions Coppola shouted through a megaphone suffused the footage, dialogue was generally inaudible. Synchronous sound therefore rarely appears in *Apocalypse Now* as released. Almost all dialogue is dubbed. What Murch searched for that morning was a sound to use during the first interior scene. His idea was that he could attribute the sound of an

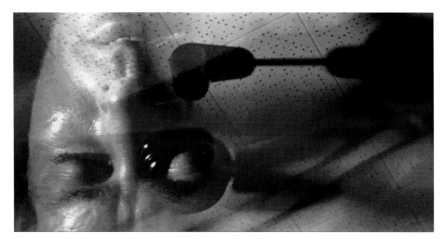

The shot Murch created to say all this in sound makes a composite of Captain Willard's head, upside down, with a ceiling fan rotating from what appears to be his right eye socket.

invisible helicopter to the ceiling fan. Sounds from different sources fusing indistinguishably, Murch reasoned, would convey a theme of *Apocalypse Now*—that reality speaks, but indecipherably, like the tracings children leave when they scribble on a magic slate. Willard hears the helicopter. He sees the fan. Bewildered, Willard (whose name we do not yet know) becomes the modern Everyman.

Murch explains what he did in a documentary about editing, *The Cutting Edge* (2004):

> **You have been hearing helicopter sounds and now you see this ceiling fan, and what you're hearing is the wha-wha-wha-wha-wha sound of a helicopter. Is that coming from his dream? Is it a reality? Is somehow that sound coming from the fan? I remember when I was assembling those images almost jumping away from the editing machine**

when I put that sound with that image because it seemed to me that that fan was making that sound, even though I knew it was impossible. If it was convincing me it was doing it, it surely would convince others. Now they begin to coalesce, and they turn into a real helicopter...coming from a fan? No. And then you hear a real helicopter fly over the room. Willard gets up out of bed, goes over to the window, and says, 'Saigon. Shit.' All of that—the narration, and the helicopter flying over, and the napalm jungle is concocted into something that is a powerful beginning to a film, not only powerful in and of itself, but powerful in the way that it sets the stage for the journey that this particular film is going to take.

Viewers sometimes suppose that making a movie is a purely commercial, formula-driven activity from which we should exclude our deepest convictions in favor of showing car crashes, knife fights, and cleavage. There are certainly movies that succeed on those terms. But the sound track Walter Murch created for *Apocalypse Now* conveys something more—the eternal truth that opposites unite. Helicopter blade begins as ceiling fan blade just as the rudiments of Kurtz are already in Willard. Antitheticals turn into each other. The sound he mixed evokes the psychedelic haze of the 1960s, Murch maintains. And it does. But it does more, too. Music or sound that counterpoints an image gives the pleasure that metaphor in poetry gives. A dark joy therefore pervades the movie.

"The function of music is to be in a kind of parallel, harmonic relationship with the film, rather than to be right on the same tracks," Murch says. The helicopter/fan sound sets Willard traveling inward to his inner man, Kurtz. "It was no accident that I got to be the caretaker of Colonel Walter E. Kurtz's memory any more than being back in Saigon was an accident," Willard says in voice-over. "There is no way to tell his story without telling my own." So the sound mix sets the key for the movie.

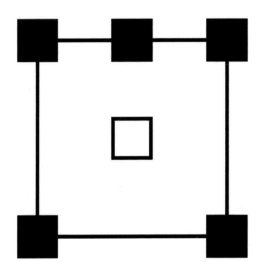

Five-track stereo. Three speakers behind the screen, one on the left, one on right surround the audience. Each speaker plays a dedicated sound track. Audiences of the '30s sat before the music. Contemporary audiences sit in it.

Above: Carmine Coppola musical cue for *Apocalypse Now*.

Rejecting both a first sound track featuring primarily songs by the Doors and a second one featuring synthesizer music composed by Isao Tomita, Francis Ford Coppola evolved a dense, five-track, stereophonic sound track for *Apocalypse Now* from bits of music—cues—composed by himself and by his father, Carmine Coppola.

"As we struggled with bringing the cues to picture, we had Carmine's writing—he'd walk in with the written page—I would perform what Carmine had written on the piano in loose sync to the picture. Francis would react to that. So that became a way to generate the actual cues for the movie... We had all been encouraged to be as creative as we possibly could by Francis, and to just try anything. There was also a level of just sheer competitiveness that was so difficult because there was people just wanting to take over the score and be the guy who got to say, "Yeah, I have all the bright ideas. I'm the one who is making this work. And I want the credit for this."
Shirley Walker, *Apocalypse Now* synthesizer keyboardist.

Murch's work on *Apocalypse Now* shows how sound mixing can work. In the 1930s, movie sound editors could aspire primarily to clarity and audibility. Monaural sound tracks emerged as a single source from behind the screen. Sound editors could distinguish foreground sound from background sound by making them loud or soft. Doing as little as that, they added depth to movies. Much can be made of little by artists of genius—using contrasting glazes Attic potters were able to depict the human spirit as the place where darkness meets light.

A surround sound five-track sound mix like Murch's, fusing helicopter blade noise and Wagner and popular music and ordinance, suggests something similar. The angel is the shadow of the beast.

Monaural sound tracks on the 1930s distinguish foreground and background with the clarity of this vase from the red figure Attic period (530-300 BC).

Wrestlers make a "there" in an otherwise featureless cosmos.

Diana and her nymphs spied upon by satyrs. Jan Brueghel (1568-1625) watercolor.

Like Brueghel's watercolor (left), Murch's sound track for *Apocalypse Now* seeps layer into layer, sounds flowing together in increments so imperceptible that background and foreground are indistinguishable.

This mix makes audible Coppola's worldview. Murch seems embarked on the "journey into the nature of man, and his relationship to the Creation" that Coppola described as his goal for this movie.

Murch's mix for theatrical exhibition directed five streams of stereophonic sound to speakers behind and around cinematographer Vittorio Storaro's widescreen footage. Now commonplace, the five-track system was revolutionary in 1976, when Dolby Laboratories introduced Dolby Stereo 70 mm six-track surround sound (five channels of sound and a sub-woofer). The Dolby system reduced noise and added low-frequency speakers to the Todd-AO 70 mm magnetic sound stereo system Mike Todd introduced in 1955.

Francis Ford Coppola spent August 1977 to August 1979 post-producing *Apocalypse Now*. Murch and others spent the last nine months mixing the synchronous, wild, and Foley sounds into a unified sound track. The ceiling fan shot expresses the method in the madness.

EXERCISE TWENTY-ONE: MIXING SOUND

What this exercise teaches:

● **How to create, modify, and move multilayered sound tracks**

● **How to modify, enhance, and transform sound files using track effects**

"Wherever we are, what we hear is mostly noise. When we ignore it, it disturbs us. When we listen to it, we find it fascinating."

John Cage, "The Future of Music: Credo"

You Did It Then: **Try it yourself. Create your own version of the opening interior scene of** *Apocalypse Now*, **using a silent shot of a ceiling fan, a shot of a young man's face, helicopter sounds, sound effects, a voice-over, and a room interior. Step-by-step instructions and the files you can use are in the digital cutting room at http:// makefilmhistory.com.**

You Do It Now: **Go back to your Voice-over movie you created for Chapter 19 and re-mix the sound tracks. If you used a score, try a different one. If you gave Jack the voice-over, take it away and give it now to Jill. Trust your ear. Trust your intuition.**

PRODUCTION Make Film History
DIRECTOR
CAMERA
DATE   SCENE   TAKE
21

MONTAGE REINVENTED:
Cinema Paradiso (1988)

"since feeling is first/who pays any attention/to the syntax of things/will never wholly kiss you..."

e. e. cummings

With thematic montage, filmmakers sometimes crack open the door of narrative so that feelings, like cats, may enter. A thematic montage is a sequence of shots that temporarily interrupts the flow of story in a movie to make room for mood. What score does for the ear, thematic montage does for the eye—it sets intuition vaulting over words. Narrative filmmakers frequently employ thematic montages. *Hugo* (2011), for instance, begins with one. A sequence of shots showing clockwork gears superimposed on a shot of streets surrounding the Arc de Triomphe invokes the mind of the namesake of the movie who sees in an automaton a path to reach his deceased father.

After Soviet filmmakers largely abandoned it in the 1930s, thematic montage served three functions in western narrative movies. It communicated mood. It knit together story lines to join them in a point. It invoked the mind of a character. In numerous experimental Super 8 and 16 mm movies of the university film society circuit that began roughly 1945 and continues today, thematic montage did more—it *was*, in essence, the movie. Whether they are narrative

The Birthday (1915). Oil on cardboard. Marc Chagall.

or experimental filmmakers, editors cutting thematic montages cut for the same reason the haiku poet Basho counted syllables—not to argue logically but to imitate the sounds of temple bells. Thematic montage is where movies most resemble poetry.

Cinema Paradiso (1988), dir. Giuseppe Tornatore.
Without giving himself a cast credit, *Cinema Paradiso* director Giuseppe Tornatore plays the projectionist in the final scene. The casting is ironic. Tornatore peers through the projection window to screen for the actor playing "the director" the thematic montage that Tornatore himself created.

The thematic montage that concludes *Cinema Paradiso* (1988) performs all three functions of thematic montage.

As the film begins, viewers learn that an obscure, childless man, Alfredo, has died of old age in distant Sicily. With an affection approaching love, Alfredo had mentored and virtually fathered the film's protagonist, Salvatore Di Vita—"Savior of Life." Di Vita is now a grown man, a famous film director living in Rome, but people still call him by his childhood diminutive, "Toto." In Sicily, the childless man and the fatherless child had found what each needed in the other. Alfredo had projected movies in the now long defunct

Cinema Paradiso, and Toto, the child, had shadowed him. When a nitrate print ignited in a projector, Toto rescued Alfredo from the fire. The fire blinded the projectionist, and the child stepped into his job. Years passed. Toto passes into adolescence. He falls in love with a classmate. When she seems to spurn him, Toto flees his hometown forever. Only the death of Alfredo brings him home.

Toto returns to Sicily to attend Alfredo's funeral. The sight of his old familiars works on him, "like chisels scraping the rust off his soul and bringing old feelings to light again," Tornatore writes in the film script. Toto rediscovers in his memories the small boy living to win the approval of the projectionist who is now beyond conferring it. But after the funeral, the projectionist's widow presents him a canister containing film. It is a gift for Toto from Alfredo.

"Salvatore examines the can," Tornatore writes in the script, and "wonders what it can be. He opens it: inside is a reel of film, wrapped in a plastic bag, well preserved. Those objects bring a pang to his heart... but he feels disappointed, as if he expected to find something else."

After the funeral, Toto arrives at a film studio in Rome where a different projectionist waits for the canister of film in order to screen it. What the film in the canister contains remains unknown. Toto has kept it sealed. Giuseppe Tornatore, the actual director and writer of *Cinema Paradiso*, plays the man who will project the mysterious gift. In a movie that treats the act of projecting a movie as a metaphor for living itself, this casting is resonant.

The director hands the projectionist the film can. The projectionist says—the voice is dubbed and might be anyone's—"Right. And I liked your film. Terrific." As the real director of this movie playing the projectionist of the movie-in-the-movie, Tornatore is on all sides of this transaction. Concentric circles on the cover of the film might even suggest Dante's conclusion to *Paradiso*:

> "as in a wheel whose motion nothing jars
> by the Love that moves the sun and other stars."

The projectionist switches on the projector.

All 125 minutes of *Cinema Paradiso*—or all 173 minutes of the director's cut—lead entirely to this moment.

Viewers view the footage at the same time Toto does. It is thematic montage. Playing before us are cinched, scratched outtakes from movies of the '30s, '40s, and '50s. Someone—Alfredo—has spliced them together. They show couples embracing, but they pass in no discernible order, as fleeting and familiar as dreams. In the context of this movie about people and movies, they express the love binding people to people. They are the love that Alfredo, from across the grave, vouchsafes Toto.

Earlier, in a flashback, viewers witness the parish priest-censor alone inside Cinema Paradiso, previewing a film before Alfredo exhibits it. Just above his ear, the priest rings a bell to ward off caresses he deemed too fervid. In effect, the priest acted as an editor. The shot the priest requires excised and all the others excised over the years reappear in this thematic montage, scratched but still vivid. The shot excised by the priest comes from Jean Renoir's *The Lower Depths* (1936). In dialogue before the censored kiss, actress Suzy Prim had been telling actor Jean Gabin, "Pepe, one day we'll have it all. We'll go away together, live the easy life where no one knows us." The woman's statement would ring like a tocsin if only the mesmerized Toto could hear it. Toto and his adolescent love had yearned but failed to escape together like that. But Toto the director is now beyond comprehending words. He drinks in the screen, communing with it. The clips play inaudibly, orchestral music from the outer movies filling the sound track of the inner one.

The director and the viewer behold 47 such shots—all excised over the years by the priest's bell. This montage assembled by Alfredo annuls the priest's cuts. Some shots bear white emulsion scratches. Some bear black back scratches. Some are fingerprinted and some,

The top shot shows Toto in the preview theater waiting for Tornatore to project Alfredo's film reel. It reverses an earlier one (below) that sets the Sicilian priest, facing away from the camera and towards the screen of the movie theater, Cinema Paradiso.

flared. Director, priest, clips, audience and projectionist join like fingers of a single hand. This bringing together of elements remote in time and space is the goal of thematic montage. It creates a place in a movie where time stops. Seeing now what he never saw then, Toto slumps in his seat. He sees these kisses—this gift from Alfredo—as kisses from eternity.

The shots crack open the shell of narrative and let in pure feeling. Like Buster Keaton descending from the projection booth in *Sherlock Jr.* (1924) and entering the movie he is projecting, they lead inward. The grown man, Salvatore Di Vita, smiles. He no longer feels empty. Peering through the projection window, Tornatore, the real author of this vision is, in effect, looking on from above at the actor playing him. We go to movies to mingle with the souls of everyone else, Tornatore suggests.

Thematic montage in movies excites "the spontaneous overflow of powerful emotions" by drawing attention to "similitude in dissimilitude," as Wordsworth described how poetry works. Independent moviemakers and some avant-garde musicians of the 1960s saw thematic montage as the tool of the visionary, which many of them aspired to be. Montage was and remains a tool of numerous "counter-cultural," "trance," visionary, "avant-garde," "New American Cinema" experimental Super 8, 16 mm movie makers. Many saw in montage during the '50s and '60s what avant-garde musician John Cage heard in music in 1949: "Music is edifying, for from time to time it sets the soul in operation. The soul is the

Beholding clips of excised kisses is the director, Salvatore Di Vita.

Toto (meaning "as a whole, entirely, uncut") is a name with overtones that echo and re-echo in *Cinema Paradiso*. The protagonist shares the nickname with another Toto, a comedian beloved by Italian moviegoers in the 1940s and '50s. That Toto appears on screen at turning points in this movie.

Bisected by a scratch in Alfredo's reel of clips is this frame showing Italian comedian Toto (1898-1967). Toto the comedian passed from Naples and poverty to inherited noble titles. This Toto lost his sight in 1956, as Alfredo does in *Cinema Paradiso*. Bulging eyes and an immobile nose endowed him with a masklike Janus face. The Cinema Paradiso burns down, blinding Alfredo, when Alfredo attempts to project *The Firefighters of Viggiù* (1949) to a wall outside the theater. Toto headlined that film.

gatherer-together of the disparate elements (Meister Eckhart), and its work fills one with peace and love."

Mothlight (1963) by Stan Brakhage exemplifies what montage meant to spiritually inclined filmmakers of the 1960s. Leaves, spores, and moth wings take on a virtual life by seeming to twitch silently for three minutes fifteen seconds between the

black-on-white hand-painted title—"Moth Light"—and the white-on-black scratched credit, "by Brakhage." Brakhage hand-built the movie out of dead translucent things, compressing them between strips of clear plastic. He used an optical printer, Brakhage says, to lend them "life again, to animate them again, to try to put them into some sort of life through the motion picture machine."

As Brakhage joined moth wings and Bergman joined minds, Tornatore joins excised and antiqued kisses in montage to bring *Cinema Paradiso* to a point of peak experience. In the script, he describes his montage this way: "In rapid sequence the passionate kisses between actors and actresses, names famous and names unknown in the history of movies. Greta Garbo, Gary Cooper, Alida Valli, Rudolph Valentino, Ingrid Bergman, Clark Gable, Anna Magnani, Humphrey Bogart, Marlene Dietrich, Amedeo Nazzari, Luisa Ferida, Vittorio De Sica, Rita Hayworth, Tyrone Power, Doris Durante, Massimo Gironi, Marta Abba, Fred Astaire and Ginger Rogers, Assia Noris..."

Absent from Tornatore's list is Toto. He is the sixteen kisser, the twenty-fourth kisser, and perhaps the final kisser in the montage, who, like lightning in a thundercloud, by electrifying one scratch, illuminates all of them. Lending his name, he lends as well his blindness and joy to the thematic montage that concludes *Cinema Paradiso*.

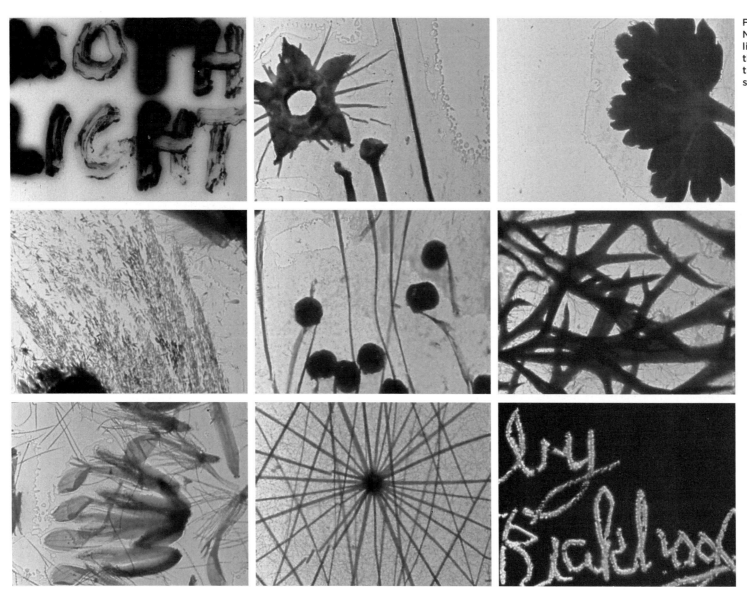

Frames from *Mothlight* (1963). Not kisses, but scraps of the living world flow motion from the hand proclaiming the name to the hand scratching the signature.

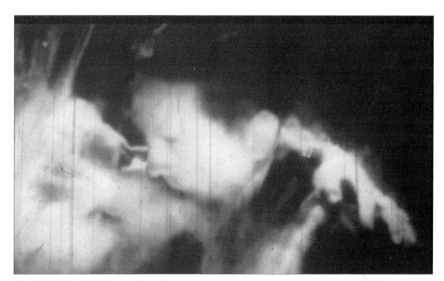

The final kiss of *Cinema Paradiso.*

Waking and dreaming are hard to distinguish from the threshold of montage-land. Ingmar Bergman begins *Persona* (1966) with thematic montage. Bergman's montage evokes, among other things, the world of movies as it intersects the minds of the primary characters—an actress and a nurse who, without always speaking them aloud, exchange memories and thoughts. The montage concludes when a boy in a featureless place reaches toward what seems a movie screen.

EXERCISE TWENTY-TWO: REINVENTED MONTAGE

What this exercise teaches:

- **How to "hard cut" shots to state a theme**

- **How movies can allude and quote, as literature can**

- **How pace in movies, like tempo in music, establishes theme**

- **How repetition in movies, like harmonic notes in music, creates mood and theme**

"A finished work is exactly that, requires resurrection."

John Cage, "Forerunners of Modern Music," *The Tiger's Eye*, March 1949

You Do It Now: In 2000, Kar-wai Wong created *Hua Yang De Nian Hua* [*Enchanting Years*], a two minute twenty-eight second montage of shots of women appearing in nitrate prints of "lost" Chinese movies. In this exercise, you do something similar.

The film clips for this chapter's exercise show someone passing through a doorway. From all or some of these clips build a montage. Join them so that action beginning in the first clip concludes in the last, even though the actor changes. Synchronize the cutting to a sound track. In montage, the dancer is the dance. Step-by-step instructions and the files you can use are in the digital cutting room at http://makefilmhistory.com.

"REALITY" TO CHROMA KEY:
Forrest Gump (1994)

Compositing a chroma key shot, an editor—or more exactly, the editor's editing software—lays a shot of a person or object filmed before a green or blue screen over a separate shot filmed in a different place and time. Since it transforms a shot made *here* into action seemingly occurring *there*, this sleight of hand does what poet John Donne says love does: it "makes one little room an everywhere."

A chroma key shot steps off towards the invisible. It carries action that never happened into a place it never was. Documentaries purporting to achieve precisely the opposite—reveal unvarnished truth—often work as chroma key shots do, albeit unintentionally. Had she known of it, poet and early film critic Marianne Moore might have used the image she invented to describe poetry— imaginary gardens with real toads in them—to describe the chroma key shot.

In the 1940s technicians laboriously created chroma key shots using cameras and multiple intermediate shots, but software now vastly simplifies the process. A filmmaker selects a shot of action filmed before an evenly illuminated green or blue screen—a horse rearing, a model airplane flying, a couple embracing. Using

Odilon Redon, *Eye-Balloon* (1878)

As the eye in this Odilon Redon lithograph does, the eye viewing a chroma key shot enters the imaginary through a fissure in the visible.

What Méliès started in his *féerie* (fairy tale) movies, George Lucas continues now at Industrial Light & Magic.

In this image of 1865, Félix Nadar (Gaspard-Félix Tournachon) and his wife Ernestine only *seemed* to ride in a wicker basket hanging apparently from Nadar's famous balloon, *Le Géant*. In reality, Nadar and wife posed for the camera before a painted muslin backdrop in Nadar's glass windowed photographic studio at 35 Boulevard des Capucines, Paris. Nadar's assistants stand beside the backdrop. The shot was to depict not the reality of flight but the idea.

Viewing this nineteenth-century photo or viewing *Forrest Gump* (1994), the eye does not lie. It merely asks no questions.

Filmmakers daub the real with the brush of the imaginary. Chroma key restores the painted backdrop to twenty-first-century filmmaking.

Vaslav Nijinsky & Tamara Karsavina before a backdrop in a gesture from the Ballets Russe production of *Giselle* (1910).

In 2008, dance aficionados thrilled to what a YouTube user posted as a never-seen fragment of a movie showing Nijinsky dancing as the faun in Debussy's *L'après-midi d'un faune*. But Nijinsky never appeared in a movie. A French artist "created" Nijinsky's performance from photographs of Nijinsky dancing made in 1912 by photographer Adolph de Meyer. The YouTube poster eventually explained, "I work as an alchemist in animated cinema."

Chroma key-like digital technologies now turn "givens" into "maybes."

Shot 1. Actress before green screen. Stock footage c. 2009. Cinematographer Unknown

Shot 2. Frame from *Hawaii* (1966) Cinematographer Russell Harlan

Chroma key shot. Actress is now "in" Hawaii.
Cinematographer Russell Harlan shot 100 movies—including *To Kill a Mockingbird*, *Red River*, *Gun Crazy*, and *Blackboard Jungle*. But the actress here was born long after Harlan retired. A chroma key shot composites a green screen shot of her (above left) with a shot from Harlan's *Hawaii (above center),* and her tresses fly where they never really were.

digital editing software, the filmmaker superimposes that shot over another showing an unrelated action or a distant or imaginary location—a helium mine on the moon, the sky above Belize, dancers on a planet in a distant universe. Set to ignore the specific hue of blue or green that constitutes the background of the foreground shot—blue and green are the colors most dissimilar to human skin tones—editing software superimposes whatever is not blue or green in the foreground shot. The images fuse.

Blue screens predominated when film-based cameras predominated—blue differs most from human skin tones and pre-computer age special effects technicians therefore employed blue screen image matting processes. Contemporary digital video cameras respond most sensitively to green. Either backdrop functions effectively in most digital editing software, as would any other monochromatic background. Editors working in grayscale create similar effects with "luminance key" shots. A pixel brighter or dimmer than a target brightness level turns transparent in a luminance key shot. On a layer "below" the now invisible pixels, elements of a separate shot appear. The filmmaker adjusts the shots, tweaking exposures, brightness, contrast, saturation, and color gain to stitch foreground and background together seamlessly. The actor who, in reality, stands before a green screen in a warehouse in Seattle now peers out from a blockhouse on the Maginot Line.

Contemporary digital chroma keying simplifies the pre-digital techniques of the '30s and '40s. The traveling mattes Linwood Dunn invented for *Flying Down to Rio* (1933) exemplify how early chroma keying worked. Dun photographed foreground action

Flying Down to Rio (1933), dir. Thornton Freeland. These dancers performed not on the wings of airplanes in flight but rather on motionless props in the RKO studio in Culver City, California. Linwood Dunn earned no screen credits for this sleight-of-hand.

chroma-keyed a fantasy world using optical printers and multiple intermediate negatives. Butler's "traveling mattes" shots lent the power of flight to Korda's djinn. At a time when computers had nothing to do with movies, Ray Harryhausen was hand crafting live and animated model scenes for *The Beast from 20,000 Fathoms* (1953). Arthur Widmer was devising what he called then the "Ultra Violet Traveling Matte Process" to cast an opalescent horizon behind Spencer Tracy wrestling a marlin in *The Old Man and the Sea* (1958).

before a blue screen and then re-photographed it successively first through a blue filter and then through combined red and green filters to create intermediate images. When double-exposed over background footage, these intermediate images created the illusion of motion before a background. The process—called then a traveling matte shot—required precision. But it worked, certainly more convincingly than the simpler rear screen projection method Fox Films had introduced in 1930. (Actors played rear projection scenes, especially those ubiquitous moving car scenes, in front of backgrounds—"plates." Synchronized to the camera, studio projectors projected from behind unto large translucent screens. Think Bogie and Bergman driving down the Champs-Élysées in *Casablanca*.)

Others emulated Dunn. For Alexander Korda's version of *The Thief of Bagdad* (1940)—the second of many versions—Lawrence Butler

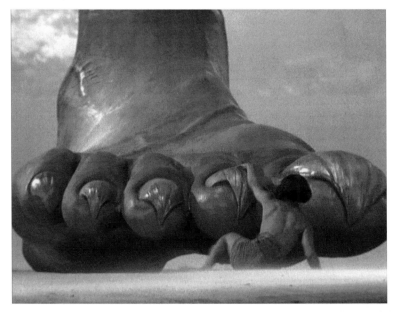

The Thief of Bagdad (1940), dir. Michael Powell, Ludwig Berger, and Tim Whelan. "You shall see that with me, nothing is impossible. You shall see and believe!" the djinn tells Abu, the thief, at the moment of the djinn's liberation. Lawrence Butler used traveling mattes to superimpose the image of the boy thief on the toe of the djinn, whose words express the spirit of the chroma key shot.

Detail of the *Birth of the Virgin* by Cennino Cennini, c 1385.

The artist's aim, Cennino Cennini asserted 600 years ago in *The Craftsman's Handbook,* "is to discover things not seen, hiding themselves under the shadow of natural objects, and to fix them with the hand, presenting to plain sight what does not actually exist." Filmmakers have sought to do that since the first days of moviemaking.

Zelig (1983), dir. Woody Allen.

Cinematographer Gordon Willis interjects Woody Allen (center) as Zelig and, in this frame, Mia Farrow into footage from various decades, especially the 1920s. Matte shots, 1920s-era lens, and intentionally crumpled and heated 1980s footage create the illusion. Zelig acquires the look and personality of whoever surrounds him. The name Zelig suggests the 1920s-era Al Selig, Fox Studios publicity man who fabricated the faux "identity" of actress Theda Bara.

In contemporary parlance, however, chroma-keying happens in nonlinear digital editing software that, in moments, renders what technicians in the 1940s labored months to achieve. In films like *Inception* (2010), chroma key shots move into the multiplex the shamanic idea that mind helps make reality and that perception *is* thought. In essence, they are new tools for achieving an ancient aspiration.

Chroma keying illustrates a truth about all movies: the mind of the filmmaker shapes what the viewer sees. Consider the ethnographic

documentary, ostensibly the antithesis of chroma keying. Director/explorer Robert Flaherty, for instance, represented *Nanook of the North* (1922*)* as a year in the life of Inuits of Canada. The action begins when Nanook, the protagonist, paddles in a kayak towards the camera. Traditional furs swaddle him. Later in the film, Nanook probes a phonograph record with his teeth to determine its qualities. He harpoons a seal and a walrus. He averts disaster for his

The Mysterious Portrait (1899), dir. Georges Méliès.

Allakariallak, represented to the world by Robert Flaherty as "Nanook."

Alice Nuvalinga, represented to the world by Robert Flaherty as "Nyla."

The Invisible Man (1933), dir. James Whale.

Georges Méliès duplicates himself in the second take of *The Mysterious Portrait* (1899) by inserting himself into the picture frame he had earlier draped with black cloth in a previous take. Technicians working on *The Invisible Man* (1933) did something similar. Over shots of terrified villagers—"Look! He's all eaten away!"—they matted a shot of protagonist Claude Rains gesturing before a black velvet background while dressed only in black (save his white shirt). These shots show what the mind can picture, not merely what the eye can see.

family by crafting together an emergency igloo. "Its people, as they appear to the spectator, are not acting, but living," a reviewer wrote in praise of the realism of *Nanook of the North* on its first release in 1922.

But Flaherty, the original ethnographic filmmaker, created, in part, what he supposedly discovered. Nanook—meaning "Polar Bear"— was a screen name Flaherty invented for his protagonist, an Inuit named Allakariallak. (Changing an actor's name was 1920s-style star marketing: for example, Ola Cronk from Cawker City, Kansas, had morphed into Hollywood star "Claire Windsor" the previous year.) Flaherty hired Allakariallak to play the protagonist of his "story of life and love in the actual arctic." In an intertitle, Flaherty describes him as "Chief of the Itivimuits, and... a great hunter famous through all Ungava." But Allakariallak no longer lived the life of a hunter-gatherer nomad. He processed nitrate film footage for Flaherty in a makeshift lab in a Canadian settlement.

Ola Cronk from Cawker City, Kansas, labored as an anonymous extra in four movies when she arrived in Hollywood in 1919, aged 27. She reported her age as 21. Renamed "Claire Windsor" in 1920 by director Lois Weber, Windsor suddenly became "The Patrician Beauty." Her image appeared on the cover of both *Motion Picture* and *Picture-Play Magazine* the summer Flaherty premiered *Nanook*. Windsor therefore regarded press reports in 1922 linking her in 1922 to the murder of director William Desmond Taylor as ruinous, since she reputedly personified "refinement."

Created by William Hope in 1923, the photograph above purportedly shows a man and the spirit of his deceased second wife. Investigators exposed Hope's chicanery in February 1922, but exposure made scant impression on Hope's believers.

As a chroma key shot does, Flaherty's movie abounds in simulation. By virtue of stop action cinematography, five Inuit and a dog emerge from Nanook's kayak (like clowns emerging from a trick car in a circus). Flaherty staged for the camera Allakariallak's tussle with a seal. (In 1917, Chaplin jigged up a mackerel in a similarly comical way in *The Immigrant*.) The igloo Nanook constructs to save his "family" was a semi-circle double the size of a normal igloo. It was as open to the wind as an ant farm under glass is open to observing eyes. Flaherty needed room for the tripod of his Akely "pancake" camera. In effect, Flaherty commissioned a stage

In the late nineteenth and early twentieth centuries, "spirit photographs" like those made by William Hope preyed on the credulous with double exposures "documenting"—that is, fabricating—"spirit extra" visitations.

Arthur Conan Doyle, author of the Sherlock Holmes series, brandished before a May 8, 1922, capacity crowd in Carnegie Hall a photograph allegedly taken by Hope in his studio in 1922. Supposedly the photo showed British writer/editor spiritualist W.T. Stead, who had perished when the Titanic sank ten years before. Forming a border around Hope's photo of Stead were words allegedly uttered by Stead to a friend before the Titanic sailed, "I will try to keep you posted." In response to this evidence, bursts of applause rippled from the audience.

In a 1927 Fox newsreel, Doyle describes how séance participants "heard the sound of a vanished voice and felt the touch of a vanished hand."

Chroma keying is twenty-first-century spiritualism. It enables us to see in movies what is not and never was.

set. Nyla (Alice Nuvalinga) and Cunayo, "wives," were not Nanook's wives. They were Flaherty's mistresses. Flaherty transformed what he actually found in Inukjuak (Port Harrison), Quebec, into what he insisted on encountering, which was purity of heart and a mind impervious to desolation. The motorized kayaks and motorboats then visiting Port Harrison appear nowhere in Flaherty's movie. Allakariallak—so-called Nanook—perished in 1923. He did not starve alone hunting deer as Flaherty romantically implied to newspapers. He ingloriously succumbed to tuberculosis in Port Harrison.

A CGI ("Computer-Generated-Imagery") shot created for but ultimately excised from *Forrest Gump* (1994) illustrates how chroma key makes the never-was visible. The shot was to consist of two elements.

One element was 8 mm Kodachrome footage showing Ambassador to China George H.W. Bush in 1975 playing ping-pong with a member of an American ping-pong team visiting China. In the footage, the visitor accidentally pings Bush. The second element was Tom Hanks in 1993 facing a blue screen and whacking ping-pong balls. Hanks wore a blazer and khakis precisely matching the original player's. He gestured before the blue screen in 1993 exactly as Bush's visitor had gestured 18 years earlier. Ping-pong balls hung on wires from the ceiling, replicating where in the air the visitor's paddle had encountered the ball when the visitor played with Bush. Hanks whacked them precisely as the visitor had whacked his. These two elements were to meld in chroma key, the Industrial

Shot 1. Archival footage c. 1975. George H.W. Bush plays ping-pong with a visitor.

Shot 2. Tom Hanks "plays" ping pong before a blue screen on December 17, 1993.

Shot 3. George H.W. Bush "plays" ping-pong with Forrest Gump. In this composited shot, even the original paddle pad has vanished from the hand of Bush's opponent. Hanks' is red. The original was green.

Light & Magic computer ignoring the blue screen behind Hanks. When the computer combined the two moving images, Hanks was to supplant the original player. CGI effects in a 2009 movie like *Avatar* simplify the mechanics of this compositing process of 1994 but do not fundamentally change it.

Shooting chroma key action now requires nothing like the complex apparatus pre-digital technicians used. Filmmakers create or acquire a chroma key background—a plastic sheet, a muslin, or chroma key video paint applied to a flat wall and illuminate it brightly, evenly, and obliquely to minimize shadows. They may render an actor partially or entirely invisible with a chroma key

suit. The actor performs roughly five feet before the chroma key background to minimize shadows. Three-point lighting—key light (primary illumination), back light (illumination from behind the subject), and fill lighting (reducing shadows)—balances on the actor to cast no shadow on the screen. The filmmaker shoots and exports the shot into digital editing software, setting the action upon background footage, identifying the chroma key color and correcting as necessary.

"The eye, like a strange balloon, drifts up to the infinite," Odilon Redon inscribes the lithograph he made of "Eye-Balloon." Redon's inscription also describes the chroma key process itself.

EXERCISE TWENTY-THREE: CHROMA KEY

What this exercise teaches:

- **How to combine a green-screen foreground shot with a real or CGI background**

- **How chroma key shots digitize effects Méliès & others made a century ago**

"Teeming city, city full of dreams,
Where ghosts by daylight grab the passer's sleeve!"

Charles Baudelaire

You Did It Then: **You can do like Redon. Chroma key a world using *Make Film History* crowd footage and green-screened "speaker" footage to recreate the Washington Monument crowd scene of *Forrest Gump*. Step-by-step instructions and the files you can use are in the digital cutting room at http://makefilmhistory.com.**

PRODUCTION Make Film History
DIRECTOR _____
CAMERA _____
DATE   SCENE   TAKE
23

PERSON AND ROLE:
Being John Malkovich (1999)

What an actor does and represents on screen defies simple explanation because an actor on screen is many and one—many minds expressing themselves invisibly off screen through the one visibly before us. When Marlene Dietrich lifts her chin to puff a cigarette in *Shanghai Express* (1932), we see Dietrich's face. But director Josef von Sternberg and cinematographer Lee Garmes composed this shot using high key light to elevate Dietrich's cheekbones and suffuse her with a numinous glow. Depicted this way, Dietrich appears ethereal. In the star somewhere is the person Dietrich was. Von Sternberg once remarked about Dietrich, "In my films Marlene is not Marlene. I am Marlene, she knows that better than anyone." Von Sternberg was stating the enigma that film acting represents.

Filmmakers sometimes used themselves, as von Sternberg used Dietrich, to express the protean identity of the actor on screen. In 1900, Méliès had already distributed himself into each of seven members of his band in *L'Homme Orchestre* (1900*)*, and Buster Keaton did much the same in *The Playhouse* (1921), filling every seat on stage and every seat in the auditorium with versions of himself. What poet John Keats says in a letter regarding poets—"A Poet is the most unpoetical of anything in existence, because he

Marlene Dietrich in *Shanghai Express* (1932).
"That's the light up there I'd like to use...up there," Dietrich would instruct cinematographer Charles Lang, who lit and shot her in *Desire* (1936) and three other films.

Edison employees dance while William K.L. Dickson fiddles. *Dickson Experimental Sound Film* (1894).

As Theodosia Burr Goodman, the daughter of a tailor from Cincinnati (above left), she was pearls, white feathers, and a Russian wolfhound named Galloper. By 1916, Fox press agents had recreated her as "Theda Bara," supposedly the daughter of "an Arab sheik and a French woman born in the Sahara" and released the vamp who lived inside of her. Above right, Theda Bara plays the lead in a now lost 1917 Fox feature, *Cleopatra*.

The Dancing Pig (1907) Pathé Frères.

has no Identity, he is continually filling some other body"—could apply as well to film actors. Even screen names express, as masks do, not who an actor is but what he is meant to portray. Betty Perske, Archie Leach, Harlean Carpenter, and Lucille LeSueur walk into a casting room and emerge as Lauren Bacall, Cary Grant, Jean Harlow, and Joan Crawford. Before she dubbed herself Marlene, Dietrich was Marie. Greta Garbo was Greta Gustaffson. Rock Hudson was Roy Scherer. Kirk Douglas was Issur Demsky. Whoopi Goldberg was Caryn Johnson.

Actors of the nineteenth century stage, where actors declaimed and gesticulated, were the original models for acting in movies. The nineteenth century movie camera regarded humans as did the

Greek God Zeus, who was privy to human feelings but attentive only when people signaled dramatically. Cameramen first took only long shots, so movie acting was first gestural. Early movie actors often dance—a long shot shows how a body sways but not how feelings pass across a face. Dancers and fighters were therefore premier subjects in early movies.

In 1894, William Dickson had already staged the so-called *Leonard-Cushing Fight* (1894) in Edison's Black Maria studio. Two lightweights from Brooklyn pummel each other before five "ringside fans" and a "referee." Stage star Sarah Bernhardt sword fighting in an 1899 Phono-Cinéma film of *Hamlet* illustrates the performance-as-semaphore stage of movie acting. Bernhardt and her opponent thrust and parry in profile, but the long shot blots the face from each swordsman. The actors combat, different but barely distinguishable people. Stabbing herself while she performs as Hamlet, Berhardt raises her hand to her brow in a pantomime of agony, collapses with her arms aloft, and dies. Bernhardt would have deemed this "Delsarte" acting, the acting style of nineteenth century operatic tenors hurling high C to furthest tier of the balcony.

The first era ended in roughly 1910. Most actors of that era had pantomimed anonymously. But actors of the next era evolved into stars by maintaining a consistent identity from movie to movie. The silent star phase of movie acting began in approximately 1910 and continued until synchronous sound films supplanted silent movies. When D.W. Griffith's personal representative claimed in an ad that Griffith had introduced the close-up, he also claimed that Griffith introduced "restraint in expression." His claim joining *mise-en-scène* and acting is reasonable—close-ups and a modicum of restraint did help professionalize acting and create the silent movie star. But commercial factors also helped.

Florence Lawrence on the cover of *Photoplay* November 1914.

In *The Broken Oath* (1910), Florence Lawrence became the first actor identified in a credit. In 125 films at Biograph from 1908-1910, she had played anonymously. When she quit for better terms, Carl Laemmle, her new employer at the Independent Motion Picture Company [IMP], determined that her value as an individual exceeded her value as "the Biograph Girl," as Biograph then dubbed her. To "bring her back" to life on screen with fanfare, Laemmle's touts earlier that year had circulated the canard that Lawrence had been killed by a streetcar. When she subsequently arrived by train in St Louis as a publicity stunt, fans mobbed her.

In 1912, Adolph Zukor started marketing stage actors associated with European theater—such as Sarah Bernhardt—as the distinguishing feature of his Famous Players Film Company. Competing studios then created competing stars, who began appearing on postcards and playing cards. As early as 1911 and until 1980, when the magazine ceased publishing, *Photoplay* ran movie star profiles.

By the end of the silent era, actors could convey emotion with intimate gesture because, in part, directors shot them, as Chaplin shot the final shot of *City Lights*, closely enough to show thought

The Gold Rush (1925), dir. Charlie Chaplin. Left, Georgia Hale and Charlie Chaplin.

In Chaplin's movies, the star's persona pervaded the set and determined how supporting characters performed. Georgia Hale, Chaplin's love interest in *The Gold Rush* (1923), remembered years later his instructions. "He always said just before the camera would go, 'Now do this scene poorly. Walk through it.' And then he would get it." Hale's character existed to draw forth his performance, Chaplin meant. Every character in a Chaplin film is an arm or leg of the Tramp. During rehearsal, Chaplin mimed out every role. Virginia Cherill, the flower girl in *City Lights* (1931), described the experience of taking his direction. "You found yourself saying that he was you."

Masaccio, *Expulsion from the Garden of Eden*, detail (1425).

King Vidor, dir. *The Crowd* (1928).

Hand shielding her face, Eleanor Boardman expresses embarrassment, shame, or exultation in the course of *The Crowd*. "Feeling overwhelms me here," Boardman communicates with the gesture.

in an eye twitch. Eleanor Boardman's hands, for instance, show Boardman passing in King Vidor's *The Crowd* (1928) from outrage to reconciliation with her philandering husband. From rubbing a cheek with a hand in anxiety, for instance, she passes to rubbing both hands on her midriff, telling us thereby that she is pregnant. Her acting summoned feeling because it played in the mind's eye theater where the viewer supplies half the story.

But what the silent camera found in this kind of acting, the sound camera missed. A sophisticate in the silent *Gigolo* (1926), actor Rod La Rocque became buffoonish in the white cowboy hat, black scarf, and white pants of a sound film, *The Delightful Rogue* (1929). "I'm in love," Norma Talmadge shrieked in *Du Barry, Woman of Passion...* in her native Brooklynese. Like numerous silent movie

Norma Talmadge enunciates into "The Microphone—The Terror of the Studios" on the cover of *Photoplay* in December 1929. *Time* panned her in *Du Barry, Woman of Passion* (1930). "In her first attempt she talked like an elocution pupil; this time she talks like an elocution teacher."

On the basis of this two-minute monologue in which, stifling her tears, she feigns happiness at the remarriage of her former husband while she "speaks" with him, Austrian actress Luise Rainer (above) won the 1936 Oscar for Best Actress. Acting the part of an actress acting at acting, Rainer worked up her monologue by studying Jean Cocteau's *La Voix humaine*. But her performance seems unrehearsed, since the words seem to come not from a script but unbidden. "Aloow Floh…" she purrs, glossing her grief with mitteleuropean pathos, "Yez, yez, Anna…"

players, Eleanor Boardman disappeared from the screen when sound came in. James Murray, who played her husband in *The Crowd*, fared worse. Lost and forgotten once sound transformed movie acting, he mysteriously drowned in 1936. Silent movie actress Lina Basquette, whose husband, Sam Warner, had ushered in the sound movie era, acidly remarks about a once familiar actress: "Claire Windsor was marshmallow soft, exquisitely beautiful, blond, stately, and serene—until she opened her mouth." Synchronous sound terminated the second era of movie acting.

The new players of the sound era packed a soul into a voice. Numerous stars had formerly performed on Broadway or the European stage. They migrated to Hollywood carrying calling card voices. Mae West delivered dialogue that winked. Demure in silents and a brassy blonde in talkies, Jean Arthur crackled. Garbo was *weltshmerz*.

Character actors were likewise voices or faces impossible to forget attached to names difficult to recall. Eugene Pallette had been a character actor in silent films, but his low pitched croak in talkies like *Shanghai Express* (1932) and *My Man Godfrey* (1936) and *The Lady Eve* (1941) identified him instantly as a bullfrog shape-shifted into human form. Thomas Mitchell, Scarlett's father in *Gone With the Wind* (1939), was a railroad car of characters sharing one elfin face. Dorothy Lee screeched comically like a macaw from atop a piano in *Syncopation* (1929), "O hawnee, o hawnee, I wonder why you act so funny..." Stars played themselves, and contract players played as many types as they could master, as both had in the 1920s, but movies created to show their foxtrots or tears now also showcased their wit or their endearing stutter.

"Method acting" entered movies when location shooting began supplanting studio shooting during the 1950s. One realism required another. Method actors attempt to "become" their characters. A performance is as out of place as a prom dress at a picnic unless it emerges from the inner life of the actor, method actors say. Method actors try for intimacy, authenticity, and spontaneity rather than pantomime or conventionalized gesture. Actors must act what they feel, method-acting instructors say. But "method acting" describes not a single technique but a constellation of ideas and practices. Truth takes the stage in the heart that is open, coaches and method actors generally affirm. Your character is *your* character. Truth is memory. Trust instinct. Step into your light. Meet your shadow. Be your wild animal. Follow your conflict to its core.

Lee Strasberg (undated photo).
Strasberg's raised hands resemble Eleanor Boardman's, but his face remains unshielded. "Be open," method coaches insist.

But these exhortations resemble Zen koans, easy to state but difficult to fully understand.

The "method" began in the nineteenth century as a training program for actors devised by German aristocrat-director Duke Georg of Saxe-Meiningen. Saxe-Meiningen sought naturalism in the theatrical productions he toured to European capitol cities. His troupe played in Moscow in 1890, where Constantin Stanislavski, then a young actor/director, took copious notes. Stanislavski formed the Moscow (Repertory) Art Theater in 1897, emphasizing there the actor's capacity to enter the skin of his character.

Production still: *On the Waterfront* (1954). Eva Marie Saint and Marlon Brando. Two method actors work together in the actress's first film.

Once a pupil and colleague of Stanislavski, Michael Chekhov eventually diverged from Stanislavski's dictum that an actor finds his character by reliving his own past experiences, the process Stanislavski dubbed "Affective Memory." Chekhov taught actors instead to search for characters within their own imagination, and he insisted that gesture effectively expresses a character to an audience. Film actors who studied with Chekhov included Yul Brynner, Gregory Peck, Marilyn Monroe, Anthony Quinn, Clint Eastwood, and others. Though they never studied with Chekhov, numerous contemporary actors, for instance, Daniel Day-Lewis and Johnny Depp, continue the method tradition.

Acting the role of a psychiatrist in *Spellbound* (1945) above, Chekhov advises his junior colleague, played by Ingrid Bergman, to subject affection she feels for the amnesiac she loves to her professional judgment as a psychiatrist. Chekhov externalizes his character's conflict in a gesture. About to light his pipe, Chekhov fumbles the character's matches. "Doctor told me not to smoke in the morning, but I am too excited," Chekhov then says. What a character desires, he also resists, Chekhov taught. The fumble expresses the character's conflict.

Eva Marie Saint in 1949, then unknown, up against the wall at a casting call. Photo by Cornell Capa.

The Italian quick-change actor Leopoldo Fregoli anticipated Malkovich when movies were beginning. In his own movies, "Fregoligraphs," and in Méliès' 1899 movie, *L'Homme Protée (The Lightning Change Artist),* Fregoli seemed to "become" other beings. His name endures as a psychiatric diagnosis. Someone stricken with the "Fregoli syndrome" thinks that everyone around him is one person ceaselessly changing his disguise or his appearance.

"There are no small parts, only small actors," Stanislavski told his actors, as the Russian actor, Mikhail Shchepkin, had earlier stated. Stanislavski taught his actors to analyze the implicit wishes and desires of the characters they play. Struggle makes character, Stanislavski reasoned. To act, you journey inward.

Stanislavski's thinking took root abroad. Lee Strasberg discovered it when Stanislavski brought a touring company to Manhattan in 1923. At the Actors Studio in Manhattan, where he served as Artistic Director beginning 1950, Strasberg eventually taught Paul Newman, Marilyn Monroe, Al Pacino, Eva Marie Saint and numerous others to apply the method to performance before a camera. Others spread the gospel. Analyze. Improvise. Remember. Feel. Commit yourself to the fiction. Sanford Meisner taught students to "live truthfully under imaginary circumstances."

Being John Malkovich (1999) places the inward journey of "The Method" at the center of the story. It returns film acting, too, to its roots. In this movie, the actor John Malkovich, playing the actor John Malkovich, enters a "portal" leading to his own inner world and finds that everyone is a variant of himself. Malkovich's partner at a dinner table, for instance, is himself as a woman murmuring, "Malkovich?" A menu lists entries, all "Malkovich." To order, Malkovich can only howl, "Malkovich." (Actors wearing rubber masks create the other Malkoviches.) The movie illustrates a central point the method-acting gurus make—the actor on screen is searching both to enter and escape himself.

Being John Malkovich (1999), dir. Spike Jonze. The actor John Malkovich playing the character "John Malkovich" dines in a restaurant occupied only by other "John Malkoviches." In rubber masks that turn their faces into his, faux Malkoviches are indistinguishable from the real.

"Everybody wants to be Cary Grant. Even I want to be Cary Grant," Cary Grant once allegedly said. But that irony enfolds another. When Leo McCarey directed him in *The Awful Truth* (1937), some say, Cary Grant (birth name Archibald Alexander Leach) discovered in McCarey's stride and suave mischief the primal "Cary Grant."

Being is to acting as walking is to dancing. The walker presses forward towards a destination. The dancer, going nowhere, eventually arrives at himself. When he gets there, he has become someone else. "I'm essentially the result of other people's imagination," the actor John Hurt says.

EXERCISE TWENTY-FOUR: PERSON AND ROLE

What this exercise teaches:

● **How to evaluate an actor's performance for style, presence, personality, command**

● **How an actor delivers text or subtext or both**

● **How an actor's body speaks**

● **How the actor's face can be the mask of a director**

"Please arrange for the executives...to see the test of Fred Astaire. I am a little uncertain about the man, but I feel, in spite of his enormous ears and bad chin line, that his charm is so tremendous that it comes through even in this wretched test."

David O. Selznick, January 26, 1933

"I don't know how you focus. You just focus.... You gotta take all your emotions, all your anger, all your love, all your hate, and push it way down here into the pit of your stomach and then let it explode like a reactor. Pow!"

"The Subway Ghost" in *Ghost* (1990)

You Did It Then: Cast *Hamlet*. Consider how six movie actors of the past interpreted the speech beginning, "To be or not to be." (Seventy-five actors have played the role on film since 1900.) Step by step instructions and the component shots are in the *Make Film History* digital cutting room: http://makefilmhistory.com.

You Do It Now: Audition five actors to play a Hamlet-like role. Record how each delivers a page of script, what casting directors call a "side." Cast the actor who brings life to the lines. If you like, you can use this speech:

I would have told you about my problem, sir, but I didn't think you wanted to hear about it. I am sorry, truly sorry, for any grief I may have caused. It's just, sir, I'm incapable of speaking truthfully when I'm up against it. In the last analysis, sir, it's every man for himself, I think. We have such fine faces in the sunshine but when the dark comes the owls start hooting in the forest and the night comes alive with fears. I am a creature of darkness, so you can find me there.

PRODUCTION Make Film History
DIRECTOR
CAMERA
DATE   SCENE   TAKE
24

DOCUMENTARY
"Reality" (2007)

"Reality is that which, when you stop believing in it, doesn't go away."
    Phillip K. Dick, *How to Build a Universe that Doesn't Fall Apart Two Days Later* (1978)

Imagination discovers new expressions but never changes the face of reality. The entire twentieth century separates *Repas de Bébé* (1895) from *Charlie Bit My Finger—Again!* (2007), but each depicts, for a similar reason, a moment that transpires with little variation wherever humans exist. Each movie runs for less than

a minute. Each is "artless." Each treats a child. These films are, respectively, the work of a world-famous uncle (Louis Lumière) and a father living privately (Howard Davies-Carr). Neither would apply the term to what he did, but each made a documentary movie. Each made his movie to document a moment devoid of special significance except when beheld with familial love. Reality is best perceived that way. The purpose of the documentary movie is to show the face of reality.

Louis Lumière, *Repas de Bébé* (1895). Auguste Lumière, elder of the two inventors of the cinématographe, feeds his daughter, Andrée Lumière. The baby smiles at her father when she bites on a biscuit. The meal took place sometime after March 22 and before June 10, 1895. The fiction film suspends the river of time. The documentary flows with it. At the time of this feeding, Andrée Lumière was one year old.

As she grew, Andrée Lumière became a poster girl for the autochrome color on glass plate photographic image process marketed by the Lumières when they abandoned movie production. She died in 1918, aged 24.

Charlie Bit My Finger—Again! (2007) Howard Davies-Carr. The video features Harry and Charlie Davies-Carr, the filmmaker's children. As Lumière's film of his child did in his century, the Davies-Carr film of two children has found a worldwide audience.

Indochina: Namo Village, Panorama Taken from a Rickshaw (1900) Gabriel Veyre.

The Lumières included this movie in their show of cinématographe films at the Paris Exhibition of 1900.

Postcard from Saigon, French Indochina c. 1907.

Documentaries show real people in real places taking real actions. Since 1895, documentarians have successively sought to witness the world (actualité), then shape it ('30s documentary), then present it as a specimen for others to judge (*cinéma vérité*), then share it as a gift (YouTube).

Indochina: Namo Village, Panorama taken from a Rickshaw typifies documentary in its first Lumière phase—48 seconds of haiku-like imagery. (You can hold your breath under water for the length of a Lumière cinématographe film, and the feeling of immersion in a pleasurable experience that must end soon is similar.) Shot from the rear of a rolling rickshaw, the cinématographe records a jubilant scene. Boys and girls joyous as tails beneath a kite chase behind the rickshaw. Their racing ends when the cinématographe exhausts its film. A pair of porters carrying what must have been a member of the cameraman's party—the cameraman was a Lumière contract employee named Gabriel Veyre—trip behind this exultation of children.

Indochina: Namo Village, Panorama taken from a Rickshaw is the world as seen from the colonist's veranda, turn-of-the-century postcard reality. The Lumière catalogue called such films "*actualitiés*," meaning "news" or "what is happening." Those films record

John Grierson's *Night Mail* (1936) typifies the second phase of documentary—the drum-rolling ceremonial of the 1930s that lauds right action or delivers an indictment. In Grierson's movie, a night train speeds northward from London to Glasgow while *en route* postal workers sort mail. Wild and synchronous sound, location and studio footage depict a northbound train that, with darkness as thread, stitches dusk to dawn. As Grierson constructs it, this northward passage seems to signify the wish of the British people to rediscover their commonality. The film largely uses what Grierson liked to call "unstaged reality" to amplify the muffled cry of humanity.

Second phase documentarians like Grierson, notwithstanding the "realism" of the documentary, offer judgments explicitly. With narration and montage, Grierson casts the postal worker as a modern Hermes. Grierson himself delivers, or intermittently shouts, the *Night Mail* narration—"4 million miles every year! 500 million letters every year!"—and as the train approaches Glasgow, W.H. Auden takes over to race through a poem of couplets—"Letters of thanks/Letters from banks/Letters of joy/From the girl and the boy..." A score by Benjamin Britten syncopates everything.

The second phase documentary was often the work of an agency or government office. *Night Mail* was an institutional promo intended to raise morale and preserve the post office against efforts to privatize it. In the United States, Pare Lorenz created similar orchestral-scored government-commissioned movies—*The*

Self-portrait, Gabriel Veyre, Casablanca, 1908.
Former Lumière cameraman Gabriel Veyre journeyed to Morocco in 1901, where he settled in Casablanca. Starting 1907, he recorded Morocco on Lumière autochrome (color) glass plates.

what single cameraman witnessed when he opened his cinématographe to the world. Inscriptions like "Je ne t'oublie pas" ("I'll never forget you") passed into Paris mail pouches on picture postcards like this. A writer pitching a story idea speaks like this kind of documentary—"A prince has one night in Paris to capture the wizard who enchanted him a century before." You see it in a flash. It is a vision.

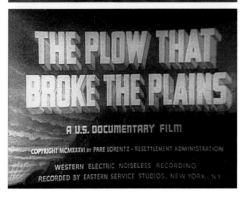

Above, block letter titles for *Night-mail* crawl up from the bottom of the screen, perhaps to convey that, ascending together from shadows, the "masses" were rising. Titles frequently rose *en masse* in '30s documentaries, as if to depict '30s political theory in machined typography.

Leni Riefenstahl uses a similar effect to introduce *Triumph of the Will* (1935), as does Pare Lorenz to introduce *The Plow that Broke the Plains* (1936).

Plow that Broke the Plains (1936) and *The River* (1937). As propagandists seek to do—see Hitler arriving from the clouds to begin Leni Riefenstahl's *Triumph of the Will* (1935)—second phase documentarians, by accident, from enthusiasm, or to inspire some action, reshaped the foot of reality to fit their shoe. A socialist, Grierson identifies the people in the movie as "workers of the traveling post office " and "workers of the L.M.S. railroad." Out of railroad signals and reciprocating pistons and slender men sorting mail—no women appear in this movie—he constructs the train, as he constructs his "reality," as a single living being, a beneficent "Anonymous" engaged in compassionate works running in dusk and darkness past dogs and workmen in workmen's caps and sleeping towns.

Grierson judges this activity and finds it good. Documentarians of the second phase make unashamed judgments. They render verdicts with the certainty of a gavel. Shot by shot, declarative sentence by declarative sentence, they advance towards truth in "voice-of-God" narratives. Even poets drafted into documentary making during the Second World War wrought scripts exhorting engagement with reality. "Morning is breaking over Wales at war... against the men who would murder Man," Dylan Thomas wrote in a narration for in *Wales: Green Mountain, Black Mountain* (1942).

Particularly during World War II, propagandists during the second documentary phase commandeered the documentary but ignored its central purpose—to witness truth—in order to roll in tanks over reality. Depending on a filmmaker's disposition toward reality, a second phase documentary could bear witness to truth or torture facts into submission. John Huston's *Battle of San Pietro* (1945) shows American infantrymen in combat that kills many of them. Fritz Hippler's *Feldzug in Polen (Campaign in Poland)* (1940) shows German infantrymen happily advancing while a narrator cants, "The German regiments are renewing their unforgettable fame. Their immense marching efficiency, their power of resistance in suffering fatigue and hardship are as astonishing as their fighting capacity."

The third phase of documentary was the *cinéma-vérité* ("film truth") documentary of the 1960s. The *cinéma-vérité* filmmaker—sometimes called in America the "Direct Cinema" filmmaker—seeks above all unmanipulated reality and therefore passes with as light a tread as possible into the world he is filming. A documentarian must wait quietly, the *cinéma-vérité* documentarian says. He resembles the Lumière cameraman but differs from him in sensing that reality delivers ambiguous testimony. You cannot act in reality without transforming it, anymore than you can study the nightlife of the woods by shining a light on it.

Cinéma-vérité documentarians generally resist narration on the grounds that viewers are or should be, like the documentarians themselves, authors of the reality they inhabit. *Cinéma-vérité* abounds in caffeinated speculation about what we know and how we know it. *Chronique d'un été* (1960) by Jean Rouch and Edgar

Morin, an early example, takes as its subject Rouch's thought that the camera transforms what it records. Rouch speculates about how sincere a person can be before a camera recording him. He interrogates people in Paris and St. Tropez on camera about their lives, then shows his interlocutors the assembled footage and records that, too. "Reality TV" derives, in essence, from *cinéma-vérité*. If *cinéma-vérité* philosophizing is a locomotive pulling a freight train of "buts," the movies themselves are simple. They

"Show, don't tell," is a precept that *cinéma vérité* filmmakers share with writers of fiction. Documentaries are works of imagination, but *cinéma vérité* documentaries seek to dispel illusion.

Titicut Follies (1967), dir. Frederick Wiseman, indicts cruelty and incompetence at a Massachusetts prison for the criminally insane, offering as evidence acts and words of supervisors, guards, and inmates. Above (left), an inmate rants. Below (left), inmates and staff sing on stage together in the institution's annual show, *The Titicut Follies*. Wiseman recorded sound and cinematographer John Marshall shot the 16 mm film. After a superior court judge order all prints destroyed in 1968, the Supreme Court of Massachusetts authorized the film for viewing by medical, legal, and social work students and professionals. A superior court judge released the film for general viewing in 1991.

take place far from Hollywood. They are simply lit. They are acts of creative witness. They show real people answering telephones or working out the details of a surgery, what you would see about you if you paid attention to the dancing bones of the face of reality.

To shoot this kind of documentary, the filmmaker shoulders the camera, beats back the impulse to issue directions, and follows the world wherever it leads. This is documentary filmmaking as pick-up-sticks: the filmmaker is able to continue taking what he needs so long as he is able to leave the material undisturbed. Shooting a *cinéma-vérité* movie, the filmmaker floats like a cork on the river of life, to employ the metaphor for artistic creation filmmaker Jean Renoir attributes to his father, the impressionist painter. This kind of filmmaking is an exercise in waiting. The cameraman stays open to the world in a mental state approximating prayer.

To cut a *cinéma-vérité* documentary, the editor works much as the cameraman does. The cameraman finds, the editor—who is usually the cameraman or producer himself—makes, and a movie emerges in stages the way photos in darkrooms formerly appeared. *Cinéma-vérité* documentarians in the 1960's spent months running 16 mm rushes through Moviolas to accomplish what today digital cameras and non-linear editing software accomplish in days. But the machine matters less than what it captures.

The fourth stage of the documentary, where we are today, resembles the first. More than four hundred twenty million viewers have now viewed, smiled at, and passed along Howard Davies-Carr's YouTube

Gimme Shelter (1970), dir. Albert Maysles, David Maysles, and Charlotte Zwerin. Recollecting *Gimme Shelter* in 2011, Al Maysles asserts the *cinéma vérité* aesthetic: "We didn't alter any events." *Cinéma vérité* was the classroom of a generation of filmmakers—George Lukas, for instance, shot the last shot of *Gimme Shelter* and Walter Murch worked on sound tracks.

video, possibly the most beloved home movie of the twenty-first century. (The number of viewers grows exponentially and will be higher when you read this.) Production costs could hardly have exceeded $20. The movie runs 56 seconds, about two breaths longer than *Repas de Bébé*, the Lumière film it resembles. A single shot shows an interior. A pair of brothers snuggle on a couch when, lifting his eyes to the camera, one of them addresses it. Howard

Davies-Carr, the children's father who made the movie, is a software salesman born the year a man first walked on the moon. He may be the second millennium Everyman. "Nobody in our household thinks they are famous and life goes on as normal. Thankfully we do not get recognized in the street nor do we ever expect to," he writes on YouTube. This family lives a half hour's drive from Iver Heath in Great Britain, where Michael Powell shot *Black Narcissus* with a Technicolor camera as large as Davies-Carr's couch.

When he released this movie May 22, 2007, Davies-Carr anticipated that his audience would fit in a minivan. Instead, 2.6 million pilgrims found their way to it in the first eight months after he released it. Viewship swelled to 470 million by July 2012. People visit here ceaselessly. Visitors outnumber the millions who, since Davies-Carr posted his video, have passed through London's Heathrow Airport. The movie is obviously attracting vast numbers of viewers with simple truths that affect them. They send out Davies-Carr's movie across the Internet accompanied by notes written in English, Portuguese, Spanish, Danish, Tamil, and other languages. The movie treats thoughts and feelings more than a half billion viewers feel to be true and important.

The older boy addresses the younger in the foreground. "Charlie!" he says, before raising his chin to the camera to announce, "Charlie bit me!" The biter swells with glee, regards the camera, and chomps down when Harry offers him his index finger. "Ow. Ouch! Ouch Charlie! Ow! Charlie!" Eyes draw together. "Charlie! That really hurt!" One year old, Charlie speaks not in words but in gesture. He seems to rejoice at the pain he caused, his head jerking back in jubilation. Harry repeats to the camera, "Charlie bit me." Like an actor facing an audience while addressing Yorick's skull, Charlie says climatically, "And that really hurt, Charlie, and it still hurts."

People revere this video as if it were a conversation of angels. It sees the world with simple eyes that see universal truth: Consciousness begins in pain. Grief is the twin of love. Babies are adorable. But these are not conclusions that viewers share in the notes they leave beneath the video. "I love how Charlie's laughing when his brother is close to tears ;)" one says. The movie inspires joy.

The Davies-Carr movie is a contemporary documentary. In legal proceedings, "documentary" is an adjective denoting evidence and refers to bills, documents, written and other records. Filmmaker John Grierson was first to describe a movie as "documentary" when he slipped the term into a review of Robert Flaherty's *Moana* (1926) "*Moana*, being a visual account of events in the daily life of a Polynesian youth, has documentary value," Grierson wrote. By two years, Flaherty anticipates anthropologist Margaret Mead's claim that adolescents in Polynesia live free of neurosis because they live beyond the constraints of western oppressive culture. Flaherty sees selectively, romanticizes and manipulates, but real people, not actors, advance his case. He thinks that he is moving within reality, not making it, showing what he believes the world is doing when no one is looking.

Regarded by many as the father of the documentary, Grierson eventually came to define documentary as "the creative treatment of actuality," perhaps to distinguish between transcribing testimony, as a court reporter does, and assessing it as a jury does. The key word in that definition remains "creative." The documentary filmmaker seeks to turn the world seen into the world understood. Documentary filmmakers don't usually set out to distort. They attempt to find what is true and real. That quest is difficult. The doors of perception open always on the same room—reality—but documentary filmmakers cannot easily enter there, any more than anyone can.

Koyaanisqatsi: Life Out of Balance (1982), dir. Godfrey Reggio.

The reason is simple. Documentaries give reality a name, and what we name, we change. This naming continues the work we begin at birth and continue as we grow old—our increasingly powerful imperative to engage with reality, comprehend our mortality, and lead lives of significance and singularity. Making a documentary is not a slog through a battlefield. It's bird watching. The filmmaker sees what he seeks only as it shifts among trees or when it sings within the leaves.

A filmmaker needs no vast budget to make inspired documentary. Howard Davies-Carr shot *Charlie Bit My Finger—Again!* on the couch in his living room. Godfrey Reggio, a former monk, created *Koyaanisqatsi* (1982), his documentary proclaiming the oneness of the world, out of footage shot by one or two collaborators. History begins as perception and ends as memory. Imagination refreshes it. The realist drinks from the well of the mystic. Documentary puts imagination to the service of reality, as you are doing by making film history.

EXERCISE TWENTY-FIVE: DOCUMENTARY

What this exercise teaches:

- **How to scan, classify, discard, highlight and select shots**

- **How to find your story line in events that "just happen"**

- **How to stay honest and express a point-of-view**

- **How to format a digital release**

- **How to identify an audience**

"In the documentary the basic material has been created by God, whereas in the fiction film the director is a God; he must create life."

Alfred Hitchcock, quoted by François Truffaut in *Hitchcock* (1984)

You Did It Then: **You're ready to start making film history. Your job is to pull a documentary out of unedited archival footage. Step-by-step instructions and the files to use are in the digital cutting room at http://makefilmhistory. com.**

You Do It Now: **Shoot a 5-10 minute documentary. Put everything you learned in *Make Film History* into it.**

The Answer Print

We're there...the answer print stage of the filmmaking process. Before you release it, you cast a calm cool eye over your movie. It is the pause backstage before the curtain reopens for applause.

Maybe there are retakes to make, dissolves to retime, a sound track that still requires tinkering. But in the answer print, you see a movie. It's yours, but it no longer belongs just to you. In the answer print, your movie enters the minds and lives of others. Your movie expresses your thoughts as the experience of everyone.

Consider where *Make Film History* has led you. You looked at movies emerging from nineteenth century cameras. Movies passed as a needle through the twentieth century, and, retroactively, your own hand made the thread sink and rise. You made still images move. You gave them the illusion of reality. You made birds rise from canisters that could not contain them. You joined shots. You mixed sounds, paced shots, made simple and elaborate montages. You thought about movies from the point of view of the censored and the censor and looked at movies from the point of view of the camera viewfinder. You passed a flight of people through a doorway. You met directors, stars, moguls, extras, Ola Cronk from Cawker City, Kansas, and a boy named Charlie. You thought about the enigma of the actor, who, walking across the screen, leaves no tracks. You thought about why it's better to be a person than a character. You can see in but they can't see out.

The answer print is in your hands because the work began in your imagination. Moviemaking is creation. To create is to remake yourself, and to remake yourself is to begin remaking the world.

So what do you want to do with the answer print? Retime the fourth shot to darken it? Re-cue the voice-over? Cut a frame where Harry glances at Sally and says...? Or go for lunch and think about all this later? It's your call. You decide.

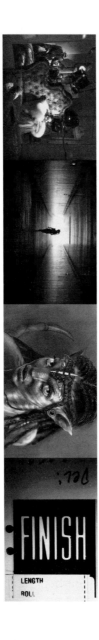

Two millennia ago, Pliny the Younger wrote to a friend, "Create something and shape it, so that it becomes yours for ever. Whereas all else will pass to a succession of owners, this will never cease to be your own from the moment it begins to exist."

That's a wrap. Make film history.

Credits

The author acknowledges the copyright owners of the following motion pictures from which single frames have been used in this book for purposes of commentary, criticism and scholarship under the Fair Use Doctrine.

7th Heaven. DVD. Directed by Frank Borzage. 1927; Beverly Hills, CA: Hollywood's Attic, N.D.

Adaptation. DVD. Directed by Spike Jonze. 2002; Culver City, CA: Sony Pictures Home Entertainment, 2003.

Ali Baba and the Forty Thieves. In *The Movies Begin—A Treasury of Early Cinema*. DVD. Directed by Segundo de Chomón. 1907; New York, NY: Kino International, 2002.

An American in Paris. DVD. Directed by Vincente Minnelli. 1951; Burbank, CA: Warner Home Video, 2000.

Annabelle's Serpentine Dance. In *The Movies Begin—A Treasury of Early Cinema*. DVD. Directed by William K.L. Dickson & William Heise. 1895; New York, NY: Kino International, 2002.

Apocalypse Now: Redux. DVD. 1979. Santa Monica, CA: Lionsgate, 2010.

Battleship Potemkin (*Bronenosets Potyomkin*). DVD. Directed by Sergei Eisenstein. 1925; New York, NY: Kino International, 2007.

Being John Malkovich. DVD. Directed by Spike Jonze. 1999; Universal City, CA: Universal Studios, 2003.

Big Night. DVD. Directed by Campbell Scott and Stanley Tucci. 1996: Culver City, CA: Sony Pictures Home Entertainment, 2002.

Black Narcissus. DVD. Directed by Michael Powell & Emeric Pressburger. 1947; New York, NY: Criterion Collection, 2010.

Black Swan. DVD. Directed by Darren Aronofsky. 2010; Los Angeles, CA: Fox Searchlight Pictures, 2011.

Breaker Morant. DVD. Directed by Bruce Beresford. 1980; New York, NY: Fox Lorber, 2004.

Breathless (À bout de souffle.) DVD. Directed by Jean-Luc Godard. 1960; New York, NY: Criterion Collection, 2007.

Cabiria. DVD. Directed by Giovanni Pastrone. 1914; New York, NY: Kino International, 2000.

Call Her Savage. DVD. Directed by John Francis Dillon. 1932; Century City, CA: Fox Film Corporation, 2006.

Casablanca. DVD. Directed by Michael Curtiz. 1942; Burbank, CA: Warner Home Video, 2010.

Chungking Express (Chongqing Senlin.) DVD. Directed by Kar-wai Wong. 1994; New York, NY: Criterion Collection, 2008.

Cinema Paradiso. DVD. Directed by Giuseppe Tornatore. 1988; Burbank, CA: Buena Vista Home Entertainment, 2011.

City Lights. DVD. In *The Chaplin Collection, Volume Two*. Directed by Charles Chaplin. 1931; Burbank, CA: Warner Home Video, 2004.

Dark Passage. DVD. Directed by Delmer Daves. 1947; Burbank, CA: Warner Home Video, 2006.

Dark Victory. DVD. Directed by Edmund Goulding. 1939; Burbank, CA: Warner Home Video, 2005.

Fantasmagorie. In *Saved From The Flames—54 Rare and Restored Films 1896-1944*. DVD. Directed by Émile Cohl. 1908; Los Angeles, CA: Flicker Alley, 2008.

Fight Club. DVD. Directed by David Fincher. 1999; Century City, CA: Twentieth Century Fox, 2002.

Flying Down to Rio. DVD. Directed by Thornton Freeland. 1933; Atlanta, GA: Turner Home Entertainment, 2006.

Free and Easy. In *Buster Keaton Collection*. DVD. Directed by Edward Sedgwick. 1928; Burbank, CA: Warner Home Video, 2004.

Gimme Shelter. In *The Rolling Stones: Gimme Shelter*. DVD. Directed by Albert Maysles, David Maysles, and Charlotte Zwerin. 1970. New York, NY: Criterion Collection, 2000.

Gold Diggers of 1937. In *The Busby Berkeley Collection, Volume Two*. DVD. Directed by Lloyd Bacon. 1937; Burbank, CA: Warner Home Video, 2006.

Gone With the Wind. DVD. Directed by Victor Fleming. 1939; Burbank, CA: Warner Home Video, 2009.

Hamlet. DVD. Directed by Laurence Olivier. 1948; New York, NY: Criterion Collection, 2000.

Hearts of Darkness—A Filmmaker's Apocalypse. DVD. Directed by Fax Bahr, George Hickenlooper, and Eleanor Coppola. 1991; Los Angeles, CA: Paramount, 2007.

Hollywood Sound—Music for the Movies/Max Steiner, Franz Waxman, David Raksin. DVD. Directed by Joshua Waletzky. 1995; West Branch, NJ: Kultur Video 2007.

Indochina: Namo Village, Panorama Taken from a Rickshaw (1900) Gabriel Veyre. In Michelle Aubert and Jean-Claude Seguin, *La production cinématographique des frères Lumière*. DVD. Directed by Gabriel Veyre. 1900; Paris, France: Bibliothèque du Film, 1996.

Kid Auto Races at Venice. In *Chaplin At Keystone: An International Collaboration of 34 Original Films*. DVD. Directed by Henry Lehrman. 1914; Los Angeles, CA: Flicker Alley, 2010.

Koyaanisqatsi - Life Out of Balance. DVD. Directed by Godfrey Reggio. 1983; Santa Monica, CA: MGM Home Entertainment, 2002.

La Strada (The Criterion Collection.) DVD. Directed by Federico Fellini. 1954; New York, NY: Criterion Collection, 2003.

L'arrivée en gare d'un train à La Ciotat. In *Landmarks of Early Film*. DVD. Directed by Louis Lumière. 1897; Chatsworth, CA: Image Entertainment, 1997.

L'Atalantide. In *Rediscover Jacques Feyder*. DVD. Directed by Jacques Feyder. 1921; Chicago, IL: Home Vision Entertainment, 2006.

Le Plaisir. DVD. Directed by Max Ophüls. 1952; New York, NY: Criterion Collection, 2008.

Lifeboat. DVD. Directed by Alfred Hitchcock. 1944; Century City, CA: Twentieth Century Fox, 2005.

Lumière 407. In Michelle Aubert and Jean-Claude Seguin, *La production cinématographique des frères Lumière*. DVD. Directed by Unknown. N.D.; Paris, France: Bibliothèque du Film, 1996.

Mabel's Strange Predicament. In *Charlie Chaplin: 57 Classics*. DVD. Directed by Mabel Normand. 1914; Newbury Park, CA: BCI/Eclipse, 2004.

Man with a Movie Camera. DVD. Directed by Dziga Vertov. 1929; Hollywood, CA: Image Entertainment, 2002.

Master and Commander: The Far Side of the World. DVD. Directed by Peter Weir. 2003; Century City, CA: Twentieth Century Fox, 2004.

Mothlight. In *by Brakhage: an anthology*. DVD. Directed by Stan Brakhage. 1963; New York, NY: Criterion Collection, 2003.

Motion Painting No. 1. In *Oskar Fischinger: Ten Films*. DVD. Directed by Oscar Fischinger. 1947; Los Angeles, CA: Center for Visual Music, 2006.

Murder. In *The Alfred Hitchcock Box Set*. DVD. Directed by Alfred Hitchcock. 1930; Santa Monica, CA: Lionsgate, 2007.

Murder at the Vanities. In *Pre-Code Hollywood Collection*. DVD. Directed by Mitchell Leisen. 1934; Universal City, CA: Universal Studios, 2009.

Murder on the Orient Express. DVD. Directed by Sidney Lumet. 1974; Los Angeles, CA: Paramount, 2004.

Murnau and Borzage at Fox—The Expressionist Heritage. DVD. Directed by Janet Bergstom. 2007; Munich, Germany: Edition Filmmuseum, 2008.

Mutiny on the Bounty. DVD. Directed by Frank Lloyd. 1935; Burbank, CA: Warner Home Video, 2004.

Nanook of the North. DVD. Directed by Robert J. Flaherty. 1922; New York, NY: Criterion Collection, 1999.

Napoléon. DVD. Directed by Abel Gance. 1927; Barcelona, Spain: Magna Films, N.D.

Night Mail. In *The Plow that Broke the Plains and Night Mail*. DVD. Directed by John Grierson. 1936; Sandy Hook, CT: Video Yesteryear, 2008.

Persona. DVD. Directed by Ingmar Bergman. 1966; Santa Monica, CA: MGM Home Entertainment, 2004.

Portrait of Jennie. DVD. Directed by William Dieterle. 1948; Century City, CA: MGM, 2004.

Prix de Beauté. DVD. Directed by Augusto Genina. 1930; New York, NY: Kino Video, 2006.

Repas de bébé. In *Landmarks of Early Film*. DVD. Directed by Louis Lumière. 1895; Chatsworth, CA: Image Entertainment, 1997.

Saboteur. DVD. Directed by Alfred Hitchcock. 1942; Universal City, CA: Universal Studios, 2007.

Scarface. DVD. Directed by Howard Hawks & Richard Rosson. 1932; Century City, CA: United Artists, 2007.

Seeing Is Believing. In *Forrest Gump: Two-Disc Special Collector's Edition*. DVD. Los Angeles, CA: 2001.

Se7en. (Seven.) In Seven. DVD. Directed by David Fincher. 1995: Los Angeles, CA: New Line Home Video, 2004.

Shadow of the Vampire. DVD. Directed by E. Elias Merhige. 2000; Santa Monica, CA: Lionsgate, 2003.

Shanghai Express. DVD. Directed by Josef von Sternberg. 1932; Universal City, CA: Universal Studios, N.D.

Signs. DVD. Directed by M. Night Shyamalan. 2002; Burbank, CA: Buena Vista Pictures, 2003.

Spellbound. DVD. Directed by Alfred Hitchcock. 1945; Los Angeles, CA: MGM, 2008.

Stella Maris. DVD. Directed by Marshall Neilan. 1918; Chatsworth, CA: Image Entertainment, 2000.

Sunrise—A Song of Two Humans (Limited Edition.) DVD. Directed by F.W. Murnau. 1927; Century City, CA: Twentieth Century Fox, 2003.

The Awful Truth. DVD. Directed by Leo McCarey. 1937; Culver City, CA: Sony Pictures Home Entertainment, 2003.

The Big Sleep. DVD. Directed by Howard Hawks. 1946; Burbank, CA: Warner Home Video, 2006.

The Big Swallow. In *The Movies Begin—A Treasury of Early Cinema*. DVD. Directed by James Williamson. 1901; New York, NY: Kino International, 2002.

The Big Trail. In *The Big Trail (Two Disc Special Edition)*. DVD. Directed by Raoul Walsh. 1930; Century City, CA: Twentieth Century Fox, 2008.

The Birth of a Nation: Deluxe Edition. DVD. Directed by D.W. Griffith. 1915; New York, NY: Kino International, 2011.

The Burglar on the Roof. In *Edison-The Invention of the Movies: 1891-1918*. DVD. Directed by Stuart Blackton. 1898; New York, NY: Kino International, 2005.

The Cabinet of Dr. Caligari (Das Cabinet des Dr. Caligari.) DVD. Directed by Robert Wiene. 1920; Chatsworth, CA: Image Entertainment, 1997.

The Cameraman. In *Buster Keaton Collection*. DVD. Directed by Edward Sedgwick & Buster Keaton. 1928; Burbank, CA: Warner Home Video, 2004.

The Crowd. DVD. Directed by King Vidor. 1928; Hong Kong, China: Boyng, N.D.

The Cutting Edge—The Magic of Movie Editing. DVD. Directed by Wendy Apple. 2004; Burbank, CA: Warner Home Video, 2005.

The Earrings of Madame de.... DVD. Directed by Max Ophüls. 1954; New York, NY: Criterion Collection, 2008.

The End of the Affair. DVD. Directed by Neil Jordan. 1999; Culver City, CA: Sony Pictures Home Entertainment, 2000.

The Evidence of the Film. In *Thanhouser Collection*. DVD. Directed by Lawrence Marston & Edwin Thanhouser. 1913; Spicewood, TX: Marengo Films, 2003.

The Gold Rush. DVD. Directed by Charlie Chaplin. 1925; Burbank, CA: Warner Home Video, 2003.

The Great Train Robbery. In *Landmarks of Early Film*. DVD. Directed by Edwin S. Porter. 1903; Chatsworth, CA: Image Entertainment, 1997.

The Great Ziegfeld. DVD. Directed by Robert Z. Leonard. 1936; Burbank, CA: Warner Home Video, 2004.

The Invisible Man. DVD. Directed by James Whale. 1933; Universal City, CA: Universal Studios, 2009.

The Jazz Singer. DVD. Directed by Alan Crosland. 1927; Burbank, CA: Warner Home Video, 2007.

The Lives of Others (Das Leben der Anderen.) DVD. Directed by Florian Henckel von Donnersmarck. 2006; Culver City, CA: Sony Pictures Home Entertainment, 2007.

The Making of The Birth of a Nation. In *The Birth of a Nation*. DVD. Directed by Robert G. Beecher. 1993; London, UK: Eureka Video, 2002.

The Mysterious Portrait. In *Georges Méliès: First Wizard of Cinema 1896-1913*. DVD. Directed by Georges Méliès.1899; Los Angeles, CA: Flicker Alley, 2008.

The Plow That Broke the Plains. In *The Plow that Broke the Plains and Night Mail*. DVD. Directed by Pare Lorentz. 1936; Sandy Hook, CT: Video Yesteryear, 2008.

The Return (Vozvrashchenie.) DVD. Directed by Andrey Zvygintsev. 2003; New York, NY: Kino International, 2003.

The Scarlet Empress. DVD. Directed by Josef von Sternberg. 1934; New York, NY: Criterion Collection, 2001.

The Tales of Hoffmann. DVD. Directed by Michael Powell & Emeric Pressburger. 1952; New York, NY: Criterion Collection, 2005.

The Thief of Bagdad. DVD. Directed by Ludwig Berger, Michael Powell and Tim Whelan. 1940; New York, NY: Criterion Collection, 2008.

The Toll of the Sea. In *Treasures from American Film Archives*. DVD. Directed by Chester M. Franklin.1922; Chatsworth, CA: Image Entertainment, 2000.

Three Little Pigs. In *Disney Animation Collection Two*. DVD. Directed by Burt Gillett. 1933; Burbank, CA: Walt Disney Video, 2009.

Three Little Wolves. In *Disney Animation Collection Two*. DVD. Directed by David Hand. 1936; Burbank, CA: Walt Disney Video, 2009.

Titicut Follies. DVD. Directed by Frederick Wiseman. 1967; Cambridge, MA: Zipporah Films, 2007.

Triumph of the Will (Special Edition.) DVD. Directed by Leni Riefenstahl. 1935; Romulus, MI: Synapse Films, 2006.

Trouble in Paradise. DVD. Directed by Ernst Lubitsch. 1932; New York, NY: Criterion Collection, 2003.

Zelig. DVD. Directed by Woody Allen. 1983; Santa Monica, CA: MGM, 2001.

The author acknowledges the institutions that have provided the following images.

Chapter One

"Photographed by MUYBRIDGE..."   Library of Congress Prints & Photographs Online Catalog
Zoöpraxiscope glass disc   Library of Congress Prints & Photographs Online Catalog
Man views a Kinetoscope movie   Library of Congress Prints & Photographs Online Catalog
Peter Bacigalupi's Kinetoscope Parlor   Library of Congress Prints & Photographs Online Catalog

Chapter Four

Gold Miners and Packers on Dyea Trail   Library of Congress Prints & Photographs Online Catalog
Sensational and Startling "Hold Up"   Library of Congress Prints & Photographs Online Catalog
Princess Theater   Library of Congress Prints & Photographs Online Catalog

Chapter Five

Charlie Chaplin at desk   Library of Congress Prints & Photographs Online Catalog
Mac Sennett at Keystone Studio   Los Angeles Public Library Photo Collection

Chapter Six

Cabiria Poster   Library of Congress Prints & Photographs Online Catalog

Chapter Seven

D.W. Griffith directing   Library of Congress Prints & Photographs Online Catalog
Dorothy Gish, D.W. Griffith, Lillian Gish Library of Congress Prints & Photographs Online Catalog

Chapter Eight

While czarists and Bolsheviks clashed   Library of Congress Prints & Photographs Online Catalog
"The road is covered..."   New York Public Library Digital Gallery
"Days of Revolution..."   Library of Congress Prints & Photographs Online Catalog

Chapter Nine

Stacia Napierkowska   Library of Congress Prints & Photographs Online Catalog

Opening night at Grauman's Egyptian   Los Angeles Public Library Photo Collection

Comedy producer Joe Rock   Los Angeles Public Library Photo Collection

Chapter 10

The William Fox Studio   The Kobal Collection

The Brown Derby Restaurant   UCLA Library Digital Collections

Near midnight of the silent movie era   The Kobal Collection

William Fox Studio School Room   Los Angeles Public Library Photo Collection

North from the Hollywood Club   Library of Congress Prints & Photographs Online Catalog

Los Angeles Car Show (1)   UCLA Library Digital Collections

Los Angeles Car Show (2)   UCLA Library Digital Collections

Chapter 14

Federation of Women's Clubs   Library of Congress Prints & Photographs Online Catalog

Will H. Hays   Library of Congress Prints & Photographs Online Catalog

Joseph Breen and Harold Huth   Getty Images

Chapter 15

Menzies storyboards for *Gone With the Wind*   The Kobal Collection

Chapter 16

Max Steiner composing   The Kobal Collection

Chapter 18

Jack Cardiff, cinematographer   The Kobal Collection

Chapter 25

Eva Marie Saint in 1949   Magnum Photos

Acknowledgements

Thanks to my students at Massachusetts College of Art and Design, both those I teach in the classroom and those I teach online, for inspiring me to develop this hands-on way to assimilate film history. Their experiences have enriched this book. To my supportive and imaginative colleagues at Mass Art I feel deep gratitude. To the Massachusetts College of Art Foundation I am particularly grateful. Their grant enabled me to undertake travel and research that have sharpened and deepened this work.

Thanks to Jeffrey Stoiber at the L. Jeffrey Selznick School of Film Preservation of the George Eastman House in Rochester, New York, for sharing his expertise.

To institutions that maintain collections of images that document the history of film I feel especial gratitude. In particular, I express my thanks to the Library of Congress for their Prints & Photographs Online Catalog, to the New York Public Library for their Digital Gallery, to the Los Angeles Public Library for the Photo Collection, to the UCLA Library for their Changing Times: Los Angeles in Photographs, 1920-1990 Collection, and to the Margaret Herrick Library of the Academy of Motion Picture Arts and Sciences. Images from their collections enrich this book. Their efforts help preserve the history of the movies.

I am grateful to Richard Wilbur, John Logan, Leslie Fiedler, Norman Holland, and Frank Brogan, poets, scholars, and teachers who taught me that all lives converge to some center and helped me find my own.

Thanks to Al Fiering, who first taught me back at Polymorph Films how to cut work print, how to see through the eyepiece of an Auricon camera, and how to hear the world in a Nagra tape recorder.

Make Film History has benefited immeasurably from the enthusiasm, guidance, and imagination of Michael Wiese and Ken Lee at Michael Wiese Productions. Thank you Michael and Ken for your faith in this project and for your faith in me.

To Leon Steinmetz and Inga Karentnikova, thank you—*Spasiba*—for all those translations from the Russian, and to Felix Kaputu, thank you—*Merci*—for helping me translate from the French.

To my stepdaughter, Morgan, for her years of support and loyalty, and to my son, Andrew, whose insight and suggestions improved this book, I express my heartfelt thanks.

But all these thanks are but preface to the essential—my gratitude to Angela, my wife, whose faith and encouragement make all else live. Without her, there would be nothing.

About the Author

Robert Gerst, Ph.D., has taught film aesthetics and film history to thousands of designers, artists, and young filmmakers in the United States and, in online courses at Massachusetts College of Art and Design, to film students around the world. A veteran teacher who first cut movies standing at a Moviola, he brings a hands-on perspective to the history of the movies. He chairs the Liberal Arts Department at Massachusetts College of Art and Design in Boston.

Contact Robert Gerst at robert@makefilmhistory.com.

THE MYTH OF MWP

In a dark time, a light bringer came along, leading the curious and the frustrated to clarity and empowerment. It took the well-guarded secrets out of the hands of the few and made them available to all. It spread a spirit of openness and creative freedom, and built a storehouse of knowledge dedicated to the betterment of the arts.

The essence of the Michael Wiese Productions (MWP) is empowering people who have the burning desire to express themselves creatively. We help them realize their dreams by putting the tools in their hands. We demystify the sometimes secretive worlds of screenwriting, directing, acting, producing, film financing, and other media crafts.

By doing so, we hope to bring forth a realization of 'conscious media' which we define as being positively charged, emphasizing hope and affirming positive values like trust, cooperation, self-empowerment, freedom, and love. Grounded in the deep roots of myth, it aims to be healing both for those who make the art and those who encounter it. It hopes to be transformative for people, opening doors to new possibilities and pulling back veils to reveal hidden worlds.

MWP has built a storehouse of knowledge unequaled in the world, for no other publisher has so many titles on the media arts. Please visit www.mwp.com where you will find many free resources and a 25% discount on our books. Sign up and become part of the wider creative community!

Onward and upward,

Michael Wiese
Publisher/Filmmaker